Tortilla Mastery

230 Authentic Recipes of Burritos, Chimichangas, Quesadillas, Tacos, Tostadas, Enchiladas, Casseroles, Chilaquiles, Tamales, and Much More!

MARISSA MARIE

TABLE OF CONTENTS

MEXICAN COOKING FUNDAMENTALS

Cooking Mexican food in an authentic way can seem like a daunting task, but like everything else in life, some guidance and a bit of practice is all you need. I'll take care of the guidance part, and I will leave it to you to take care of the rest!

Mexican food has an insane variety, and the taste easily covers a wide spectrum of flavours. Most American cooks can cook great Mexican food, but are sometimes a little off the mark from authentic Mexican flavour. The primary objective of this book is to enable an average non-Mexican cook to cook authentic Mexican food using the tools and ingredients easily available in any corner of the world.

In this section, we will look at some of the ingredients, equipment, and techniques you will need to know about before you can achieve great results with Mexican cooking. Keep at it, and you'll be preparing full-course Mexican dinners in no time!

THE FLAVOURS OF MEXICO

All regional cuisine has its distinct flavour, and Mexican food is no exception. You can tell when Mexican food is cooking nearby just by the smell. Mexican food gets its distinct flavour from the combination of ingredients that are commonly used in Mexican food. A few of these ingredients are: cilantro, cumin, chiles, garlic, etc. Once you get a hang of the Mexican flavour and ingredient combinations, you will be able to give a Mexican twist to pretty much every recipe in the world!

Latin markets are great places to stock up on supplies for cooking Mexican food. If you're in the USA or UK, you probably have such a market in close vicinity. You can easily find nearby markets using Google. If there is an ingredient, you're having problem finding, amazon.com is always a great last resort.

I will try my best to keep things simple, and will only use ingredients that are easy to source.

MEXICAN STAPLES

In order to achieve close to authentic Mexican flavour, you will need to have full understanding of the ingredients that make food taste Mexican. In this section we will talk about a few of the

Mexican staples that you will absolutely need to include in your kitchen pantry, if you're serious about Mexican cooking.

Feel free to buy canned/preserved versions of the ingredients if you can't find fresh ones.

CHILE

Chile is an indispensable ingredient for Mexican cooking, and we use a wide variety of these here in Mexico. The recipes in this book call for wide variety of these, so make sure you know where to source them. A nearby Latin market or store is a great place to look, or you can always find these online on www.amazon.com , or www.mexgrocer.com .

ANCHO

This dried poblano sports a deep, smoky flavour that couples great with beef and appears in an quite a few Mexican soups and salsas. It needs to be reconstituted.

ARBOL

Less hot, but just as flavourful as the habanero, this brittle, dried chile doesn't need reconstituting when added to soups, pots of pinto beans, or tequila.

GUAJILLO

Fragrant, earthy, and rather spicy, this dried chile is essential to moles and is commonly used as a purée in red chile sauces.

HABANERO

Deliciously fruity and super spicy (up to 350,000 Scoville units), this usually orange, lantern-like pepper is an essential ingredient of bottled hot sauces, tongue-singeing sauces, soups, and salsas.

JALAPEÑO

This most common of chile peppers is picked while green and usually used fresh in pretty much everything Mexican.

MORITA (DRIED CHIPOTLE)

This slightly fruity, dried chile is a smoke-dried jalapeño. When dried, it needs reconstituting. When canned and sold as chipotle en adobo, both the chile itself and its amazingly useful sauce can lend smoky depth to the recipes it is used in.

POBLANO

This mild, dark-skinned chile pepper turns into ancho when dried. When fresh, it can be roasted or turned into a vessel for Chiles Rellenos.

SERRANO

Smaller and hotter than a jalapeño, this important fresh pepper is commonly included raw into relishes and salsas. It is sometimes used roasted.

HERBS AND SPICES

ACHIOTE PASTE

Made using super-hard annatto seeds, this paste adds a smoky, peppery flavour to marinades and sauces. It's usually diluted using sour orange and serves as an important ingredient in quite a few Mexican recipes.

ALLSPICE

These peppercorn-looking berries are usually toasted and ground to impart warmth to salsas, moles, and stews. To save time, buy it ground.

BAY LEAVES

Thinner than other varieties, Mexican bay laurel adds its amazing flavour to marinades, soups, and stews.

CILANTRO

This self-seeding annual is used fresh across Mexican salsas, rice dishes, soups, and moles. It's also commonly used to garnish tacos.

CINNAMON

Mexican cinnamon, or Ceylon cinnamon, is quite unlike the cinnamon normally used in the United States—it's headier and warmer than its American counterpart. It can be found in Mexican markets as sticks or ground. If you can't find Mexican cinnamon, use whichever version you have on hand.

CUMIN

Strong, earthy cumin seeds, for which there is no equivalent, are commonly toasted and ground and used in stews and soups.

MARJORAM

Usually used with thyme and oregano to flavour stews, this fragrant herb also appears as a component of pickled vegetables.

OREGANO

Different from the Mediterranean variety, the Mexican herb is often used dry in pozole and tomato-based soups, or in main dishes.

SESAME (AJONJOLÍ)

An important ingredient in moles, these nutty seeds are also used in baked goods, including on sandwich rolls.

THYME

This aromatic perennial is often used to pickle vegetables and to dry and use in combination with oregano and marjoram for flavouring stews and other slow-simmered dishes.

OTHER INGREDIENTS

AVOCADOS

This mild fruit finds is a common ingredient in many Mexican recipes. Simply halve, pit, and peel.

CAJETA

Similar to dulce de leche, this caramel sauce is a common ingredient in multiple desserts and is used to top ice cream. Look for Coronado brand, which is made from goat's milk and has a full, rich flavour. Cow's milk versions can also be used.

CHEESE

Cheese is a staple in the Mexican kitchen. A few of the popular kinds of cheese in Mexico are: cotija, queso Oaxaca, queso fresco, and Chihuahua.

CHOCOLATE

Mexican chocolate is indispensable for moles. Unsweetened cocoa is great as a background note for sauces and stews, because it lends wonderful depth.

CORN

Sweet corn is indispensable for on-the-cob elotes, as well as in salads and soups.

GARLIC

Whether roasted or used raw in salsas, these cloves are a vital ingredient in Mexican Cooking.

HOT SAUCE

Popular hot sauces among Mexican cooking newbies are: mild Tapatío or Valentina; Cholula; and El Yucateco's Salsa Picante de Habanero.

LIMES

Keep plenty of limes on hand—they're indispensable for adding a spritz of citrusy brightness to finished dishes, as well as to salsas and cocktails.

ONIONS

Red and white/yellow onions are vital ingredients in Mexican cooking. Red ones are used for pickling and using fresh, while white/yellow ones are used in blended salsas as well as soups, stews, and pretty much everything else savory.

TORTILLAS

You can buy these or make your own. I will show you how in the next section.

VINEGAR

White, apple cider, and sometimes sugarcane vinegar add acidic pungency to pickled vegetables, vinaigrettes, and one-pot meals. Fruit vinegars are called for in quite a few Mexican recipes too.

EQUIPMENT

Improvisation is a talent every good cook has. Don't have an ingredient or appliance that a recipe calls for? Just improvise! However, too much improvisation can take a toll on the final result, which is why I will recommend having at least a few basic things in your kitchen if you are serious about Mexican cooking.

THE ESSENTIALS

COMAL

Any old cast iron or non-stick griddle will do the job. If you don't have any of these, you can get a comal, which is the traditional Mexican griddle used to make tortillas, sopes, quesadillas, etc. It is also a handy tool for dry roasting.

DUTCH OVEN

This little appliance is great for slow-cooking, and if you don't have one yet, you would do well to invest in one. If you don't know where to look, just pick up one from amazon.

MOLCAJETE

Mexican recipes sometimes require you to crush stuff. Might as well do it using a traditional Mexican tool. If you don't wish to invest in one, any old crushing tool will do the job.

STEAMER

Quite a few Mexican staples such as *tamales* require steaming. There are many ways of steaming if you don't have a steamer and don't wish to invest in one, just google them.

TORTILLA PRESS

If you ever get tired of rolling out tortillas and other stuff using a rolling pin, just remember that you can always make your work much easier by investing in a tortilla press. These are cheap, and easily available online, and in stores.

THE TIME-SAVERS

All the appliances in this section exist purely to save time. If you have a lot of free time on your hands, feel free to skip to the next section.

BLENDER OR IMMERSION BLENDER

Mexican sauces, drinks, salsas, etc. call for quite aa lot of puréeing and pulsing. Having an electric appliance that does the job at the press of a button sure helps.

FOOD PROCESSOR

Mexican food has a LOT of chopped up stuff. If you don't wish to do the chopping manually, invest in an electric food processor.

PRESSURE COOKER

Pressure cooking is the most efficient cooking method known to man. It is quick, cheap, and doesn't allow for much wastage of energy. It would be a good idea to invest in an electric or traditional pressure cooker if you don't have one already.

SLOW COOKER

Slow cooking really allows the flavours to be incorporated into the dishes, and is a great tool to have in your kitchen.

BASIC TECHNIQUES

If you've been cooking for a while, you will know all the basic techniques mentioned in this section. If you're a newbie, read through this section, and also watch a few videos on YouTube if you don't understand the procedure.

BLISTERING

To blacken and blister chiles, roast them directly over a gas flame for approximately five minutes, turning using tongs until charred and blistered. Another method is to broil them 4 inches beneath a preheated broiler for approximately ten minutes. Then, place them in a bowl, and cover the bowl using a kitchen towel to steam. After about five minutes, remove and discard the stem and seeds, and peel away and discard the blackened skin.

BRAISING

Using an enameled cast iron Dutch oven, which retains and uniformly distributes heat, sear seasoned meat on all sides in shimmering-hot oil on moderate to high heat to accomplish deep caramelization. If sautéing vegetables, remove and reserve browned meat before this step (and return it to the pot once done). Deglaze the pot by pouring in the braising liquid, using a wooden spoon to scrape the browned, tasty bits from the bottom of the pan, as they will enhance the flavour of the dish. Place the meat back into the pot, along with any juices that accumulated while it was resting. Bring the liquid to a simmer, cover the pot, and move it to a preheated 325°F oven to finish cooking until it becomes fall-apart tender.

DRY ROASTING

Dry roasting means applying heat to "dry" foods, such as unpeeled garlic, tomatoes, tomatillos, onions, or chiles. It can be done using a skillet, cast iron skillet, or comal.

GRILLING

Grilling is called for in quite a few Mexican recipes. The process is simple, as long as you have a grill. Keep it clean, well oiled, and preheat it before you throw the food on it.

GRINDING

You can do this in three ways. The most popular method is to pulverize them using a mortar and pestle, or molcajete, a kitchen tool you can also use to bruise herbs and mash ingredients for guacamole. The second way is to use a spice grinder, perfect for larger jobs. Finally, a third option is a Microplane, great for grating nutmeg, cinnamon, chocolate, citrus zest, and garlic.

RECONSTITUTING

Dried chiles have an incredible depth of flavour, and they're something you'll use a lot when cooking Mexican recipes. While ground, dried chiles may sometimes be used as a substitute, just follow this procedure. For up to eight peppers, fill a small saucepan with water and bring to the boiling point over high heat. Take the pan off the heat, and immerse the peppers in the hot water. Let them reconstitute for about half an hour. Drain, discard the water, and use in recipes as required.

STEAMING

My favourite steaming method is using a covered Dutch oven or pot with a tight-fitting rack placed inside. To steam tamales, use a large covered pot outfitted with either a rack or a perforated steamer basket that sits above the water line. Bring the water to the boiling point, place the tamales in the basket, cover, and steam until the masa dough becomes firm and easily pulls away from the corn husk. The process takes approximately ninety minutes.

TOASTING SPICES

This technique enhances the flavour of spices, while mellowing them out at the same time. In a skillet over moderate heat, toast spices just until aromatic, shaking the pan once in a while to avoid burning. Then, move them to a mortar, or molcajete, for grinding.

SALSA, SAUCES, & SEASONINGS

Fresh homemade salsa is the best salsa. Restaurants may or may not use fresh ingredients, and store-bought ready to eat salsa is hardly salsa, as it is laden with preservatives.

So, if you're preparing a full-course Mexican meal, make sure you make your own salsa. In this section we will cover a few of the most popular Mexican sauces and seasonings. Let us dive straight into the recipes!

Achiote Paste (RECADO COLORADO)

This spicy red seasoning is perfect for adding punch to your meat recipes!

Yield: Approximately ¾ Cup

Ingredients:

- ¼ cup olive oil
- ½ cup freshly squeezed lemon juice (about 5 lemons)
- ½ cup freshly squeezed orange juice
- ½ teaspoon whole cloves
- 1 tablespoon black peppercorns
- 10 garlic cloves
- 2 tablespoons salt
- 2 teaspoons cumin seeds
- 3 habanero peppers, seeded
- 5 tablespoons achiote (annatto) seeds
- 8 whole allspice berries

Directions:

1. Use a food processor to pulse-grind the achiote seeds, peppercorns, cumin, allspice, and cloves until thoroughly powdered. Put in the orange juice, habaneros, garlic, and salt and blend until the desired smoothness is achieved. Mix in the lemon juice and olive oil until a paste is achieved.
2. Cover tablespoon-sized portions of the paste using plastic and place it in your freezer for no more than a month.

Ancho and Chile De Árbol Salsa

An insanely delicious rustic salsa from Mexico's interior!

Yield: About 2 cups

Ingredients:

- 1 ancho chile, toasted and rehydrated, 1/3 cup of the soaking water reserved
- 1 teaspoon agave nectar or sugar
- 1 teaspoon salt
- 1 tomato (about 1/2 pound), roasted
- 1/2 cup finely chopped white onion
- 1/2 pound tomatillos, husked and rinsed
- 4 chiles de árbol, toasted and rehydrated

Directions:

1. Put the tomatillos in a small deep cooking pan, submerge them in water, bring them to its boiling point, and simmer until they are tender but not falling apart, about five minutes. Drain and save for later.
2. Finish the salsa. Put the chiles in a blender and put in the reserved 1/3 cup of soaking water. Put in the tomatillos, tomato, agave nectar, and salt to the blender and blend until thoroughly puréed. Pour the salsa into a serving dish and mix in the onions.

Ancho Chile Jam

This jam has a complex sweet & spicy flavour. It can be enjoyed mixed into soups, as a chutney with meat recipes, and much more!

Yield: 2 ½ Cups

Ingredients:

- ½ teaspoon salt
- 2 cloves garlic, peeled
- 2 ounces ancho chiles, approximately 5
- 2 tablespoons honey

- 2 tablespoons white or red wine vinegar
- 6 tablespoons any kind of red jam or jelly

Directions:

1. Use scissors to cut the ancho chiles open, discard the stems, and shake out all the seeds. Put the chiles in a container and add sufficient boiling water to immerse the chiles. Put a small plate on top of the chiles to immerse them. Soak for half an hour, then drain, saving for later 1 cup of the chile soaking water.
2. Put the chiles, garlic, jam, honey, vinegar, and salt in a blender. Put in the 1 cup reserved chile soaking water and pulse on high speed to blend for a minute. Move the jam to an airtight container and place in your fridge for maximum half a year.

Ancho Chile Sauce V2

This delicious spicy sauce goes with pretty much everything!

Yield: Approximately 2½ Cups

Ingredients:

- ¼ cup chopped onion
- ¼ cup raisins
- ½ teaspoon ground cumin
- 1 tablespoon vegetable oil
- 1 teaspoon dried or 1 tablespoon fresh oregano
- 2 ancho chiles
- 2 cups chicken broth
- 2 tomatoes, chopped

Directions:

1. Take the stems and seeds of the chiles and soak them in hot water for about ten minutes. Take the chiles and cut them.
2. In a big deep cooking pan, heat the vegetable oil using high heat. Put in the chiles and onion and sauté until tender, about five minutes. Put in the broth, tomatoes, raisins, oregano, and cumin and bring to its boiling point. Lower the heat and allow to simmer until the tomatoes are cooked, another ten minutes.

3. Cautiously pour all of the contents into a food processor or blender and process until the desired smoothness is achieved. Serve instantly, or store in a firmly sealed container in your fridge for maximum one week.

Arizona-Style Salsa

This salsa from the Mexican state of Sonora goes great with chips or antojitos!

Yield: About 1 cup

Ingredients:

- 1 (8-12 ounce) tomato, roasted
- 1 dried Anaheim (California) chile, or a mild, dried New Mexico chile, toasted and rehydrated
- 1/2 tablespoon rice vinegar
- 1/2 teaspoon salt
- 3 chiles de árbol, toasted and rehydrated

Directions:

1. Throw all ingredients into your blender and pulse for a couple of minutes, or until the desired smoothness is achieved.

Banana Salsa

Tastes great as an appetizer on its own, or as a dip with chips!

Yield: 2 Cups

Ingredients:

- ¼ cup chopped fresh cilantro, leaves and tender stems
- ½ teaspoon salt
- 1 red bell pepper, stemmed and seeded
- 1 serrano chile, thoroughly minced, including the seeds
- 1 whole green onion, minced
- 2 firm yellow skinned bananas

- 2 tablespoons light brown sugar
- 2 tablespoons minced fresh ginger
- 3 tablespoons freshly squeezed lime juice

Directions:

1. Peel the bananas and cut along the length into long strips. Cut across the strips so that the banana is in ½-inch cubes. Mince the red bell pepper and green onion.
2. Mix the bananas with the bell pepper, green onion, cilantro, ginger, chile, lime juice, brown sugar, and salt in a medium container. Press plastic wrap directly across the surface. The salsa can be made twelve hours before serving and placed in the fridge in an airtight container. Allow to reach room temperature and stir before you serve.

BANANA SALSA VARIATION 1: MANGO SALSA

Substitute the bananas with 3 perfectly ripe mangoes. Remove the skin of the mangoes. Cut off the flesh in big pieces, and then cut coarsely to yield 2 to 3 cups. Mix the mango with the rest of the ingredients as directed in the "Banana Salsa" recipe.

BANANA SALSA VARIATION 2: PAPAYA SALSA

Substitute the bananas with 2 firm, underripe Hawaiian papayas or a 3-inch-thick slice of Mexican papaya. Peel, seed, and cut the fruit to yield 2 to 3 cups. Mix the papaya with the rest of the ingredients as directed in the "Banana Salsa" recipe.

BANANA SALSA VARIATION 3: TROPICAL SALSA

Replace the bananas with a mix of chopped fruits— avocado, papaya or mango, strawberries, and kiwi—to yield 2 to 3 cups. Mix the mixed fruit with the rest of the ingredients as directed in the "Banana Salsa" recipe.

BANANA SALSA VARIATION 4: PINEAPPLE SALSA

Replace the bananas with 2 to 3 cups chopped fresh pineapple. Omit the lime juice. Mix the pineapple with the rest of the ingredients as directed in the "Banana Salsa" recipe.

Cebollas En Escabeche (PICKLED ONIONS)

Yield: About 2 cups

An insanely delicious garnish and relish from Yucatán state, this recipe goes great with tacos, seafood, meats, and poultry.

Ingredients:

- 1 (12-ounce) red onion, cut into 1/3-inch rings
- 1 bay leaf
- 1 clove garlic, peeled and smashed
- 1 small habanero chile, cut in half (not necessary)
- 1 teaspoon dried leaf oregano
- 1/2 cup rice vinegar
- 1/2 tablespoon extra-virgin olive oil
- 1/4 cup water
- 1/8 teaspoon salt
- 1/8 teaspoon whole dried thyme

Directions:

1. Make the onions. Put all the ingredients apart from the onion in a big deep cooking pan and simmer for about three minutes.
2. Put the onions in a nonreactive container and pour the hot liquid over them.
3. Allow the onions to sit at room temperature for about two hours, stirring occasionally. Place in your fridge.

Chile Pequín Salsa

Yield: About 1 cup

Don't put too much of this fiery salsa into your mouth in one go. This salsa goes great with steak, seafood, and pork.

Ingredients:

- 1 big or 2 small cloves garlic, minced
- 1 big tomato (approximately eight ounces)
- 1 tablespoon chile pequín
- 1/2 cup chopped white onion
- 1/2 teaspoon rice vinegar
- 1/2 teaspoon salt
- 1/8 teaspoon ground cloves

Directions:

1. Bring sufficient water to cover the tomato to its boiling point and put in the tomato, onion, and garlic. Simmer for about ten minutes, or until the tomato is fairly tender.
2. Peel the tomato and discard the skin. Put the tomato, onion, and garlic in a food processor, put in the rest of the ingredients, and pulse until puréed. Allow about fifteen minutes for the chiles to rehydrate, and process again before you serve.

Chile-Tomatillo Salsa

Poblano chile and tomatillo is an insane combination!

Yield: 2½ Cups

Ingredients:

- ¼ cup packed fresh cilantro, leaves and tender stems
- ½ teaspoon salt
- 1 poblano chile
- 1 serrano chile
- 3 cloves garlic, peeled
- 8 small green tomatillos, husks removed

Directions:

1. In a dry, heavy frying pan on moderate to high heat, mildly char the tomatillos. Char the poblano and rub off the blackened skin. Then discard the seeds and stem. Chop the tomatillos into quarters. In the same dry, heavy frying pan using high heat, mildly brown

the garlic and serrano chile. Chop the garlic and chiles a few times so they are in slightly smaller pieces.

2. Put the poblano chile, tomatillos, garlic, serranogarlic mixture (including the seeds), cilantro, and salt in a blender. Blend until the desired smoothness is achieved. If you don't like this method, if you have the time, finely cut the salsa ingredients by hand for a more interesting texture. Taste and calibrate the seasonings for salt. This can be stored for three days refrigerated in an airtight container. Allow to reach room temperature before you serve.

Chimichurri Sauce

Yield: About 3/4 cup

An Argentinian sauce with a Mexican twist! This sauce goes great with meat dishes!

Ingredients:

- 1 tablespoon dried leaf oregano
- 2 teaspoons chile flakes
- 4 teaspoons red wine vinegar
- 6 cloves garlic, very finely chopped or put through a garlic press
- 1/2 cup extra-virgin olive oil
- 1/2 teaspoon salt
- 1/4 cup finely chopped parsley
- 1/4 teaspoon freshly ground black pepper

Directions:

1. Put the olive oil, garlic, oregano, and chile flakes into a small microwave-safe dish and microwave to approximately 135°-150°F on an instant-read thermometer, approximately half a minute on High. You want to heat the garlic just sufficient to release its flavour, but not so much that it actually cooks or makes the oil turn cloudy. Let the oil cool to room temperature.
2. Mix in the vinegar, salt, pepper, and parsley and let the flavours meld for a couple of hours before you serve.

Cranberry-Jalapeño Jelly

Adjust the amount of jalapeño to adjust the hotness of this fiery recipe to your taste!

Yield: 1-1¼ cups

Ingredients:

- 1 cup fresh cranberries
- 1 small jalapeño, stems and seeds removed, very finely chopped
- 1/2 cup sugar
- 1/2 cup water
- 1/4 cup finely chopped dried apricots
- Grated zest from 1/2 orange
- Pinch of salt

Directions:

1. Cook the water and sugar on low-moderate boil for five minutes.
2. Put in the cranberries, apricots, salt, and jalapeño and cook them on low-moderate simmer for about six minutes, at which time the cranberries should be breaking apart. Put in the orange zest and carry on simmering, stirring, until thick, approximately one minute.

Dog's Snout Salsa

A hot and tangy salsa from Yucatán state!

Yield: About 2 cups

Ingredients:

- 1 habanero chile, stemmed, seeded, veins removed, and very finely chopped
- 1/4 cup finely chopped cilantro
- 1/4 heaping teaspoon salt
- 1-1/3 cups chopped tomatoes
- 2/3 cup finely chopped red onion

- 4 tablespoons sour orange juice, or substitute 2 tablespoons freshly squeezed lime juice and 2 tablespoons freshly squeezed orange juice

Directions:

1. Lightly toss together everything apart from the salt. Let the salsa marinate, stirring intermittently, for a couple of hours at room temperature. Mix in the salt before you serve.

Fresh Tomatillo Salsa

This salsa is a bite of pure freshness, and looks absolutely amazing!

Yield: About 1-1/4 cups. Nutrition information is for 1 tablespoon.

Ingredients:

- 1 heaping teaspoon salt
- 1 medium-sized serrano chile, stem removed, finely chopped
- 3 tablespoons chopped cilantro
- 3 tablespoons chopped white onion
- 3/4 pound fresh tomatillos, husked, rinsed, dried, and cut into quarters

Directions:

1. Put all the ingredients in a blender and pulse just until the sauce is dense and lumpy but not thoroughly puréed.

Guacamole

Yield: 2 to 3 Cups

Easily one of the most popular Mexican recipes in the world, Guacamole is easy to prepare, but also just as easy to screw up. The avocado is the most important ingredient in this recipe, so make sure it is fresh and ripe, and preferably Mexican.

Ingredients:

- ½ teaspoon salt

- 1 serrano chile, minced, including the seeds
- 2 cloves garlic, minced
- 2 tablespoons chopped fresh cilantro, leaves and tender stems (not necessary)
- 2 whole green onions, chopped
- 3 ripe avocados
- Freshly squeezed juice of 2 limes

Directions:

1. Chop the avocados in half and remove the pits. Use a spoon to scoop out the flesh. Then purée the avocados using the tongs of a fork. Mix the avocados with the green onions, garlic, chile, cilantro, lime juice, and salt in a medium container. Taste and calibrate the seasonings for salt, lime juice, and chile.
2. If making this more than an hour in advance, squeeze some lime juice over the surface, then secure the surface using plastic wrap. The guacamole will stay perfectly green for a couple of days stored this way in your fridge.

VARIATION

Decorate using crumbled goat cheese, queso fresco, or crema.

Habanero Salsa

An easy to make salsa from Yucatán packing some serious heat.

Yield: About 3/4 cup

Ingredients:

- 1 teaspoon salt
- 1/2 cup cider vinegar
- 1/2 cup pineapple juice
- 4 cloves garlic, unpeeled
- 5 habanero chiles, seeds and veins removed, roughly chopped

Directions:

1. Put the chiles, vinegar, and pineapple juice in a small deep cooking pan, bring to its boiling point, and simmer, covered, for about twelve minutes. Let the liquid and chiles cool.
2. Roast the garlic. Put the garlic in a small frying pan on moderate heat and cook, flipping frequently, until it is slightly charred on the outside and very tender inside, 8-ten minutes. When the garlic is sufficiently cool to handle, peel and roughly cut it.
3. Pour the chiles and their cooking liquid into a blender, put in the garlic and salt, and blend to a purée, approximately one minute. Allow the sauce to cool and the acids to tone down the chile's heat for two to three hours before you serve. Serve with Yucatecan dishes.

Jalisco-Style Pico De Gallo

Famously enjoyed with fajitas all over the world!

Yield: About 3 cups

Ingredients:

- 2 tablespoons freshly squeezed lime juice
- 1/2 cup peeled, seeded, and chopped cucumber, 1/2-inch pieces
- 1/2 cup mango, chopped into 1/2-inch pieces
- 1/2 cup pineapple, chopped into 1/2-inch pieces
- 1/2 cup orange or tangerine segments, cut into 1/2-inch pieces
- 1/2 cup peeled and finely chopped jícama
- 1/2 cup thinly sliced red onion
- 1 teaspoon pure ancho chile powder, or 1/2 teaspoon powder made from chile de árbol
- 1/8 heaping teaspoon salt

Directions:

1. Make the salsa. Mix everything apart from the salt and chile powder.
2. Mix in the salt and chile powder and place in your fridge for thirty minutes to let the flavours blend before you serve.

Manual Salsa Mexicana

This salsa takes time to make, and only works if you have vine-ripened tomatoes on hand.

Yield: 4½ Cups

Ingredients:

- ¼ to ½ cup coarsely chopped fresh cilantro, leaves and tender stems
- ½ teaspoon salt
- 1 to 2 serrano chiles, minced, including the seeds
- 2 whole green onions, minced
- 3 cloves garlic, minced
- 4 cups chopped vine-ripened tomatoes, including skins and seeds

Directions:

1. In a large container, mix the chopped tomatoes with the cilantro, green onions, chiles, garlic, and salt.
2. Taste and calibrate the seasonings, especially for salt and chile flavour. This can be made three days ahead and placed in the fridge in an airtight container.
3. Allow to reach room temperature before you serve.

Mexican Chile Sauce

This sauce tastes insane with grilled meat!

Yield: 3 Cups

Ingredients:

- ¼ cup lightly packed light brown sugar
- ½ teaspoon ground cumin
- ½ teaspoon salt
- 1 serrano chile
- 1 teaspoon dried oregano, or 2 teaspoons minced fresh oregano, preferably Mexican
- 1½ ounces guajillo chiles, approximately 6
- 2 big vine-ripened tomatoes, 12 to 16 ounces
- 4 cloves garlic, peeled

Directions:

1. Chop the stem ends off the guajillo chiles and shake out the seeds. Put the guajillos in a container and cover with boiling water (put a small plate on top of the chiles to immerse them). Soak for half an hour, then drain, saving for later 1 cup of the chile soaking water.
2. Chop the stems off the tomatoes and slice them in half horizontally. Put a dry cast-iron frying pan on moderate to high heat. When hot, mildly brown the garlic, tomatoes, and serrano chile, five minutes. Discard the tomato skins.
3. In a blender, put in the guajillo chiles, garlic, tomato, serrano, brown sugar, cumin, oregano, salt, and the 1 cup reserved chile water. Blend until liquefied. Taste and calibrate the seasonings. This can be stored safely in a fridge for about ninety days stored in an airtight container.

Pasilla Chile Salsa

This salsa goes great with seafood and grilled meat!

Yield: About 2 cups. Nutrition information is for 1 tablespoon.

Ingredients:

- 1 teaspoon canned chipotle chile, or to taste
- 2 teaspoons extra-virgin olive oil, or cooking spray to coat the garlic
- 2 very big pasilla chiles, or 2½ medium to big ones, toasted and rehydrated
- 3 cloves garlic, unpeeled
- 2/3 cup minced white onion
- 1/4 teaspoon dried leaf oregano
- 1-1/4 pounds tomatoes, roasted (about 2 big or 3 medium)
- 3/4 teaspoon salt

Directions:

1. Preheat the oven to 350°F.
2. Brush or spray garlic with some of the olive oil, wrap in foil, and bake until soft, about forty minutes. Peel and reserve the garlic.
3. Combine the ingredients. Put the rehydrated pasilla chiles, the chipotle chile, one of the tomatoes, the oregano, garlic, and salt in a food processor and pulse until a smooth

purée is achieved. Put in the rest of the tomato and pulse until it is blended with the other ingredients, but leave the salsa with some texture.

4. Put the rest of the olive oil in a frying pan on moderate heat, put in the onions, and sauté until they are just starting to become tender. Mix the onions with the rest of the salsa in a container.

Pico De Gallo Salsa

Pico de gallo translates to "beak of the rooster." This recipe is a Mexican favourite and has hundreds of versions. This is probably the most popular version out there. Serve it as a side with tortilla chips!

Yield: 4 Cups

Ingredients:

- ½ medium onion
- 1 jalapeño pepper
- 1 packed cup coarsely chopped fresh cilantro, stems cut
- 1 teaspoon freshly ground black pepper
- 1 teaspoon ground cumin
- 1 teaspoon salt
- 2 garlic cloves
- 2 limes
- 2 pounds Roma or vine-ripened tomatoes

Directions:

1. Cut the tomatoes into little cubes and put them into a large container.
2. Use a food processor to pulse the onion until it is finely chopped (make sure you don't over-process or it'll become gooey). Scrape it into the container with the tomatoes.
3. In the same processor, put in the cilantro and pulse until chopped. Put in to the container with the tomato and onion.
4. Chop the jalapeño in half, along the length, discarding the stem (discard the seeds and veins if you think it'll be too spicy). Pulse the jalapeño and garlic using your processor until thoroughly minced. Scrape into the container with the other vegetables.

5. Chop the limes in half and squeeze their juices into the tomato mixture. Put in the cumin, black pepper, and salt, adding a little extra salt to your taste. Toss together before you serve.

Ranch-Style Salsa (SALSA RANCHERA)

Salsa Ranchera has multiple versions floating around in the world. This version doesn't have an overly strong flavour, and goes great with eggs and meat.

Yield: About 2 cups

Ingredients:

- 1 big guajillo chile, stemmed, seeded, toasted, and rehydrated, 1/2 cup of the soaking water reserved
- 1 clove garlic, minced
- 1 pound tomatoes (about 2 medium to large), roasted
- 1 tablespoon extra-virgin olive oil
- 1/2 teaspoon salt
- 1½ cups chopped white onion

Directions:

1. Combine the tomatoes and chiles. Put the chiles, tomatoes, and the 1/2 cup chile soaking water in a blender and purée thoroughly, a couple of minutes.
2. Heat a big deep cooking pan on moderate heat, put in the oil and onions, and sauté them until they are tender but not browned, about five minutes. Put in the garlic and cook one more minute.
3. Pour the tomatoes and chiles into the deep cooking pan with the onion and garlic and mix in the salt. Bring to a simmer and cook for five to ten minutes, or until the sauce holds together. If it becomes too thick, put in some more water.

Red Enchilada Sauce (SALSA ROJA)

You will never buy enchilada sauce from a store after you make your own!

Yield: 2½ Cups

Ingredients:

- ¼ cup chili powder
- ¼ teaspoon ground cinnamon
- ¼ teaspoon sugar
- ½ teaspoon salt
- 1 tablespoon flour
- 1 teaspoon dried or 1 tablespoon chopped fresh oregano
- 1 teaspoon ground cumin
- 2 cups chicken broth
- 3 tablespoons garlic powder
- 3 tablespoons vegetable oil
- Two 5-ounce cans tomato sauce

Directions:

1. Heat the vegetable oil in a moderate-sized deep cooking pan on moderate heat. Put in the flour and stir, smoothing it out to make a roux, and cook for about one minute. Put in the chili powder and cook for an additional half a minute. Put in the broth, tomato sauce, garlic powder, oregano, cumin, salt, sugar, and cinnamon and stir until blended.
2. Raise the heat and bring to its boiling point, then decrease the heat to moderate and cook until the flavours deepen, an additional fifteen minutes.
3. Turn off the heat and use in your favorite enchilada recipe, pour over burritos to make them "wet," or to make tamales. If you're not using the sauce immediately, store it in a glass jar with a firmly fitting lid in your fridge for maximum one week.

TOMATE VERDE *(SALSA VERDE)*

One of the most popular tomato-bases salsa out there!

Yield: 3 Cups

Ingredients:

- 1 bunch fresh cilantro, stems cut

- 1 jalapeño, stemmed and halved
- 1 small (or ½ medium) onion, quartered
- 1 teaspoon salt
- 1½ pounds (12 to 15) tomatillos, husked and washed
- 4 or 5 garlic cloves

Directions:

1. Preheat your broiler.
2. Chop the tomatillos in half and place them, cut-sides down, on a foil-lined baking sheet. Put under a broiler until the skins are fairly blackened on top, about eight to ten minutes.
3. Cautiously pierce the tomatillos using a fork and put them in a food processor or blender. Put in the onion and garlic and pulse until blended. Put in the cilantro, jalapeño, and salt and pulse until puréed.
4. Go ahead; taste it before you serve and add a little extra salt, if required.

Roasted-Tomato and Pumpkin Seed Salsa

A simple and delicious salsa that tastes insane with grilled meat!

Yield: About 2½ cups

Ingredients:

- 1 medium to big serrano chile
- 1 teaspoon salt, or to taste
- 1/2 cup toasted and ground pumpkin seeds (pepitas) (from 2/3 cup raw hulled pumpkin seeds)
- 1/2-inch slice of white onion
- 2 cloves garlic, peeled
- 3 or 4 tomatoes, for a total of about 1½ pounds

Directions:

1. Put the tomatoes and chile on a baking sheet as close to your broiler as possible and broil until the tomatoes have become tender and barely start to char, about ten to fifteen minutes. Put in the onion and garlic and carry on cooking until the onion is slightly charred and the garlic is soft, an additional five to ten minutes. Ensure that the tomatoes

are thoroughly cooked and fairly tender. Take the vegetables out of the oven, put them in a food processor, put in the salt, and pulse until the sauce is smooth.

2. As the vegetables broil, heat a nonstick frying pan on moderate heat and toast the pumpkin seeds, stirring regularly, until most of them have popped. Don't allow them to scorch. Grind the toasted seeds to a powder in a spice or coffee grinder. Put in 1/2 cup of the ground seeds and the salt to the processor and pulse with the other ingredients until everything is well blended.

Romesco Sauce

Insanely nutritious and delicious, this sauce goes with pretty much everything.

Yield: About 1 cup

Ingredients:

- 1 cup cherry tomatoes
- 1 small to moderate canned chipotle chile, seeded and chopped
- 1 tablespoon sherry vinegar (or freshly squeezed lime or lemon juice)
- 1/2 heaping teaspoon salt
- 1/2 teaspoon sweet smoked Spanish paprika
- 1/3 cup extra-virgin olive oil
- 2 tablespoons minced parsley
- 2 tablespoons roasted and skinned whole almonds
- 3 garlic cloves, peeled and cut in half along the length

Directions:

1. Dry roast the tomatoes, nuts, and garlic. Heat an ungreased frying pan on moderate to high heat until it is very hot. Put the tomatoes, almonds, and garlic in the frying pan and cook, stirring continuously, until the tomatoes are blackened and just beginning to deflate. It is okay if the nuts and garlic seem burned; that just augments the flavour. Do make sure that the garlic is thoroughly cooked.
2. Finish the sauce. Put the tomatoes, almonds, and garlic in a food processor, put in the rest of the ingredients, and process in pulses until the sauce is thick but still has some texture.

Salsa De Chile (Chile Sauce)

One of the most versatile salsa recipes in this book, chile sauce will go with pretty much everything.

Yield: About 2½ cups

Ingredients:

- 1 tablespoon extra-virgin olive oil
- 1 teaspoon dried leaf oregano
- 1 teaspoon rice vinegar
- 2 bay leaves
- 3/4 teaspoon salt, or to taste
- 4 cloves garlic, chopped
- 8 mild to moderate-hot New Mexico dried red chiles, 12 guajillo chiles, or 4 medium-sized ancho chiles, stemmed, seeded, toasted, and rehydrated, 4 cups soaking water reserved

Directions:

1. Combine the sauce ingredients. Put the chiles in a blender, put in the garlic, oregano, and 2 cups of the reserved chile soaking water, and blend for a couple of minutes, or until comprehensively puréed. Put in the rest of the 2 cups chile soaking water and blend one more minute.
2. Cook the sauce. Heat a big deep cooking pan on moderate heat, put in the olive oil, and mix in the blended sauce ingredients. Put in the vinegar and bay leaves, bring to its boiling point, and cook on a moderate simmer until the sauce is barely sufficiently thick to coat the back of a spoon, or the consistency of a very thin milkshake, about fifteen minutes. If the sauce becomes too thick, put in some more water. If it is too thin, cook it a bit longer. Put in the salt and simmer one more minute.

Salsa De Molcajete

A traditional Mexican salsa. Salsa doesn't get more authentic than this!

Yield: About 1 cup

Ingredients:

- 1 chile de árbol, toasted in an oil-filmed frying pan until crisp but not burned
- 1 small jalapeño chile, roasted and peeled
- 1 tomato, broiled and peeled
- 1 very small pasilla chile, toasted in an oil-filmed frying pan until crisp but not burned
- 2 chiles pequín, toasted in an oil-filmed frying pan until crisp but not burned
- 2 cloves garlic
- 2 tablespoons finely chopped white onion
- 2 teaspoons toasted sesame seeds
- 2/3 of 1 small ancho chile, toasted in an oil-filmed frying pan until crisp but not burned
- 3/4 teaspoon salt
- Water as needed to get the consistency you want

Directions:

1. Put in the salt to the molcajete.
2. Put in the ingredients one at a time, grinding each one to the texture you want before you put in the next.

Salsa Fresca

A great all-round salsa!

Yield: About 1 cup

Ingredients:

- 1/2 teaspoon salt
- 1/4-ounce serrano chile (about 1-1/4 inches) long, cut into 1/3-inch pieces
- 1/4 cup loosely packed, roughly chopped cilantro
- 1/4 cup very finely chopped white onion
- 1/4 cup water (not necessary)
- 4 ounces tomatillos, husked, rinsed, dried, and cut into 3/4-inch pieces
- 6 ounces Roma tomatoes, cut into 3/4-inch pieces

Directions:

1. If you have a meat grinder, grind together into a container the tomatillos, tomatoes, chile, and cilantro.
2. Mix in the onion and salt. If you are using a food processor, put the tomatillos, tomatoes, chile, and cilantro into the work container, put in 1/4 cup water, and pulse until everything is finely chopped (as if it had been put through a meat grinder).
3. Mix in the onions and salt.

Smoky Chipotle Salsa (SALSA CON CHIPOTLE)

This moderately spicy salsa tastes great with a side of chips.

Yield: Approximately 5 Cups

Ingredients:

- ½ teaspoon freshly ground black pepper
- 1 onion, chopped
- 12 garlic cloves, sliced
- 2 tablespoons freshly squeezed lime juice
- 2 tablespoons olive oil
- 2 tablespoons salt
- 3 cups chipotle peppers in adobo sauce
- 8 Roma tomatoes, coarsely chopped

Directions:

1. Heat the olive oil in a big frying pan using high heat. Put in the garlic and onion and allow them to brown, stirring only a couple of times (about 2 minutes). Put in the chipotle with adobo sauce and the tomatoes and cook for another three to four minutes until thoroughly heated.
2. Cautiously pour the mixture into a blender or food processor. Put in the salt, lime juice, and black pepper and blend until the desired smoothness is achieved.
3. Serve instantly or save it in your fridge for a few days.

Tangerine-Serrano Salsa

Are tangerines in season? This is the salsa to try!

Yield: 3 to 4 Cups

Ingredients:

- ¼ cup chopped fresh cilantro, leaves and tender stems
- ¼ cup freshly squeezed lime juice
- ¼ cup lightly packed light brown sugar
- ½ cup chopped red onion
- ½ teaspoon salt
- 1 serrano chile, minced, including the seeds
- 1 tablespoon finely grated tangerine zest
- 2 tablespoons minced fresh ginger
- 3 cloves garlic, minced
- 4 tangerines, peeled, segments separated and chopped

Directions:

1. Mix the tangerine zest and segments, onion, cilantro, chile, garlic, ginger, lime juice, brown sugar, and salt in a medium container.
2. This can be made one day in advance and placed in the fridge in an airtight container. Allow to reach room temperature before you serve.

The Ultimate Mojo De Ajo Sauce

Mojo de ajo (garlic sauce) is enjoyed with seafood all over Mexico.

Yield: About 3/4 cup. Nutrition information is for 1 tablespoon.

Ingredients:

- 1½ tablespoons dried cilantro
- 3 chiles de árbol, seeded and coarsely chopped, or substitute a finely chopped canned chipotle chile
- 4 sun-dried tomatoes (not packed in oil), very finely chopped
- 1/2 cup extra-virgin olive oil
- 1/2 tablespoon freshly squeezed lime juice

- 1/2 teaspoon salt
- 1/4 cup minced white onion
- 1/4 heaping teaspoon freshly ground black pepper
- 1/4 cup garlic chopped into 1/8-inch or slightly larger pieces

Directions:

1. Make the sauce. Put the chiles, tomatoes, garlic, onion, salt, oil, and pepper in a small deep cooking pan on moderate to low heat and cook until the oil just starts to bubble. Keep adjusting the heat so that the mixture cooks at the barest simmer, with just a few bubbles.
2. Cook until the garlic is very tender and just starting to brown, about forty minutes, stirring every five minutes or so. Put in the cilantro and lime juice and simmer an additional ten minutes, or until the garlic just starts to take on a golden hue.

Watermelon Relish

A refreshing, crunchy, and spicy relish!

Yield: 3 Cups

Ingredients:

- ¼ cup freshly squeezed lime juice
- ¼ cup lightly packed light brown sugar
- ½ serrano chile, minced, including the seeds
- ½ teaspoon salt
- 2 tablespoons chopped fresh cilantro, leaves and tender stems
- 2 tablespoons chopped fresh mint leaves
- 2 tablespoons minced fresh ginger
- 3 pounds seedless red watermelon

Directions:

1. Remove all the rind from the melon and chop the melon into ½-inch cubes. You should have about 6 cups. Put 4 cups of the watermelon in a blender. Put in the ginger, chile, lime juice, brown sugar, and salt. liquefied. Move to a big deep cooking pan. Bring to a

rapid boil on moderate to high heat and boil until reduced to 1 cup. Move to a container and let cool to room temperature.

2. Mix in the rest of the 2 cups chopped watermelon, the cilantro, and mint. This can be made 2 days ahead and placed in the fridge in an airtight container. Serve at room temperature.

Yucatán-Style Tomato Salsa

A tomato salsa spiced up with habanero chiles!

Yield: About 1-1/4 cups

Ingredients:

- 1 habanero chile, cut in half
- 1 pound (about 2 medium-sized) tomatoes
- 1/2 cup chopped white onion
- 1/8 heaping teaspoon salt
- 1½ tablespoons extra-virgin olive oil
- 2½ cups water

Directions:

1. Bring the water to its boiling point and put in the tomatoes and chiles. Simmer for about four minutes, or until the tomatoes are starting to become tender. Take the tomatoes and chiles from the pan; let the tomatoes cool down a little then remove and discard their skins and put the tomatoes in a food processor with the steel blade. Reserve the cooking liquid for a future cook. Reserve the chiles separately.
2. Cook the onions and purée the sauce. Heat a frying pan on moderate heat, put in 1/2 tablespoon of the oil and the onions, and sauté, stirring regularly, until the onions barely start to turn golden. Put the onions in the food processor with the tomatoes and process for a minute. Put the sauce through a strainer or food mill to remove the seeds.
3. Cook the tomato sauce. Heat a small deep cooking pan on moderate heat, put in the rest of the tablespoon oil, the sauce, and the salt. If you think the sauce needs more heat, put in back the habanero halves. Bring the sauce to its boiling point and simmer until it is thick enoigh to hold its shape, about three minutes. If you used the chiles, remove and discard them.

Three Zigzag Sauces

Here are three amazing Mexican sauces that are more versatile than a swiss knife. These are commonly used to garnish dishes, topping them in a zig-zag manner. What you do with these is completely up to you!

Chipotle Chile Zigzag Sauce

Yield: ¾ Cup

Ingredients:

- ¼ teaspoon salt
- ½ cup crema, mayonnaise, or sour cream
- 1 chipotle chile in adobo sauce, minced
- 1 clove garlic, minced
- 1 tablespoon freshly squeezed lime juice
- 2 teaspoons finely grated lime zest

Directions:

1. Mix all of the ingredients together in a small container or an electric mini-chop.
2. Store in your fridge in an airtight container and use within one week.

Cilantro Zigzag Sauce

Yield: ¾ Cup

Ingredients:

- ¼ teaspoon salt
- ½ cup crema, mayonnaise, or sour cream
- ½ cup fresh cilantro, leaves and tender stems
- 1 tablespoon freshly squeezed lime juice
- 1 tablespoon thoroughly minced fresh ginger

Directions:

1. Mix all of the ingredients together in a small container or an electric mini-chop.
2. Store in your fridge in an airtight container and use within one week.

Orange-Ginger Zigzag Sauce

Yield: 1 Cup

Ingredients:

- ½ cup crema, mayonnaise, or sour cream
- ½ serrano chile, minced, including the seeds
- ½ teaspoon finely grated orange zest
- ½ teaspoon salt
- 1 clove garlic, minced
- 1 tablespoon freshly squeezed lime juice
- 1 tablespoon Grand Marnier
- 2 tablespoons chopped fresh mint leaves or cilantro leaves and tender stems
- 2 tablespoons minced fresh ginger
- 2 teaspoons Worcestershire sauce

Directions:

1. Mix all of the ingredients together in a small container or an electric mini-chop.
2. Store in your fridge in an airtight container and use within one week.

OTHER MEXICAN SEASONINGS

All-Purpose Marinade for Chicken, Pork, and Seafood

Rub this all over your meat before you cook, and enjoy the ultimate Mexican flavour!

Yield: ½ Cup

Ingredients:

- ¼ cup extra-virgin olive oil
- ½ teaspoon salt

- 1 tablespoon freshly ground black pepper
- 1 teaspoon ground cinnamon, preferably Mexican
- 1 teaspoon ground coriander or cumin
- 2 teaspoons finely grated lime zest
- 2 teaspoons finely grated orange zest

Directions:

1. Mix the pepper, zests, coriander, cinnamon, and salt in a small container.
2. Rub the spice blend over the surface of the meat or seafood.
3. Next, rub the olive oil over the entire surface as well.
4. Proceed with grilling or roasting, as desired.

Refried Beans

These are a Mexican staple that can be used to give texture and flavour to main course meals.

Yield: 2 Cups

Ingredients:

- ½ teaspoon salt
- 1 cup dried black beans
- 1 medium yellow onion, diced
- 2 cloves garlic, minced
- 3 tablespoons lard

Directions:

1. Spread the beans on a plate and pick through the beans to remove any pebbles. Rinse the beans, then cover with cold water and soak overnight.
2. Drain the beans and put in to a deep cooking pan. Put in 4 cups hot water to the soaked beans. Simmer on moderate heat until tender, approximately 1½ hours. Remove and reserve 2 cups of the cooking water. If you don't like this method, follow the quick-cooking directions on the bean package.
3. In a big frying pan, melt the lard on moderate heat. Put in the onion and cook until the onion becomes golden, approximately ten minutes. Put in the garlic and cook for 1 more minute. Put in the salt and beans. Mash the beans using a fork, adding just sufficient of

the reserved cooking water to make the beans smooth. If you don't like this method, put in a food processor and process until the desired smoothness is achieved. The beans can be made up to four days in advance. Let cool and then place in your fridge in an airtight container.

DRY RUBS

These dry rubs are great on any meat that can be grilled or oven-roasted. Each rub makes about 6 tablespoons, sufficient to season 8 of your favorite steaks, or 8 chicken breasts, or 3 pounds of fish. Just rub the dry rub into the surface of the meat or seafood, then rub the meat with extra-virgin olive oil. As another option, after rubbing the meat with the dry rub, we like to rub the meat with Chinese mushroom soy sauce or Chinese dark soy sauce. This is not authentic Mexican, but it is delicious! Remember, the rub has to be massaged with vigor into the meat fibers. Then when you brush the meat with a marinade or olive oil before cooking, the rub will not dislodge from the meat during grilling.

ANCHO DRY RUB

Yield: Approximately 6 TABLESPOONS

Ingredients:

- ¼ cup lightly packed light brown sugar
- 1 (2-inch) cinnamon stick, preferably Mexican
- 1 tablespoon ancho or chipotle chile powder
- 1 tablespoon coriander seeds

Directions:

1. Put all of the ingredients in a clean electric coffee grinder or spice grinder. Grind into a fine powder.
2. Move to an empty glass spice jar, label, and store in your spice rack for maximum half a year.

CARAWAY DRY RUB

Yield: Approximately 6 TABLESPOONS

Ingredients:

- 1 (1-inch) cinnamon stick, preferably Mexican
- 1 tablespoon caraway seeds
- 1 tablespoon coriander seeds
- 1 tablespoon crushed red pepper
- 1 tablespoon cumin seeds
- 1 tablespoon salt
- 1 teaspoon whole cloves

Directions:

1. Put all of the ingredients in a clean electric coffee grinder or spice grinder. Grind into a fine powder.
2. Move to an empty glass spice jar, label, and store in your spice rack for maximum half a year.

ESPRESSO DRY RUB

Yield: Approximately 6 TABLESPOONS

Ingredients:

- 1 tablespoon coriander seeds
- 1 tablespoon crushed red pepper
- 1 tablespoon curry powder
- 1 tablespoon espresso powder
- 1 tablespoon rainbow peppercorn mix
- 1 tablespoon salt

Directions:

1. Put all of the ingredients in a clean electric coffee grinder or spice grinder. Grind into a fine powder.
2. Move to an empty glass spice jar, label, and store in your spice rack for maximum half a year.

Tortillas and tortilla dishes

Tortilla is easily one of the most versatile breads that exist on this planet. These are eaten all over the world, and are called by different names depending on the regions. Indians, for example, call it a "Roti" or a chapatti.

It is popular all over the world because of how easy and inexpensive it is to make. All you really need is flour, water, and griddle or another surface to cook it on.

Use the recipes in this section as a base, and feel free to experiment and invent your own recipes once you get a hang of it. Only then, will you truly master the tortilla.

FLOUR TORTILLAS

Yield: 12 (8 inch) tortillas

The best tortillas are those made at home. Considering how easy and inexpensive these are to make once you get a hang of it, there really is no reason to buy these at a store. Allowing the dough to rest in the refrigerator for a while will make it easier to work with, else it might be a little sticky.

Ingredients:

- ¾ cup plus 2 tablespoons water, heated to 110 degrees
- 1 teaspoon vegetable oil
- 1½ teaspoons salt
- 2¾ cups (13¾ ounces) all purpose flour
- 6 tablespoons vegetable shortening, cut into 6 pieces

Directions:

1. Mix flour and salt in big container. Use your hands to rub shortening into flour until mixture looks like coarse meal. Mix in water with wooden spoon until blended and dough forms. Turn dough out onto counter and knead for a short period of time to make smooth, consistent ball. Split dough into 12 pieces (2½ tablespoons each), roll into balls, and move to plate. Cover using plastic wrap and place in your fridge until dough is firm, minimum 30 minutes or maximum 3 days.

2. Working with 1 piece dough at a time and two 12 inch squares greased parchment paper, roll dough into 8 inch tortilla using a rolling pin. Take off the top piece of the parchment and softly reshape edges as required.

3. Heat oil in 12 inch nonstick frying pan over moderate high heat until it starts to shimmer Use a paper towel to wipe out frying pan, leaving thin film of oil on bottom. Flip tortilla onto your palm, take off parchment on bottom, and lay tortilla in frying pan. Cook tortilla until surface starts to bubble and it moves freely when pan is shaken, approximately one minute.

4. Turn the tortilla over and cook until puffed and bottom is spotty brown, approximately one minute. Move to plate and cover using a dish towel. Repeat with the rest of the tortillas and serve. (Tortillas can be layered between clean parchment paper, wrapped using plastic wrap, and placed in the fridge for maximum 3 days.)

CORN TORTILLAS

Mix the corn flour with warm water, in accordance with the directions on the package. Different brands recommend different proportions. Mix and allow the mixture to sit for approximately 5 minutes. For the rest, follow the directions for four tortillas.

BURRITOS, CHIMICHANGAS, AND QUESADILLAS

Flour tortillas filled and rolled up become burritos. They can be filled with whatever you want! We will give you a few suggestions for the fillings in this section, but don't be limited to these. Play around and experiment with your favourite ingredients!

ANCHO ORANGE PORK BURRITOS

Yield: Servings 8

Ingredients:

- ¼ cup minced fresh cilantro
- ½ cup distilled white vinegar
- ¾ cup orange juice (2 oranges)
- 1½ cups long grain white rice, washed
- 2 bay leaves
- 2 cups water
- 2 scallions, cut thin
- 2 tablespoon minced canned chipotle chile in adobo sauce
- 2 tablespoons tomato paste
- 2 teaspoons dried oregano
- 2 teaspoons ground cumin
- 4 dried ancho chiles, stemmed, seeded, and torn into ½ inch pieces (1 cup)
- 4 pounds boneless pork butt roast, trimmed and slice into 2 inch pieces
- 5 garlic cloves, lightly crushed and peeled
- 8 (10 inch) flour tortillas
- Salt and pepper

Directions:

1. Adjust oven rack to lower middle position and heat oven to 300 degrees. Whisk orange juice, vinegar, anchos, tomato paste, chipotle, garlic, bay leaves, cumin, oregano and 1 teaspoon salt together in Dutch oven. Sprinkle the pork with salt and pepper, mix into

pot, and position in single layer. Cover and cook in oven until pork is super soft, approximately 2 hours.

2. Move pork to big container using slotted spoon and allow to cool slightly. Use two forks to shred pork into bite size pieces. Strain braising liquid into fat separator, saving for later solids, and let settle for five minutes. Discard bay leaves and move solids to blender. Put in 1½ cups defatted liquid to blender and pulse until smooth, approximately one minute. Mix sauce and pork in now empty Dutch oven; before making burritos, reheat mixture on moderate heat until hot. (Pork can placed in the fridge for maximum three days or frozen for maximum 1 month.)

3. In the meantime, bring water, rice, and 1 teaspoon salt to boil in medium deep cooking pan over moderate high heat. Cover, decrease the heat to low, and cook until rice is soft and water is absorbed, approximately twenty minutes. Take the rice off the heat and allow it to sit, covered, for about ten minutes. Put in cilantro and scallions and fluff with fork to blend; cover to keep warm.

4. Cover tortillas in damp dish towel and microwave until warm and flexible, approximately one minute. Place warm tortillas on counter. Mound warm rice and pork across center of tortillas, close to bottom edge. Working with one tortilla at a time, fold sides then bottom of tortilla over filling, pulling back on it tightly to tighten it around filling, then carry on rolling firmly into burrito and serve.

BAKED BEEF AND BEAN BURRITOS

Yield: Servings 6

Ingredients:

- ¼ cup minced fresh cilantro
- ¾ cup long grain white rice, washed
- 1 (fifteen ounce) can pinto beans, washed
- 1 onion, chopped fine
- 1 tablespoon ground cumin
- 1 tablespoon lime juice
- 1 tablespoon vegetable oil
- 1 teaspoon chipotle chile powder
- 1 teaspoon dried oregano

- 10 ounces sharp cheddar cheese, shredded (2½ cups)
- 1¾ cups chicken broth
- 12 ounces 90 percent lean ground beef
- 3 garlic cloves, minced
- 3 tablespoons tomato paste
- 6 (10 inch) flour tortillas
- 6 tablespoons sour cream
- Salt

Directions:

1. Bring 1¼ cups broth, rice, garlic, and ½ teaspoon salt to boil in small deep cooking pan over moderate high heat. Cover, decrease the heat to low, and cook until rice is soft and broth is absorbed, approximately twenty minutes. Take the rice off the heat and allow it to sit, covered, for about ten minutes. Put in cilantro and fluff with fork to blend; cover to keep warm.

2. In the meantime, heat oil in 12 inch nonstick frying pan on moderate heat until it starts to shimmer Put in onion and cook until tender, approximately five minutes. Mix in tomato paste, garlic, cumin, oregano, and chile powder and cook until aromatic, approximately one minute. Put in beef, breaking up pieces with wooden spoon, and cook until no longer pink, about eight to ten minutes.

3. Using potato masher, crudely purée half of beans with remaining ½ cup broth in container, then mix into frying pan. Cook while stirring continuously, until nearly all liquid has vaporized, approximately 3 minutes. Remove the heat, mix in remaining whole beans, lime juice, and ¾ teaspoon salt; cover to keep warm.

4. Adjust oven rack 6 inches from broiler element and heat broiler. Coat baking sheet with aluminium foil. Cover tortillas in damp dish towel and microwave until warm and flexible, approximately one minute. Place warm tortillas on counter. Mound warm rice, beef mixture, and 1½ cups cheddar across center of tortillas, close to bottom edge, then top with sour cream. Working with one tortilla at a time, fold sides then bottom of tortilla over filling, pulling back on it tightly to tighten it around filling, then carry on rolling firmly into burrito.

5. Put burritos, seam side down, on readied sheet and drizzle remaining 1 cup cheddar over top. Broil until cheese is melted and beginning to brown, three to five minutes and serve.

CHICKEN BURRITOS MOJADOS

Yield: Servings 6

Ingredients:

- ½ cup Mexican crema
- ¾ cup long grain white rice, washed
- 1 (fifteen ounce) can pinto beans, washed
- 1½ cups tomatillo salsa Water, as required
- 1½ pounds boneless, skinless chicken breasts, trimmed
- 2 (8 ounce) cans tomato sauce
- 2 avocados, halved, pitted, and slice into ½ inch pieces
- 2 scallions, cut thin
- 2 tablespoons vegetable oil
- 2¼ cups chicken broth
- 3 garlic cloves, minced
- 3½ tablespoons chili powder
- 6 (10 inch) flour tortillas
- 6 tablespoons minced fresh cilantro
- 8 ounces Monterey Jack cheese, shredded (2 cups)
- Salt and pepper

Directions:

1. Bring 1¼ cups broth, rice, beans, 1½ teaspoons chili powder, and ½ teaspoon salt to boil in medium deep cooking pan oven over moderate high heat. Cover, decrease the heat to low, and cook until rice is soft and broth is absorbed, approximately twenty minutes. Take the rice off the heat and allow it to sit, covered, for about ten minutes. Put in scallions and fluff with fork to blend; cover to keep warm.
2. In the meantime, cook oil, garlic, and remaining 3 tablespoons chili powder in big deep cooking pan over moderate high heat until aromatic, one to two minutes. Mix in tomato sauce and remaining 1 cup broth and bring to simmer. Nestle chicken into sauce. Cover, decrease the heat to moderate low, and cook until chicken records 160 degrees, ten to fifteen minutes, turning midway through cooking.

3. Move chicken to cutting board and allow to cool slightly. Use two forks to shred chicken into bite size pieces. Toss chicken with ¼ cup sauce and 2 tablespoons cilantro in container. Set rest of the sauce aside.

4. Adjust oven rack to middle position and heat oven to 450 degrees. Coat baking sheet with aluminium foil. Cover tortillas in damp dish towel and microwave until warm and flexible, approximately one minute. Place warm tortillas on counter. Mound rice in center of tortillas, close to bottom edge, then top with chicken, avocado, and Monterey Jack. Working with one tortilla at a time, fold sides then bottom of tortilla over filling, pulling back on it tightly to tighten it around filling, then carry on rolling firmly into burrito. (Burritos can be held at room temperature for maximum 1 hour before you bake.) Put burritos seam side down on readied sheet, cover firmly using foil, and bake until hot throughout, twenty minutes to half an hour.

5. Before you serve, whisk salsa and 2 tablespoons cilantro together in container, cover, and microwave until hot, approximately one minute. Reheat red sauce in deep cooking pan on moderate heat until hot, approximately 3 minutes, putting in water as required to loosen consistency

6. Position burritos on separate plates. Pour tomatillo sauce over half of each burrito and pour red sauce over other half of burrito. Sprinkle with crema, drizzle with remaining 2 tablespoons cilantro, before you serve.

CHICKEN CHIMICHANGAS

Yield: Servings 4

Ingredients:

- ½ cup long grain white rice, washed
- ½ teaspoon ground cumin
- 1 (fifteen ounce) can pinto beans, washed
- 1 cup chicken broth
- 1 cup plus 2 tablespoons water
- 1 onion, chopped fine
- 1 pound boneless, skinless chicken breasts, trimmed
- 1 scallion, cut thin
- 1 tablespoon minced canned chipotle chile in adobo sauce

- 1 tablespoon plus 3 cups vegetable oil
- 2 garlic cloves, minced
- 2 tablespoons all purpose flour
- 2 tablespoons ancho chile powder
- 2 tablespoons minced fresh cilantro
- 4 (10 inch) flour tortillas
- 4 ounces sharp cheddar cheese, shredded (1 cup)
- Salt and pepper

Directions:

1. Bring 1 cup water, rice, and ¼ teaspoon salt to boil in small deep cooking pan over moderate high heat. Decrease the heat to low, cover, and cook until rice is soft and water is absorbed, approximately twenty minutes. Take the rice off the heat and allow it to sit, covered, for about ten minutes. Put in cilantro and scallion and fluff with fork to blend; cover to keep warm.

2. In the meantime, heat 1 tablespoon oil in 12 inch nonstick frying pan on moderate heat until it starts to shimmer Put in onion and cook until tender, approximately five minutes. Mix in chile powder, chipotle, garlic, and cumin and cook until aromatic, approximately one minute. Mix in broth and bring to simmer. Nestle chicken into sauce. Cover, decrease the heat to moderate low, and cook until chicken records 160 degrees, ten to fifteen minutes, turning midway through cooking.

3. Move chicken to cutting board, allow to cool slightly, then cut crosswise into super slim pieces. Continue to simmer sauce until it becomes thick and measures ½ cup, approximately ten minutes; turn off the heat. Coarsely purée half of beans in container using potato masher, then put in to sauce with the rest of the beans and cut chicken.

4. Whisk flour and remaining 2 tablespoons water together in container. Cover tortillas in damp dish towel and microwave until warm and flexible, approximately one minute. Place warm tortillas on counter. Mound rice, chicken bean mixture, and cheddar across center of tortillas. Working with one tortilla at a time, brush edges of tortilla with flour paste, then wrap top and bottom of tortilla firmly over filling and press tightly to secure. Brush ends of tortilla meticulously with paste, fold into center, and press tightly to secure.

5. Adjust oven rack to middle position and heat oven to 200 degrees. Coat plate with multiple layers of paper towels. Set wire rack in rimmed baking sheet. Heat remaining 3 cups oil in Dutch oven over moderate high heat to 325 degrees. Put 2 chimichangas,

seam side down, in oil. Fry, turning as required, until thoroughly browned on both sides, approximately 4 minutes, adjusting burner as required to maintain oil temperature between 300 and 325 degrees. Allow to drain for a short period of time using paper towels, then move to wire rack and keep warm in oven while frying remaining 2 chimichangas and serve.

CHICKEN QUESADILLAS

Yield: Servings 4

Ingredients:

- ¼ cup minced fresh cilantro
- ½ cup jarred roasted red peppers, patted dry and chopped
- 1 pound boneless, skinless chicken breasts, trimmed
- 1 teaspoon ground cumin
- 1 teaspoon hot sauce
- 2 garlic cloves, minced
- 3 scallions, white and green parts separated, cut thin
- 3 tablespoons plus 1 teaspoon vegetable oil
- 4 (10 inch) flour tortillas
- 8 ounces Monterey Jack cheese, shredded (2 cups)
- Salt and pepper

Directions:

1. Adjust oven rack to middle position and heat oven to 450 degrees. Coat rimmed baking sheet with aluminium foil and brush with 1 tablespoon oil.
2. Pat chicken dry using paper towels and sprinkle with salt and pepper. Heat 1 tablespoon oil in 12 inch nonstick frying pan over moderate high heat until just smoking. Lightly lay chicken in frying pan and cook, turning as required, until lightly golden on both sides and records 160 degrees, approximately twelve minutes. Move chicken to cutting board and allow to cool slightly. Use two forks to shred into bite size pieces.
3. Put in 1 teaspoon oil, scallion whites, garlic, cumin, and ¼ teaspoon salt to now empty frying pan and cook on moderate heat until tender, approximately 2 minutes. Move to

moderate container, put in shredded chicken, peppers, cilantro, scallion greens, hot sauce, and cheese, and toss to blend.

4. Place tortillas on counter. Spread chicken filling over half of each tortilla, leaving ½ inch border around edge. Fold other half of tortilla over top and press tightly to compact. Position quesadillas in single layer on readied sheet with rounded edges facing center of sheet. Brush with remaining 1 tablespoon oil.

5. Bake until quesadillas start to brown, approximately ten minutes. Flip quesadillas over and push softly with spatula to compact. Carry on baking until crunchy and golden brown on second side, approximately five minutes. Allow quesadillas to cool on wire rack for five minutes, then slice each into 4 wedges before you serve.

CHORIZO AND BLACK BEAN CHIMICHANGAS

Yield: Servings 4

Ingredients:

- ½ cup long grain white rice, washed
- ½ teaspoon ground cumin
- 1 (fifteen ounce) can black beans, washed
- 1 onion, chopped fine
- 1 scallion, cut thin
- 1 tablespoon minced canned chipotle chile in adobo sauce
- 1 tablespoon plus 3 cups vegetable oil
- 1 teaspoon chili powder
- 1½ cups plus 2 tablespoons water
- 12 ounces Mexican style chorizo sausage, casings removed
- 2 garlic cloves, minced
- 2 tablespoons all purpose flour
- 2 tablespoons minced fresh cilantro
- 4 (10 inch) flour tortillas
- 4 ounces sharp cheddar cheese, shredded (1 cup)
- Salt

Directions:

1. Bring 1 cup water, rice, and ½ teaspoon salt to boil in small deep cooking pan over moderate high heat. Decrease the heat to low, cover, and cook until rice is soft and water is absorbed, approximately twenty minutes. Take the rice off the heat and allow it to sit, covered, for about ten minutes. Put in cilantro and scallion and fluff with fork to blend; cover to keep warm.

2. In the meantime, heat 1 tablespoon oil in 12 inch nonstick frying pan oven on moderate heat until it starts to shimmer Put in onion and cook until tender, approximately five minutes. Mix in chipotle, garlic, chili powder, and cumin and cook until aromatic, approximately half a minute. Put in chorizo and cook, breaking up pieces with wooden spoon, until no longer pink, approximately five minutes. Coarsely purée half of beans with ½ cup water in container using potato masher, then put in to frying pan with the rest of the beans. Simmer until beans are warmed through, approximately five minutes; turn off the heat.

3. Whisk flour and remaining 2 tablespoons water together in container. Cover tortillas in damp dish towel and microwave until warm and flexible, approximately one minute. Place warm tortillas on counter. Mound rice, chorizo bean mixture, and cheddar across center of tortillas. Working with one tortilla at a time, brush edges of tortilla with flour paste, then wrap top and bottom of tortilla firmly over filling and press tightly to secure. Brush ends of tortilla meticulously with paste, fold into center, and press tightly to secure.

4. Adjust oven rack to middle position and heat oven to 200 degrees. Coat plate with multiple layers of paper towels. Set wire rack in rimmed baking sheet. Heat remaining 3 cups oil in Dutch oven over moderate high heat to 325 degrees. Put 2 chimichangas, seam side down, in oil. Fry, turning as required, until thoroughly browned on both sides, approximately 4 minutes, adjusting burner as required to maintain oil temperature between 300 and 325 degrees. Allow to drain for a short period of time using paper towels, then move to wire rack and keep warm in oven while frying remaining 2 chimichangas and serve.

MUSHROOM AND SWISS CHARD QUESADILLAS

Yield: Servings 4

Ingredients:

- ¼ cup vegetable oil
- ¼ teaspoon red pepper flakes
- 1 onion, chopped fine
- 1 pound Swiss chard, stemmed, leaves cut into ½ inch wide strips
- 1 pound white mushrooms, trimmed and cut thin
- 1 teaspoon cider vinegar
- 2 garlic cloves, minced
- 2 tablespoons minced fresh cilantro
- 2 teaspoons ground coriander
- 4 (10 inch) flour tortillas
- 8 ounces Monterey Jack cheese, shredded (2 cups)
- Salt and pepper

Directions:

1. Adjust oven rack to middle position and heat oven to 450 degrees. Coat rimmed baking sheet with aluminium foil and brush with 1 tablespoon oil.
2. Heat 2 tablespoons oil in 12 inch nonstick frying pan over moderate high heat until it starts to shimmer Put in onion and mushrooms and sprinkle with salt and pepper. Cover and cook, stirring once in a while, until mushrooms have released their moisture, about eight to ten minutes. Remove the cover and cook, stirring once in a while, until liquid has vaporized and mushrooms are thoroughly browned, about eight to ten minutes.
3. Mix in garlic, coriander, and pepper flakes and cook until aromatic, approximately half a minute. Put in chard, cover, and cook until wilted but still bright green, one to two minutes. Remove the cover and cook, stirring frequently, until liquid evaporates, four to six minutes. Remove the heat, mix in vinegar. Allow the mixture to cool slightly, then mix in Monterey Jack and cilantro.
4. Place tortillas on counter. Spread vegetable filling over half of each tortilla, leaving ½ inch border around edge. Fold other half of tortilla over top and press tightly to compact. Position quesadillas in single layer on readied sheet with rounded edges facing center of sheet. Brush with remaining 1 tablespoon oil.
5. Bake until quesadillas start to brown, approximately ten minutes. Flip quesadillas over and push softly with spatula to compact. Carry on baking until crunchy and golden brown on second side, approximately five minutes. Allow quesadillas to cool on wire rack for five minutes, then slice each into 4 wedges before you serve.

SPICY CHICKEN FLAUTAS

Yield: 4-6 Servings

Ingredients:

- ⅛ teaspoon cayenne pepper
- ¼ teaspoon dried oregano
- 1 (8 ounce) can tomato sauce
- 1 onion, chopped fine
- 1 recipe Avocado Sauce (recipe follows)
- 1 tablespoon chili powder
- 1 tablespoon plus 1 cup vegetable oil
- 12 (8 inch) flour tortillas
- 2 garlic cloves, minced
- 2 jalapeño chiles, stemmed, seeded, and minced
- 2 pounds boneless, skinless chicken breasts, trimmed
- 2 tablespoons all purpose flour
- 2 tablespoons lime juice
- 2 tablespoons minced fresh cilantro
- 2 tablespoons water
- Salt and pepper

Directions:

1. Heat 1 tablespoon oil in 12 inch nonstick frying pan on moderate heat until it starts to shimmer Put in onion and cook until tender, approximately five minutes. Mix in jalapeños, chili powder, garlic, oregano, and cayenne and cook until aromatic, approximately half a minute. Mix in tomato sauce and bring to simmer.

2. Sprinkle the chicken with salt and pepper and nestle into sauce. Cover, decrease the heat to moderate low, and cook until chicken records 160 degrees, ten to fifteen minutes, turning midway through cooking. Move chicken to cutting board and allow to cool slightly. Use two forks to shred chicken fine. Stir shredded chicken, cilantro, and lime juice into sauce.

3. Coat rimmed baking sheet using parchment paper. Whisk flour and water together in container. Cut off bottom third of each tortilla (discard or reserve for future use). Cover

tortillas in damp dish towel and microwave until warm and flexible, approximately one minute.

4. Place six warm tortillas on counter with trimmed edge facing you. Mound half of chicken filling alongside trimmed edges. Roll trimmed edge of one tortilla up over filling, then pull back on tortilla to tighten it around filling. Working with one tortilla at a time, brush remaining uncovered tortilla with flour paste, then roll it up firmly around filling. Push on edges tightly to secure; move to readied baking sheet. Repeat with the rest of the six tortillas and rest of the filling. (Flautas can be covered with damp towel, wrapped firmly using plastic wrap, and placed in the fridge for maximum one day.)

5. Adjust oven rack to middle position and heat oven to 200 degrees. Coat plate with multiple layers of paper towels. Set wire rack in second rimmed baking sheet. Heat remaining 1 cup oil in clean 12 inch nonstick frying pan over moderate high heat until 325 degrees. Put 6 flautas, seam side down, in oil. Fry, turning as required, until a golden-brown colour is achieved on all sides, three to five minutes, adjusting burner as required to maintain oil temperature between 300 and 325 degrees. Allow to drain for a short period of time using paper towels, then move to wire rack and keep warm in oven while frying remaining 6 flautas. Serve with Avocado Sauce.

AVOCADO SAUCE

Yield: 2½ CUPS

Make sure you use very ripe avocados when making this sauce.

Ingredients:

- ¼ cup water
- ½ cup sour cream
- 2 avocados, halved, pitted, and chopped coarse
- 2 tablespoons minced fresh cilantro
- 3 tablespoons lime juice (2 limes)
- Salt and pepper

Directions:

Mash all ingredients together in container with potato masher (or fork) until the desired smoothness is achieved. Sprinkle with salt and pepper to taste and serve.

SWISS CHARD AND PINTO BEAN BURRITOS

Yield: Servings 6

Ingredients:

- ¼ cup minced fresh cilantro
- ¾ cup long grain white rice, washed
- 1 (fifteen ounce) can pinto beans, washed
- 1 onion, chopped fine
- 1 pound Swiss chard, stemmed, leaves cut into an inch wide strips
- 1 tablespoon ground cumin
- 1 tablespoon lime juice
- 1 tablespoon vegetable oil
- 1 teaspoon dried oregano
- 1 teaspoon minced canned chipotle chile in adobo sauce
- 10 ounces Monterey jack, shredded (2½ cups)
- 2¼ cups vegetable broth
- 3 tablespoons tomato paste
- 6 (10 inch) flour tortillas
- 6 garlic cloves, minced
- Salt

Directions:

1. Bring 1¼ cups broth, rice, half of garlic, and ½ teaspoon salt to boil in small deep cooking pan over moderate high heat. Cover, decrease the heat to low, and cook until rice is soft and broth is absorbed, approximately twenty minutes. Take the rice off the heat and allow it to sit, covered, for about ten minutes. Put in cilantro and fluff with fork to blend; cover to keep warm.

2. In the meantime, heat oil in Dutch oven on moderate heat until it starts to shimmer Put in onion and cook until just starting to brown, approximately five minutes. Mix in tomato paste, chipotle, cumin, oregano, remaining garlic, and ½ teaspoon salt and cook until aromatic, approximately one minute. Put in chard and ½ cup broth, cover, and simmer until chard is soft, approximately fifteen minutes.

3. Using potato masher, crudely purée half of beans with remaining ½ cup broth in container, then mix into pot. Cook while stirring continuously, until liquid is nearly vaporized, approximately 3 minutes. Remove the heat, mix in lime juice and remaining whole beans; cover to keep warm.

4. Adjust oven rack 6 inches from broiler element and heat broiler. Coat baking sheet with aluminium foil. Cover tortillas in damp dish towel and microwave until warm and flexible, approximately one minute. Place warm tortillas on counter. Mound warm rice, chard bean mixture, and 1½ cups Monterey Jack across center of tortillas, close to bottom edge. Working with one tortilla at a time, fold sides then bottom of tortilla over filling, pulling back on it tightly to tighten it around filling, then carry on rolling firmly into burrito.

5. Put burritos, seam side down, on readied sheet and drizzle remaining 1 cup Monterey Jack over top. Broil until cheese is melted and beginning to brown, three to five minutes and serve.

TEQUILA LIME SHRIMP QUESADILLAS

Yield: Servings 4

Ingredients:

- ¼ cup minced fresh cilantro
- ⅓ cup tequila
- 1 teaspoon grated lime zest
- 1 teaspoon minced canned chipotle chile in adobo sauce
- 1½ pounds medium big shrimp (31 to 40 per pound), peeled, deveined, tails removed, and halved along the length
- 12 ounces Monterey Jack cheese, shredded (3 cups)
- 2 garlic cloves, minced
- 2 scallions, white and green parts separated, cut thin
- 3 tablespoons vegetable oil
- 4 (10 inch) flour tortillas
- Salt and pepper

Directions:

1. Adjust oven rack to middle position and heat oven to 450 degrees. Coat rimmed baking sheet with aluminium foil and brush with 1 tablespoon oil. Toss Monterey Jack with cilantro and scallion greens.

2. Pat dry shrimp using paper towels and sprinkle with salt and pepper. Heat 1 tablespoon oil in 12 inch nonstick frying pan on moderate heat until it starts to shimmer Put in scallion whites, garlic, chipotle, and ¼ teaspoon salt and cook until tender, approximately 2 minutes. Put in tequila amd simmer until tequila has vaporized and pan is dry, approximately five minutes.

3. Put in shrimp and cook, stirring frequently, until thoroughly cooked and opaque throughout, approximately 3 minutes. Move to container, mix in zest, and allow to cool for five minutes; drain thoroughly.

4. Place tortillas on counter. Drizzle half of cheese mixture over half of each tortilla, leaving ½ inch border around edge. Position shrimp on top in single layer, then drizzle with rest of the cheese mixture. Fold other half of each tortilla over top and press tightly to compact.

5. Position quesadillas in single layer on readied sheet with rounded edges facing center of sheet. Brush with remaining 1 tablespoon oil. Bake until quesadillas start to brown, approximately ten minutes. Flip quesadillas over and push softly with spatula to compact. Carry on baking until crunchy and golden brown on second side, approximately five minutes. Allow quesadillas to cool on wire rack for five minutes, then slice each into 4 wedges before you serve.

ENCHILADAS AND CASSEROLES

BEEF ENCHILADA CASSEROLE

Yield: Servings 8 to 10

Ingredients:

- ½ cup chopped fresh cilantro
- 1 (10 ounce) can Ro Tel tomatoes
- 1 pound Colby Jack cheese, shredded (4 cups)
- 1 tablespoon hot sauce
- 1 teaspoon ground cumin

- 1½ cups beef broth
- 2 onions, chopped fine
- 2 pounds 85 percent lean ground beef
- 2 tablespoons chili powder
- 2 tablespoons vegetable oil
- 20 (6 inch) corn tortillas
- 3 (fifteen ounce) cans tomato sauce
- 3 jalapeño chiles, stemmed, seeded, and minced
- 8 garlic cloves, minced
- Salt and pepper

Directions:

1. Adjust oven rack to middle position and heat oven to 450 degrees. Toast tortillas, one by one, in 12 inch nonstick frying pan over moderate high heat until mildly browned, approximately twenty seconds per side; move to plate and cover using a dish towel.
2. Tear 8 toasted tortillas into rough pieces and move to food processor. Put in tomatoes and their juice and ¾ cup broth and pulse until smooth; move to big container. Put in beef to now empty frying pan and cook over moderate high heat, breaking up meat with wooden spoon, until no longer pink, approximately five minutes. Drain beef in colander, then mix into processed tortilla mixture.
3. Put in oil and onions to now empty frying pan and cook on moderate heat until tender, approximately five minutes. Mix in garlic, chili powder, and cumin and cook until aromatic, approximately half a minute. Mix in tomato sauce and remaining ¾ cup broth and simmer until slightly thickened, five to seven minutes; move to container.
4. Stir half of tomato sauce mixture, 1½ cups Colby Jack, half of jalapeños, cilantro, and hot sauce into beef mixture. Sprinkle with salt and pepper.
5. Position 6 toasted tortillas in bottom of greased 13 by 9 inch baking dish, overlapping them slightly. Spread beef mixture uniformly into dish, then top with remaining 6 tortillas followed by rest of the tomato sauce mixture. Bake until filling is bubbling around edges, approximately 30 minutes. Drizzle with remaining 2½ cups Colby Jack and remaining jalapeños and carry on baking until cheese is browned, fifteen to twenty minutes. Allow the casserole to cool for about twenty minutes before you serve.

BEEF ENCHILADAS

Yield: Servings four to 6

Ingredients:

- ¼ cup red wine
- ¼ teaspoon cayenne pepper
- 12 (6 inch) corn tortillas
- 2 (fifteen ounce) cans tomato sauce
- 2 onions, chopped fine
- 2 pounds boneless beef chuck eye roast, trimmed and slice into 1½ inch cubes
- 2 teaspoons ground coriander
- 2 teaspoons ground cumin
- 3 tablespoons chili powder
- 3 tablespoons vegetable oil
- 4 garlic cloves, minced
- 8 ounces cheddar cheese, shredded (2 cups)
- Salt and pepper

Directions:

1. Adjust oven rack to lower middle position and heat oven to 300 degrees. Pat beef dry using paper towels and sprinkle with salt and pepper. Heat 1 tablespoon oil in Dutch oven over moderate high heat until just smoking. Brown half of beef well on all sides, 7 to ten minutes; move to container. Repeat with rest of the beef using fat left in pot.
2. Pour off all but 1 tablespoon fat from pot. Put in onions and ½ teaspoon salt and cook on moderate heat until tender, approximately eight minutes. Mix in chili powder, cumin, coriander, cayenne, and ¼ teaspoon pepper and cook until spices darken, approximately 2 minutes. Mix in garlic and cook until aromatic, approximately half a minute. Mix in tomato sauce, wine, and browned beef and any collected juices and bring to simmer. Cover, move to oven, and cook until meat is fork soft, 2 to 2½ hours.
3. Move beef to big container and allow to cool slightly. Use two forks to shred into bite size pieces; place in your fridge for about twenty minutes. Strain sauce through fine mesh strainer, discarding solids. Mix chilled beef, 1 cup cheddar, and ¼ cup reserved sauce in container.

4. Adjust oven rack to middle position and raise oven temperature to 450 degrees. Spread ¾ cup sauce over bottom of 13 by 9 inch baking dish. Brush both sides of tortillas with remaining 2 tablespoons oil. Stack tortillas, wrap in damp dish towel, and place on plate; microwave until warm and flexible, approximately one minute.

5. Working with 1 warm tortilla at a time, spread ⅓ cup beef filling across center of tortilla. Roll tortilla firmly around filling and place seam side down in baking dish; position enchiladas in 2 columns across width of dish.

6. Pour rest of the sauce over top to cover completely and drizzle remaining 1 cup cheddar over enchiladas. Cover dish firmly with greased aluminium foil. Bake until enchiladas are thoroughly heated and cheese is melted, fifteen to twenty minutes. Allow to cool for five minutes before you serve.

CASSEROLE OF TORTILLAS IN CHILE SAUCE (CASEROLA DE TORTILLAS EN CHILES GUAJILLO)

Yield: Servings 6

Ingredients:

The sauce

- ⅛ teaspoon cumin seeds, crushed
- ½ cup (125 ml) roughly chopped white onion
- 1 cup (250 ml) chicken broth or water
- 12 guajillo chiles, seeds and veins removed
- 2 garlic cloves, roughly chopped
- 2 tablespoons vegetable oil
- Salt to taste

The chilaquiles

- 2 big sprigs epazote
- 2 cups (500 ml) chicken broth, roughly
- 8 ounces (225 g) queso fresco, crumbled, or substitute mild cheddar, grated (approximately 1⅓ cups/335 ml), or muenster (1¼ cups/315 ml)
- eighteen tortillas, cut into strips or triangles and dried

- Vegetable oil for frying

To serve

- ¾ cup (185 ml) thinly cut white onion rings
- 1 cup (250 ml) prepared thin sour cream
- 2 chorizos (about 5 ounces/140 g), crumbled and fried
- 2 limes, cut into wedges

Directions:

1. Prepare a flameproof dish approximately 10 inches (25 cm) in diameter and 4 inches (10 cm) deep.
2. Heat the griddle and toast the chiles lightly on both sides. Be careful—they burn very swiftly.
3. Cover the chiles with hot water and VVVVVVVVVVVVVVVVVVVVVVVVV soak for approximately ten minutes, then move using a slotted spoon to a blender jar. Put in the onion, garlic, and cumin seeds and blend to a smooth sauce with ½ cup (125 ml) of the broth.
4. Heat the oil in a pan and put in the sauce through a fine strainer, pushing down to extract as much of the substance and juice as you can.
5. Put in the other ½ cup broth and allow the sauce to cook using high heat for a few minutes longer. Put in salt to taste. Set aside.
6. Heat the oil in a frying pan and fry the tortilla strips until they are a pale gold, but not too crunchy. Remove and drain using paper towels.
7. Cover the bottom of the dish with a third of the tortilla pieces, then one third of the cheese and one third of the sauce. Repeat the layers two more times.
8. Put in the 2 cups broth and bring to its boiling point. Reduce the heat and carry on cooking the chilaquiles at a brisk simmer, until most of the broth has been absorbed—about fifteen minutes. Put in the epazote one minute or so before the chilaquiles are done cooking.
9. Pour the sour cream around the edge of the dish, then top with the chorizos and the onion rings. Serve in small deep bowls with lime wedges on the side.

CHEESE ENCHILADAS

Yield: Servings four to 6

Ingredients:

- 1 onion, chopped fine
- 1 tablespoon cumin seeds
- 1 tablespoon garlic powder
- 12 (6 inch) corn tortillas
- 2 cups chicken broth
- 2 dried ancho chiles, stemmed, seeded, and torn into ½ inch pieces (½ cup)
- 2 teaspoons distilled white vinegar
- 2 teaspoons dried oregano
- 3 tablespoons all purpose flour
- 5 tablespoons vegetable oil
- 6 ounces sharp cheddar cheese, shredded (1½ cups)
- 8 ounces Monterey Jack cheese, shredded (2 cups)
- Salt and pepper

Directions:

1. Toast anchos and cumin in 12 inch frying pan on moderate heat, stirring regularly, until aromatic, 2 to six minutes. Move to spice grinder and allow to cool slightly. Put in garlic powder and oregano and grind to fine powder.
2. Heat 3 tablespoons oil in now empty frying pan over moderate high heat until it starts to shimmer Whisk in flour, ½ teaspoon salt, ½ teaspoon pepper, and ground spices and cook until aromatic and slightly deepened in color, approximately one minute. Slowly whisk in broth and bring to simmer. Decrease the heat to moderate low and cook, whisking frequently, until sauce has thickened and measures 1½ cups, approximately five minutes. Whisk in vinegar and sprinkle with salt and pepper to taste. Turn off the heat, cover, and keep warm.
3. Adjust oven rack to middle position and heat oven to 450 degrees. Spread ½ cup sauce over bottom of 13 by 9 inch baking dish. Mix Monterey Jack and cheddar in container; set ½ cup cheese mixture aside for topping. Brush both sides of tortillas with remaining 2 tablespoons oil. Stack tortillas, wrap in damp dish towel, and place on plate; microwave until warm and flexible, approximately one minute.

4. Working with 1 warm tortilla at a time, spread ¼ cup cheese mixture across center of tortilla and drizzle with 1 tablespoon onion. Roll tortilla firmly around filling and place seam side down in baking dish; position enchiladas in 2 columns across width of dish.

5. Pour rest of the sauce over top to cover completely and drizzle reserved cheese over enchiladas. Cover dish firmly with greased aluminium foil. Bake until enchiladas are thoroughly heated and cheese is melted, fifteen to twenty minutes. Allow to cool for five minutes and drizzle with remaining onion and serve.

CHICKEN CHILAQUILES

Yield: Servings 4

Ingredients:

- ¼ cup olive oil
- 1 (28 ounce) can whole peeled tomatoes
- 1 avocado, halved, pitted, and slice into ½ inch pieces
- 1 cup finely chopped onion
- 1 jalapeño chile, stemmed, seeded, and chopped
- 1 poblano chile, stemmed, seeded, and chopped
- 1½ cups chicken broth
- 1½ pounds boneless, skinless chicken breasts, trimmed
- 16 (6 inch) corn tortillas, cut into 8 wedges
- 2 radishes, trimmed and cut thin
- 3 garlic cloves, peeled and chopped
- 4 ounces queso fresco, crumbled (1 cup)
- 5 dried guajillo chiles, stemmed, seeded, and torn into ½ inch pieces (⅔ cup)
- 8 sprigs fresh cilantro plus 2 tablespoons minced
- Salt

Directions:

1. Adjust oven racks to upper middle and lower middle positions and heat oven to 425 degrees. Spread tortillas uniformly over 2 rimmed baking sheets. Sprinkle each sheet with 2 tablespoons oil and ¼ teaspoon salt and toss until uniformly coated. Bake, stirring once

in a while, until tortillas are golden brown and crunchy, fifteen to twenty minutes, switching sheets midway through baking.

2. Toast guajillos in Dutch oven on moderate heat, stirring regularly, until aromatic, 2 to six minutes. Move toasted guajillos to blender and pulse until thoroughly ground, 60 to 90 seconds. Put in tomatoes and their juice, ¾ cup onion, poblano, jalapeño, garlic, cilantro sprigs, and ¾ teaspoon salt to blender and pulse until super smooth, 60 to 90 seconds.

3. Mix guajillo tomato mixture and broth in now empty Dutch oven and bring to boiling point over moderate high heat. Nestle chicken into sauce. Cover, decrease the heat to moderate low, and cook until chicken records 160 degrees, ten to fifteen minutes, turning midway through cooking.

4. Move chicken to plate and allow to cool slightly. Use two forks to shred chicken into bite size pieces. In the meantime, increase heat to moderate and simmer sauce until it becomes thick and measures 4½ cups, approximately five minutes.

5. Mix in shredded chicken and cook until warmed through, approximately 2 minutes. Remove the heat, mix in tortillas, cover, and allow it to sit until tortillas have become tender slightly, 2 to five minutes. Move tortilla mixture to serving dish and drizzle with queso fresco, avocado, radishes, remaining ¼ cup onion, and minced cilantro. Serve instantly.

CHICKEN ENCHILADAS VERDES

Yield: Servings four to 6

Ingredients:

- ½ cup chopped fresh cilantro
- ½ teaspoon ground cumin
- 1 onion, chopped fine
- 1 pound boneless, skinless chicken breasts, trimmed
- 1 teaspoon sugar, plus extra as required
- 1½ cups chicken broth
- 1½ pounds tomatillos, husks and stems removed, washed well, dried, and halved
- 12 (6 inch) corn tortillas
- 2 scallions, cut thin
- 3 garlic cloves, minced

- 3 poblano chiles, halved along the length, stemmed, and seeded
- 3 tablespoons vegetable oil
- 8 ounces pepper Jack or Monterey Jack cheese, shredded (2 cups)
- Salt and pepper

Directions:

1. Heat 2 teaspoons oil in medium deep cooking pan on moderate heat until it starts to shimmer Put in onion and cook until golden, six to eight minutes. Mix in cumin and two thirds of garlic and cook until aromatic, approximately half a minute. Mix in broth and bring to simmer.

2. Nestle chicken into sauce. Cover, decrease the heat to moderate low, and cook until chicken records 160 degrees, ten to fifteen minutes, turning chicken midway through cooking. Move chicken to plate and allow to cool slightly. Use two forks to shred chicken into bite size pieces; place in your fridge for about twenty minutes to chill. Reserve ¼ cup cooking liquid for sauce, discarding extra.

3. In the meantime, adjust oven rack 6 inches from broiler element and heat broiler. Coat rimmed baking sheet with aluminium foil. Toss tomatillos and poblanos with 1 teaspoon oil. Position tomatillos cut side down and poblanos skin side up on readied sheet. Broil until vegetables are blackened and starting to tenderize, 5 to ten minutes. Move poblanos to container, cover using aluminium foil, and allow to steam until skins peel off easily, approximately ten minutes. Using back of spoon, scrape loosened skins from poblanos.

4. Process broiled tomatillos with any collected juices, peeled poblanos, ¼ cup reserved cooking liquid, sugar, 1 teaspoon salt, and remaining garlic inside a food processor until sauce is fairly lumpy, approximately eight pulses. Sprinkle with salt, pepper, and extra sugar to taste. Mix chilled chicken, cilantro, and 1½ cups cheese in container and sprinkle with salt and pepper to taste.

5. Adjust oven rack to middle position and heat oven to 450 degrees. Spread ¾ cup tomatillo sauce over bottom of 13 by 9 inch baking dish. Brush both sides of tortillas with remaining 2 tablespoons oil. Stack tortillas, wrap in damp dish towel, and place on plate; microwave until warm and flexible, approximately one minute.

6. Working with 1 warm tortilla at a time, spread ⅓ cup chicken filling across center of tortilla. Roll tortilla firmly around filling and place seam side down in baking dish; position enchiladas in 2 columns across width of dish.

7. Pour rest of the sauce over top to cover completely and drizzle remaining ½ cup cheese over enchiladas. Cover dish firmly with greased aluminium foil. Bake until enchiladas are thoroughly heated and cheese is melted, fifteen to twenty minutes. Allow to cool for five minutes, drizzle with scallions, before you serve.

CHICKEN ENCHILADAS WITH RED CHILE SAUCE

Yield: Servings four to 6

Ingredients:

- ¼ cup jarred jalapeños, chopped
- ¼ cup vegetable oil
- ½ cup chopped fresh cilantro
- ½ teaspoon salt
- 1 cup water
- 1 onion, chopped fine
- 1 pound boneless, skinless chicken thighs, trimmed and slice into ¼ inch wide strips
- 12 (6 inch) corn tortillas
- 12 ounces sharp cheddar cheese, shredded (3 cups)
- 2 (8 ounce) cans tomato sauce
- 2 teaspoons ground coriander
- 2 teaspoons ground cumin
- 2 teaspoons sugar
- 3 garlic cloves, minced
- 3 tablespoons chili powder

Directions:

1. Heat 2 tablespoons oil in medium deep cooking pan over moderate high heat until it starts to shimmer Put in onion and cook until tender, five to seven minutes. Mix in chili powder, garlic, coriander, cumin, sugar, and salt and cook until aromatic, approximately half a minute. Mix in chicken and coat completely with spices. Mix in tomato sauce and water, bring to simmer, and cook until chicken is thoroughly cooked, approximately eight minutes.

2. Drain mixture in fine mesh strainer set over container, pushing on chicken and onion to extract as much sauce as you can; set sauce aside. Move chicken mixture to separate container, place in your fridge for about twenty minutes to chill, then mix in cilantro, jalapeños, and 2½ cups cheese.

3. Adjust oven rack middle position and heat oven to 450 degrees. Spread ¾ cup sauce over bottom of 13 by 9 inch baking dish. Brush both sides of tortillas with remaining 2 tablespoons oil. Stack tortillas, wrap in damp dish towel, and place on plate; microwave until warm and flexible, approximately one minute.

4. Working with 1 warm tortilla at a time, spread ⅓ cup chicken filling across center of tortilla. Roll tortilla firmly around filling and place seam side down in baking dish; position enchiladas in 2 columns across width of dish.

5. Pour rest of the sauce over top to cover completely and drizzle remaining ½ cup cheese over enchiladas. Cover dish firmly with greased aluminium foil. Bake until enchiladas are thoroughly heated and cheese is melted, fifteen to twenty minutes. Allow to cool for five minutes before you serve.

CHILES RELLENOS CASSEROLE

Yield: Servings 6 to 8

Ingredients:

- ¼ teaspoon cayenne pepper
- ½ cup all purpose flour
- ¾ cup skim milk
- 1 (10 ounce) can Ro Tel tomatoes, drained
- 1 onion, chopped fine
- 1 tablespoon vegetable oil
- 1 teaspoon dried oregano
- 10 ounces Monterey Jack cheese, shredded (2½ cups)
- 2 big egg whites
- 2 garlic cloves, minced
- 2 pounds 90 percent lean ground beef
- 2 teaspoons ground cumin
- 4 poblano chiles, stemmed, seeded, and chopped

- Salt and pepper

Directions:

1. Adjust oven rack to upper middle position and heat oven to 450 degrees. Heat oil in 12 inch nonstick frying pan on moderate heat until it starts to shimmer Put in onion and cook until tender, approximately five minutes. Mix in beef, breaking up meat with wooden spoon, and cook until no longer pink, about eight to ten minutes. Using slotted spoon, move beef mixture to paper towel–lined plate. Pour off all but 2 tablespoons fat from frying pan.

2. Put in poblanos to fat left in frying pan and cook over moderate high heat until browned, about eight to ten minutes. Mix in garlic, cumin, oregano, cayenne, ¾ teaspoon salt, ½ teaspoon pepper, and beef mixture and cook until aromatic, approximately half a minute. Mix in tomatoes and cook until mixture is dry, approximately one minute. Remove the heat, mix in 2 cups Monterey Jack. Scrape mixture into 13 by 9 inch baking dish and press into even layer.

3. Mix flour, ½ teaspoon salt, and ¼ teaspoon pepper in container. Slowly whisk in milk until the desired smoothness is achieved. Using stand mixer fitted with whisk, whip egg whites on medium low speed until foamy, approximately one minute. Increase speed to moderate high and whip until stiff peaks form, approximately 3 minutes. Whisk one third whipped egg whites into milk flour batter to lighten. Lightly fold in remaining whites, 1 scoop at a time, until blended.

4. Pour batter uniformly over beef mixture. Bake until topping is light golden and puffed, approximately fifteen minutes. Drizzle with remaining ½ cup Monterey Jack and bake until a golden-brown colour is achieved, approximately ten minutes. Allow to cool on wire rack for about ten minutes and serve.

ENCHILADAS DE FRESNILLO

Yield: 12 enchiladas

Ingredients:

The sauce

- ⅛ teaspoon dried mexican oregano
- ¼ cup (65 ml) shelled peanuts, toasted and crushed

- ¼-inch (.75-cm) piece of cinnamon stick, crushed
- 1 tablespoon sesame seeds, toasted and crushed
- 1 whole clove, crushed
- 1½ cups (375 ml) cold water
- 2 tablespoons vegetable oil
- 3 ancho chiles, seeds and veins removed, mildly toasted
- 3 peppercorns, crushed
- 3 sprigs fresh marjoram or ⅛ teaspoon dried
- 3 sprigs fresh thyme or ⅛ teaspoon dried
- Salt to taste

The filling

- 1 medium white onion, finely chopped
- 8 ounces (225 g) queso fresco, crumbled (approximately 1½ cups/375 ml)
- twelve tortillas
- Vegetable oil for frying

To serve

- ¾ cup (185 ml) prepared sour cream
- 1 avocado, thinly cut
- 2 chorizos, crumbled and fried
- 6 big radishes, thinly cut

Directions:

1. Cover the chiles with hot water and VVVVVVVVVVVVVVVVVVVVVVVVV soak for approximately five minutes. Drain, then move the chiles to a blender jar, put in the rest of the sauce ingredients, and blend until the desired smoothness is achieved.
2. Heat the oil in a frying pan and cook the sauce over moderate heat for approximately 8 minutes, stirring and scraping the bottom of the pan almost continuously. Turn off the heat and keep warm.
3. One at a time, fry the tortillas lightly on both sides, drain thoroughly, and keep them warm while you do the rest.
4. Immerse the tortillas into the sauce, then fill each one with some of the cheese and onion. Roll up loosely and place side by side in the serving dish. Put in a little water to the

rest of the sauce, then bring to its boiling point and pour over the enchiladas. Top with the avocado slices, cut radishes, sour cream, and chorizos and serve instantly.

ENCHILADAS DE JALISCO

Yield: Servings 6

Ingredients:

The filling (or picadillo)

- ⅓ cup (85 ml) reserved meat broth
- ½ cup (125 ml) finely chopped white onion
- 1 pound (450 g) tomatoes
- 1 tablespoon finely chopped parsley
- 1 zucchini squash (approximately four ounces/115 g)
- 2 small carrots (approximately four ounces/115 g)
- 2 teaspoons salt, or to taste
- 3 small red bliss or waxy new potatoes (approximately eight ounces/225 g)
- 3 tablespoons lard
- 8 ounces (225 g) ground beef
- 8 ounces (225 g) ground pork
- Salt to taste

The chile sauce

- ¼-inch (.75-cm) piece of cinnamon stick, crushed
- 1 cup (250 ml) reserved meat broth
- 10 guajillo chiles (about 2 ounces/60 g), veins and seeds removed
- 2 tablespoons lard
- 2 whole cloves, crushed
- Salt to taste

The enchiladas

- ¼ cup (65 ml) lard
- 24 4-inch (10-cm) tortillas

To serve

- ¼ cup (65 ml) grated queso añejo, or substitute romano or sardo
- ½ cup (125 ml) finely chopped white onion
- Shredded lettuce
- Strips of jalapeño chiles en escabeche
- Thinly cut radishes

Directions:

1. Trim the squash and leave whole. Trim and scrape the carrots and slice into quarters along the length. Peel the potatoes and slice into halves. Cover the vegetables with boiling water in a big deep cooking pan, put in the salt, and allow them to cook for five minutes.
2. Combine the meat with salt to taste. Push firmly into two big balls and put in them, with the whole tomatoes, to the vegetables in the pan. Cover and cook all together using low heat until the vegetables are just soft—do not overcook—and the meat balls are almost thoroughly cooked—about ten minutes. Drain and reserve the broth.
3. When the vegetables are sufficiently cool to handle, cut them into little cubes and save for later.
4. Combine the tomatoes for a few seconds. Set aside.
5. Melt the lard in a big frying pan and cook the onion until translucent.
6. Crush the cooked meat balls into the pan, put in the parsley, and fry for approximately five minutes over moderate heat. Put in the mixed tomato puree and cook over brisk heat until some of the juice has vaporized. Put in the broth and vegetables and carry on cooking the mixture until it is well seasoned—about ten minutes. Put in salt as required. Set aside.
7. Heat a comal and toast the chiles lightly, turning them continuously, since they burn very swiftly. Cover the chiles with hot water in a container and let soak for approximately ten minutes. Move using a slotted spoon to a blender jar. Put in the broth, blend, and strain to remove any traces of the tough skin, return to the blender, put in the spices and salt, and blend until the desired smoothness is achieved.
8. Melt the lard and cook the sauce until it is well seasoned and a rich, dark-red color— approximately eight minutes.
9. Preheat your oven to 350° f (180° c).

10. Heat a little of the lard in a frying pan, and fry the tortillas on both sides, putting in more lard as required—they should just tenderize and heat through in the hot fat. Pile one on top of the other between sheets of toweling and keep warm.
11. Immerse the tortillas into the sauce, which should lightly cover them (if it is too thick, then put in slightly more broth). Put some of the picadillo across each tortilla and roll up. Put one layer of the enchiladas on the bottom of an ovenproof dish approximately four inches (10 cm) deep. Pour a little of the rest of the sauce over them. Then place another enchilada layer on top and pour over the remaining sauce.
12. Cover the dish and heat the enchiladas through in your oven for approximately fifteen minutes, then serve instantly, topped with the lettuce, radishes, and canned chiles, and sprinkled with the cheese and chopped onion.

ENCHILADAS PLACERAS O POLLO DE PLAZA

Yield: Servings 6

Ingredients:

The topping

- ⅓ cup (85 ml) mild vinegar
- 1 teaspoon salt
- 8 ounces (225 g) carrots (3 medium)
- 8 ounces (225 g) red bliss or waxy new potatoes (3 small ones), unpeeled

The sauce

- ¼ teaspoon dried mexican oregano
- 1 slice white onion
- 2 garlic cloves, roughly chopped
- 3 ancho chiles, seeds and veins removed
- 3 guajillo chiles, seeds and veins removed
- About 1½ cups (375 ml) water
- Salt to taste

The enchiladas

- ½ cup (125 ml) finely chopped white onion
- 12 freshly made tortillas
- 8 ounces (225 g) queso fresco, crumbled and lightly salted (approximately 1⅓ cups/333 ml)
- A 3-pound (1.35-kg) chicken, poached and slice into serving pieces
- Lard or vegetable oil for frying

To serve

- ¼ cup (65 ml) grated queso añejo, or substitute romano or sardo
- ⅔ cup (165 ml) prepared sour cream
- 1 cup (250 ml) finely shredded lettuce or raw cabbage
- Strips of canned jalapeño chiles en escabeche

Directions:

1. Wash the potatoes and cut them into little cubes; scrape the carrots and cut them into smaller cubes. Cover the carrots with boiling water, put in the salt, and cook them for approximately five minutes using high heat. Put in the potatoes and cook them for approximately 8 minutes—they should still be firm to the bite—then drain.
2. Cover the vegetables with cold water and put in the vinegar. Stir and save for later.
3. Heat a griddle and toast the chiles lightly, turning continuously so they do not burn.
4. Cover the chiles with hot water and VVVVVVVVVVVVVVVVVVVVVVVVVVV soak for ten minutes.
5. Put ½ cup (125 ml) of the water into a blender jar, put in the guajillos, and blend until the desired smoothness is achieved. Strain. Put in the remaining 1 cup (250 ml) water, the anchos, garlic, and onion and blend until the desired smoothness is achieved. Put in the guajillo puree, the oregano, and salt to taste.
6. Melt a little of the lard, and when it is sizzling, dip each tortilla into the raw sauce—it should just lightly cover it (if the sauce is too thick dilute it with slightly more water) and fry it swiftly on both sides.
7. Take out of the frying pan and put approximately 1 small tablespoon of the cheese and ½ tablespoon of the onion across each tortilla. Roll them up loosely and set them side by side on the serving dish. Keep warm.
8. In the same fat, fry the pieces of chicken until they become golden brown. Drain and place them around the enchiladas.

9. In the same fat, fry the vegetables until just starting to brown, and drain thoroughly. In the same fat, cook the rest of the sauce for a little time and pour it over the enchiladas. Cover with the fried vegetables.
10. Top with the chile strips and on each serving put in a spoonful of sour cream and a drizzling of cheese, with lettuce on the side.

GREEN ENCHILADAS (ENCHILADAS VERDES DE AGUASCALIENTES)

Yield: 12 enchiladas

Ingredients:

The sauce

- ½ cup (125 ml) sour cream, commercial or homemade
- 1 cup (250 ml) chicken broth
- 1 whole clove, crushed
- 2 big romaine lettuce leaves
- 2 tablespoons vegetable oil
- 3 poblano chiles, charred, peeled, and seeds removed (not veins;)
- Salt to taste

The filling

- 1½ to 2 cups (375 to 500 ml) cooked, shredded, and well-salted chicken
- twelve tortillas
- Vegetable oil for frying

To serve

- ½ cup (125 ml) pitted, halved green olives
- 1½ cups (375 ml) finely shredded lettuce
- 6 big radishes, thinly cut

Directions:

1. Combine the chiles with the lettuce, clove, and ½ cup (125 ml) of the chicken broth until super smooth.
2. Heat the 2 tablespoons of oil in a big frying pan, put in the sauce, and cook over quite high heat for approximately five minutes, stirring and scraping the bottom of the pan to prevent sticking. Put in the salt, sour cream, and the rest of the ½ cup chicken broth and just heat through, then take out of the heat and keep warm.
3. Heat the oil in a different frying pan and fry the tortillas, one by one, for a short period of time on both sides. Drain thoroughly and keep warm.
4. Immerse the tortillas, one at a time, into the sauce, then fill each one with some of the chicken. Roll up and place side by side on a warmed dish. Pour the rest of the sauce over the enchiladas, top with the lettuce, cut radishes, and olives, and serve instantly.

GREEN ENCHILADAS (ENCHILADAS VERDES DE SAN LUIS POTOSÍ)

Yield: 12 enchiladas

Ingredients:

The sauce

- ⅓ cup (85 ml) milk
- 1 garlic clove
- 2 cups (500 ml) cooked tomate verde, drained
- 2 tablespoons sour cream, commercial or homemade
- 2 tablespoons vegetable oil
- 3 sprigs cilantro
- 4 serrano chiles
- Salt to taste

The tortillas

- twelve tortillas
- Vegetable oil for frying

The filling

- 1½ to 2 cups (375 to 500 ml) shredded cooked chicken

To serve

- ½ cup (125 ml) prepared sour cream
- ¾ cup (190 ml) finely chopped white onion
- 3 ounces (85 g) queso fresco, crumbled (about ½ cup/125 ml)

Directions:

1. Combine the tomate verde with the chiles, cilantro, milk, garlic, and salt until the desired smoothness is achieved.
2. Heat the oil in a big frying pan and cook the sauce over quite high heat until reduced and seasoned—about five minutes. Turn off the heat, put in the sour cream, and save for later. Keep warm.
3. Heat the oil in a second frying pan and fry the tortillas, one at a time, for a short period of time on each side. Drain thoroughly and keep warm.
4. One at a time, immerse the tortillas into the sauce. Fill each one with some of the chicken, then roll and place side by side in the warmed dish. Dilute the remaining sauce, if required, and pour it over the enchiladas. Top lavishly with the onion, cheese, and sour cream and serve instantly.

GREEN ENCHILADAS (ENCHILADAS VERDES)

Yield: 12 enchiladas

Ingredients:

The sauce

- ⅓ cup (85 ml) plus ½ cup (125 ml) chicken broth
- ½ cup (125 ml) toasted (shelled), unsalted peanuts, crushed
- 1 cup (250 ml) cooked tomate verde, drained
- 2 sprigs cilantro, thick stems removed
- 2 tablespoons vegetable oil
- 3 poblano chiles, charred, peeled, and cleaned

- Salt to taste

The tortillas

- 12 freshly made tortillas

The filling

- 1½ to 2 cups (375 to 500 ml) shredded, cooked chicken
- 2 poblano chiles, prepared in rajas and fried with a little onion

To serve

- ⅓ cup (85 ml) crumbled queso fresco (about 2 ounces/60 g)
- ½ cup (125 ml) prepared sour cream
- ⅔ cup (165 ml) finely chopped white onion

Directions:

1. Combine the tomate verde with the remaining sauce ingredients, apart from the oil and ½ cup (125 ml) chicken broth, until the desired smoothness is achieved.
2. Heat the oil in a big frying pan and fry the sauce over quite high heat for five minutes, stirring and scraping the bottom of the pan occasionally to prevent sticking. Put in the remaining ½ cup (125 ml) broth and bring to its boiling point, then take out of the heat and keep warm.
3. If the tortillas are not freshly made and still warm, heat them for a short period of time in a steamer. Immerse them, one at a time, into the sauce, fill each one with a little of the chicken and a few rajas, roll loosely, and set side by side in the serving dish. Reheat the rest of the sauce, diluting it if required with a little broth or water. Pour it over the enchiladas and top with the cheese, onion, and sour cream before you serve.

GREEN ENCHILADAS FROM VERACRUZ (ENCHILADAS VERDES VERACRUZANAS)

Based on a recipe by señora josefina velázquez de león

Yield: 12 enchiladas

Ingredients:

The sauce

- ½ cup (125 ml) cooking liquid from the tomatoes
- ½ cup (125 ml) roughly chopped white onion
- ½ cup (125 ml) sour cream, commercial or homemade
- 1 cup (250 ml) cooked tomate verde, drained
- 2 tablespoons vegetable oil
- 4 poblano chiles, charred, peeled, and cleaned
- Salt to taste

The tortillas

- 12 freshly made tortillas

The filling

- 2 cups (500 ml) guacamole

To serve

- ¼ cup (65 ml) roughly chopped flat-leaf parsley
- 3 ounces (85 g) queso fresco, crumbled (about ½ cup/125 ml)

Directions:

1. Combine the tomate verde with the cooking liquid, chilies, onion, and salt until the desired smoothness is achieved.
2. Heat the oil in a frying pan and cook the sauce over quite high heat for approximately five minutes, stirring and scraping the bottom of the pan occasionally to prevent sticking. Turn off the heat and put in the sour cream, then set the sauce over a very low heat just to heat it through. Set aside and keep warm.
3. If the tortillas are not freshly made and still warm, heat them for a short period of time in a steamer. Immerse them, one at a time, into the sauce, put approximately 1½ tablespoons of the guacamole across the face of each, roll up loosely, and place side by side in the serving dish. Dilute the rest of the sauce with a little water or milk and pour over the enchiladas. Drizzle with the parsley and cheese and serve instantly.

GREEN ENCHILADAS WITH CARNITAS (ENCHILADAS VERDES CON CARNITAS)

Yield: Servings 6

Ingredients:

- 2 garlic cloves, crushed
- 3 pounds (1.35 kg) country-style spareribs
- Salt to taste

The sauce

- ¼ cup (65 ml) broth or water
- ⅓ cup (85 ml) finely chopped white onion
- 1 cup (250 ml) cooked tomate verde, drained
- 2 big romaine lettuce leaves
- 2 garlic cloves
- 2 poblano chiles, charred, peeled, seeds and veins removed
- 2 sprigs epazote
- 2 tablespoons vegetable oil
- 6 sprigs cilantro
- Salt to taste

The filling

- ¼ medium white onion, finely chopped
- 3 tablespoons vegetable oil
- 4 serrano chiles, finely chopped
- 5 big eggs
- 6 ounces (180 g) tomatoes, finely chopped (approximately 1 cup/250 ml)
- Salt to taste

The tortillas

- 2 cups (500 ml) finely shredded lettuce
- 6 big radish flowers

- **To serve**

- twelve tortillas
- Vegetable oil for frying

Directions:

1. Place the meat into a wide pan just big enough to accommodate it in no more than two layers. Barely cover the meat with water, put in the garlic and salt, and bring to its boiling point. Reduce the heat to moderate and allow the meat to cook until it is soft, the water evaporates, and the fat is rendered out. Allow the meat fry in its fat, turning it occasionally until thoroughly browned—approximately 1 hour. Set aside and keep warm.
2. Heat the oil in a frying pan and fry the onion until translucent.
3. Combine the rest of the ingredients for the sauce until the desired smoothness is achieved. Put into the onion in the pan and fry over quite high heat while stirring and scraping the bottom of the pan until it has reduced a little and is well seasoned—about five minutes. Turn off the heat and keep warm.
4. Heat the oil in a second frying pan.
5. In the meantime, beat the eggs together well, then mix in the salt, onion, tomatoes, and chiles. Pour into the hot oil and scramble them using super low heat; they must be just set and soft. Turn off the heat and keep warm.
6. Heat the oil in a frying pan and fry the tortillas, one at a time, lightly on both sides. Drain and keep warm.
7. Immerse the tortillas into the green sauce, fill each one with some of the egg mixture, then roll up and put them on the serving dish. Dilute the rest of the sauce, if required, and pour over the enchiladas. Put the pork, lettuce, and radish flowers around the dish, and serve instantly.

MOCTEZUMA PIE (BUDÍN AZTECA)

Yield: Servings 6

Ingredients:

The green tomato sauce

- 2 small garlic cloves, roughly chopped

- 2 tablespoons finely chopped white onion
- 2 tablespoons vegetable oil
- 3 cups (750 ml) cooked tomate verde (approximately 1½ pounds/680 g), drained, saving for later ½ cup (125 ml) of the liquid
- 3 serrano chiles, cooked with the tomate verde

The rajas

- ⅓ cup (85 ml) thinly cut white onion
- 3 tablespoons vegetable oil
- 7 poblano chiles, prepared in rajas
- Salt to taste

The budín

- ⅓ cup (85 ml) vegetable oil
- 1½ cups (375 ml) thick sour cream
- 1¾ cups (440 ml) grated chihuahua cheese or cheddar (approximately eight ounces/225 g)
- 18 freshly made tortillas, approximately 5 inches (13 cm) across, cut into halves
- 2 cups (500 ml) shredded, poached chicken, well salted

Directions:

1. Prepare an ovenproof dish approximately 10 inches (25 cm) in diameter and 4 inches (10 cm) deep.
2. Preheat your oven to 350° f (180° c).
3. In a blender, blend the tomate verde with the ½ cup (125 ml) reserved liquid and the chiles, garlic, and onion to a smooth sauce.
4. Heat the oil in a frying pan, put in the sauce, and cook using high heat for approximately five minutes, stirring occasionally to prevent sticking, by which time it will have thickened a little and will be well seasoned. Set aside.
5. Chop the chiles into thin strips and save for later.
6. Heat the 3 tablespoons of oil in a different frying pan, then put in the onion and fry until translucent—about one minute. Put in the chile strips and salt, cover the pan, and cook over gentle heat until the chiles are soft but not too soft—about five minutes.

7. Heat the oil in a different frying pan and fry each tortilla for a few seconds—they should not get crisp or hard. Blot off surplus oil on the next unfried tortilla.

8. Spread one third of the tortillas over the bottom of the dish. Then spread, in layers on top of them, half the chicken, half the rajas, and a third each of the sauce, sour cream, and cheese. Repeat the layers and finish off with a layer of tortillas, sprinkled with the remaining sauce, sour cream, and cheese.

9. Bake the budín for approximately twenty-five minutes, or until it is well thoroughly heated and the cheese has melted.

MUSHROOM PUDDING (BUDÍN DE HONGOS)

Yield: Servings 4

Ingredients:

The filling

- ½ cup (125 ml) thinly cut white onion
- 1 big sprig epazote or parsley, leaves only, roughly chopped
- 1 pound (450 g) mushrooms, washed and thinly cut, or roughly chopped cuitlacoche
- 2 garlic cloves, peeled and finely chopped
- 2 tablespoons vegetable oil
- 3 serrano chiles, finely chopped
- Salt to taste

The sauce

- ¼ cup (65 ml) roughly chopped white onion
- 1 garlic clove, roughly chopped
- 1 pound (450 g) tomatoes, roughly chopped (about 3 cups/750 ml)
- 1 tablespoon vegetable oil
- Salt to taste

The tortillas

- 12 5- to 6-inch (12.5- to fifteen-cm) tortillas, cut into four and dried

- 4 ounces (115 g) chihuahua cheese (see substitutes), grated (approximately 1 heaped cup/265 ml)
- Vegetable oil for frying

Directions:

1. Prepare a mildly greased ovenproof dish about 9 by 6 by 3 inches (23 by fifteen by 8 cm).
2. Heat the oil in a big frying pan and fry the onion and garlic for a couple of minutes, stirring occasionally to prevent sticking—they should not brown. Put in the mushrooms, chiles, and salt, then cover the pan and cook over moderate heat until the mushrooms are soft—about twenty minutes; they must be juicy. Put in the epazote and cook for a minute more. Set aside in a container.
3. Combine the tomatoes, onion, and garlic together until the desired smoothness is achieved.
4. Heat the oil in a frying pan and cook the sauce over quite high heat while stirring it occasionally, for approximately 4 minutes to reduce. Put in salt.
5. Heat the oil in a second frying pan and fry the tortillas, approximately one third at a time so they fry uniformly, until they are just becoming stiff but do not harden and brown. Drain using paper towels.
6. Preheat your oven to 375° f (190° c).
7. Put one third of the tortilla pieces at the bottom of the dish, then put in half of the mushroom mixture, one third of the cheese, and ⅓ cup (85 ml) sauce. Repeat the layers and top off with the remaining cheese, sauce, and any mushroom juice left in the pan. Bake until well thoroughly heated and bubbling—twenty to twenty-five minutes.

PASTEL AZTECA

Yield: Servings 6 to 8

Ingredients:

2 dried ancho chiles, stemmed, seeded, and torn into ½ inch pieces (½ cup)

- ⅓ cup chopped fresh cilantro
- 1 onion, chopped
- 1 tablespoon lime juice
- 1 tablespoon tomato paste

- 1 tablespoon vegetable oil
- 1 teaspoon ground coriander
- 1 teaspoon ground cumin
- 18 (6 inch) corn tortillas
- 2 teaspoons dried oregano
- 2 tomatoes, cored and chopped
- 2½ pounds boneless, skinless chicken breasts, trimmed
- 3 cups chicken broth
- 3 garlic cloves, minced
- 3 tablespoons all purpose flour
- 5 scallions, cut thin
- 8 ounces Monterey Jack cheese, shredded (2 cups)
- 8 ounces queso fresco, crumbled (2 cups)
- Salt and pepper

Directions:

1. Adjust oven rack to middle position and heat oven to 425 degrees. Toast anchos in 12 inch frying pan on moderate heat, stirring regularly, until aromatic, 2 to six minutes; move to blender.

2. Heat oil in Dutch oven over moderate high heat until it starts to shimmer Put in onion and cook until tender, approximately five minutes. Mix in tomato paste, garlic, oregano, cumin, coriander, 1 teaspoon salt, and ½ teaspoon pepper and cook until aromatic, approximately one minute. Mix in flour and cook until slightly deepened in color, approximately one minute. Slowly whisk in broth and bring to simmer. Decrease the heat to moderate low and cook, whisking frequently, until sauce is slightly thickened, approximately 3 minutes.

3. Put in sauce to blender and pulse until smooth, approximately half a minute; return to now empty pot. Nestle chicken into sauce, cover, and cook over moderate low heat until chicken records 160 degrees, approximately fifteen minutes. Move chicken to cutting board, allow to cool slightly, then shred into bite size pieces with the help of two forks; move to container. Put in 1½ cups sauce, two thirds of scallions, ¼ cup cilantro, and lime juice and toss to blend.

4. In the meantime, toast tortillas, one by one, in 8 inch frying pan over moderate high heat until mildly browned, approximately twenty seconds per side; move to plate and cover using a dish towel. Mix Monterey Jack and queso fresco in container.

5. Spread ½ cup rest of the sauce over bottom of 13 by 9 inch baking dish. Lay 6 tortillas into dish, overlapping them slightly. Spread ½ cup sauce over tortillas and top with half of chicken mixture and one third of cheese mixture. Repeat with 6 more tortillas, ½ cup sauce, remaining chicken mixture, and half of rest of the cheese mixture. Top with remaining 6 tortillas, rest of the sauce, and rest of the cheese.

6. Cover dish with aluminium foil and bake until sauce is bubbling and cheese is melted, fifteen to twenty minutes. Allow the casserole to cool for about ten minutes. Drizzle with tomatoes, remaining scallions, and remaining cilantro and serve.

RED ENCHILADAS (ENCHILADAS ROJAS DE AGUASCALIENTES)

Yield: 12 enchiladas

Ingredients:

The sauce

- 1 garlic clove
- 1 hard-cooked egg yolk
- 1½ cups (375 ml) hot milk
- 2 tablespoons vegetable oil
- 4 ancho chiles, wiped clean, seeds and veins removed, mildly toasted
- Salt to taste

The filling

- 1 cup (250 ml) finely chopped white onion
- 8 ounces (225 g) queso fresco, crumbled (approximately 1½ cups/375 ml)
- twelve tortillas
- Vegetable oil for frying

To serve

- 1 hard-cooked egg white, finely chopped

- 1½ cups (375 ml) finely shredded lettuce
- 6 radishes, thinly cut
- Strips of jalapeño chiles en escabeche

Directions:

1. Tear the chiles into pieces and put in to a blender jar with the milk and let soak for approximately ten minutes. Put in the salt, garlic, and egg yolk and blend until the desired smoothness is achieved. (you will have about 2 cups/500 ml of sauce; put in water if required to make up that quantity.)
2. Heat the oil in a moderate-sized frying pan, put in the sauce, and cook for approximately five minutes over moderate heat, stirring and scraping the sides and bottom of the pan occasionally. Turn off the heat and keep warm.
3. Heat the oil in a different frying pan and fry the tortillas, one at a time, for a short period of time on both sides. Drain thoroughly and keep warm.
4. Immerse the tortillas, one at a time, into the sauce. Fill each one with some of the cheese and onion, then roll and place side by side in a serving dish. Dilute the rest of the sauce, if required, and pour it over the enchiladas. Top with the chopped egg white, the lettuce, cut radishes, and chile strips and serve instantly.

ROASTED POBLANO AND BLACK BEAN ENCHILADAS

Yield: Servings four to 6

Ingredients:

- ¼ cup heavy cream
- ⅓ cup vegetable broth
- ½ teaspoon ground coriander
- ½ teaspoon ground cumin
- 1 (fifteen ounce) can black beans, washed, half of beans mashed smooth
- 1 cup fresh cilantro leaves
- 1 pound tomatillos, husks and stems removed, washed well, dried, and halved
- 1 tablespoon lime juice
- 1 teaspoon chili powder
- 1 teaspoon plus ¼ cup vegetable oil

- 1 teaspoon sugar
- 12 (6 inch) corn tortillas
- 2 onions, chopped fine
- 4 garlic cloves, minced
- 4 poblano chiles, halved along the length, stemmed, and seeded
- 8 ounces Monterey Jack cheese, shredded (2 cups)
- Salt and pepper

Directions:

1. Adjust oven rack 6 inches from broiler element and heat broiler. Coat rimmed baking sheet with aluminium foil. Toss tomatillos and poblanos with 1 teaspoon oil. Position tomatillos cut side down and poblanos skin side up on readied sheet. Broil until vegetables are blackened and starting to tenderize, 5 to ten minutes. Move poblanos to container, cover using aluminium foil, and allow to steam until skins peel off easily, approximately ten minutes. Using back of spoon, scrape loosened skins from poblanos. Chop tomatillos and poblanos into ½ inch pieces.

2. Process broiled tomatillos, 1 cup onion, ½ cup cilantro, broth, cream, 1 tablespoon oil, half of garlic, lime juice, sugar, and 1 teaspoon salt inside a food processor until sauce is smooth, approximately 2 minutes. Sprinkle with salt and pepper to taste.

3. Heat 1 tablespoon oil in 12 inch frying pan on moderate heat until it starts to shimmer Put in remaining onion and cook until tender, five to seven minutes. Mix in chili powder, coriander, cumin, and remaining garlic and cook until aromatic, approximately half a minute. Mix in mashed and whole beans and chopped poblanos and cook until warmed through, approximately 2 minutes. Move mixture to big container and allow to cool slightly. Mix in 1 cup Monterey Jack, ½ cup tomatillo sauce, and remaining ½ cup cilantro. Sprinkle with salt and pepper to taste.

4. Adjust oven rack to middle position and heat oven to 400 degrees. Spread ½ cup tomatillo sauce over bottom of 13 by 9 inch baking dish. Brush both sides of tortillas with remaining 2 tablespoons oil. Stack tortillas, wrap in damp dish towel, and place on plate; microwave until warm and flexible, approximately one minute.

5. Working with 1 warm tortilla at a time, spread ¼ cup bean cheese filling across center of tortilla. Roll tortilla firmly around filling and place seam side down in baking dish; position enchiladas in 2 columns across width of dish.

6. Pour rest of the sauce over top to cover completely and drizzle remaining 1 cup cheese down center of enchiladas. Cover dish firmly with greased aluminium foil. Bake until

enchiladas are thoroughly heated and cheese is melted, fifteen to twenty minutes. Allow to cool for five minutes before you serve.

SIMPLE ENCHILADAS (ENCHILADAS SENCILLAS)

Yield: 12 enchiladas

Ingredients:

The tomato sauce

- ½ cup (125 ml) thick sour cream, at room temperature
- 1 garlic clove
- 1 pound (450 g) tomatoes, broiled
- 2 fresh serrano chiles, toasted
- 2 tablespoons vegetable oil
- Salt to taste

The enchiladas

- 1 cup (250 ml) finely chopped white onion
- 12 freshly made tortillas
- 7 big eggs, scrambled with sufficient salt, or 1½ cups (375 ml) cooked and shredded chicken, well salted
- Vegetable oil for frying

To serve

- 1 cup (250 ml) grated chihuahua cheese or cheddar

Directions:

1. In a blender, puree the tomatoes, garlic, and chiles until the desired smoothness is achieved—you'll have about 2 cups (500 ml).
2. Heat the oil in a big frying pan and fry the sauce for approximately five minutes, or until it has reduced and thickened. Put in the salt. Set aside to cool a little.
3. Mix the sour cream thoroughly into the sauce and just heat it through lightly. Do not let the sauce come to a boil after the cream has been added or it will curdle.

4. Heat the oil in a different frying pan and fry the tortillas swiftly, one at a time, without letting them become crisp around the edges.
5. Preheat your oven to 350° f (180° c).
6. Immerse the tortillas into the warm sauce—they must be just lightly covered—then put about 2 tablespoons of the scrambled egg or shredded chicken across each tortilla and drizzle it with a little of the onion. Roll the filled tortillas up loosely and set them side by side in an ovenproof dish.
7. Cover the enchiladas with the rest of the sauce and drizzle with the cheese and remaining onion. Place the dish into the oven and just heat them through for a very short time, no more than ten minutes. Serve instantly.

SIMPLE TORTILLA CASSEROLE (CASEROLA DE TORTILLAS SENCILLA)

Yield: Servings 4

Ingredients:

The sauce

- ¼ cup (65 ml) roughly chopped white onion
- 1 big garlic clove, roughly chopped
- 1 pound (450 g) tomatoes, roughly chopped (about 3 cups/750 ml)
- 2 tablespoons vegetable oil
- Salt to taste

The filling

- ⅓ cup (85 ml) broth or hot water
- 4 ounces (115 g) chihuahua cheese (about ¾ cup/185 ml), or queso fresco (about ⅔ cup/165 ml)
- twelve tortillas cut into strips and dried
- Vegetable oil for frying

To serve

- 1 cup (250 ml) prepared sour cream

- 2 tablespoons finely chopped parsley (not necessary)

Directions:

1. Prepare a mildly greased ovenproof dish about 9 by 6 by 3 inches (23 by fifteen by 8 cm).
2. Combine the tomatoes with the remaining sauce ingredients apart from the oil until the desired smoothness is achieved.
3. Heat the oil in a moderate-sized frying pan and fry the sauce over a quite high heat to reduce and season—approximately four minutes. Turn off the heat and set in a warm place.
4. Heat the oil in a second frying pan and fry the tortilla pieces, approximately one third at a time so they will cook uniformly, until they are just stiffening but not brown. Drain thoroughly.
5. Preheat your oven to 375° f (190° c).
6. Put one third of the tortilla pieces at the bottom of the dish; drizzle with ⅓ cup (85 ml) of the sauce and one third of the cheese. Repeat with half of the rest of the tortillas, sauce, and cheese, then top off with the rest of the ingredients. Moisten the top cover with the broth. Set in the top level of the oven, uncovered, and bake for fifteen to twenty minutes, or until thoroughly heated and bubbling. (the liquid should have been absorbed and the tortilla pieces just soft, not falling apart, at the bottom and still a little chewy on top. Slight adjustments may be needed to suit the tortillas that are available to you.)
7. Serve, sprinkled with parsley, if you prefer it. Pass the sour cream separately.

TAMALE PIE

Yield: Servings 6 to 8

Ingredients:

- ¾ cup coarse cornmeal
- 1 (14.5 ounce) can diced tomatoes
- 1 (fifteen ounce) can black beans, washed
- 1 cup fresh or frozen corn
- 1 jalapeño chile, stemmed, seeded, and minced
- 1 onion, chopped fine
- 1 pound 90 percent lean ground beef

- 1 tablespoon minced fresh oregano or 1 teaspoon dried
- 2 garlic cloves, minced
- 2 tablespoons chili powder
- 2½ cups water
- 3 tablespoons vegetable oil
- 4 ounces Monterey Jack cheese, shredded (1 cup)
- Salt and pepper

Directions:

1. Adjust oven rack to lower middle position and heat oven to 375 degrees. Heat 1 tablespoon oil in 12 inch frying pan over moderate high heat until just smoking. Put in beef and cook, breaking up meat with wooden spoon, until just starting to brown, approximately five minutes.
2. Mix in onion, jalapeño, and ¼ teaspoon salt and cook until vegetables become tender, approximately five minutes. Mix in chili powder, oregano, and garlic and cook until aromatic, approximately half a minute. Mix in beans, tomatoes and their juice, and corn and simmer until most of liquid has vaporized, approximately 3 minutes. Remove the heat, sprinkle with salt and pepper to taste.
3. Bring water to boil in big deep cooking pan. Put in ¼ teaspoon salt and then slowly pour in cornmeal while whisking vigorously to stop clumping. Turn heat to moderate and cook, whisking continuously, until cornmeal thickens, approximately 3 minutes. Mix in remaining 2 tablespoons oil.
4. Stir Monterey Jack into beef mixture, then scrape into deep dish pie plate (or other 3 quart baking dish). Spread cornmeal mixture over top and seal against edge of dish. Cover with aluminium foil and bake until crust has set and filling is hot throughout, approximately 30 minutes. Allow the casserole to cool for about ten minutes and serve.

TORTILLA AND VEGETABLE CASSEROLE (CASEROLA DE TORTILLAS Y LEGUMBRES)

Yield: Servings 4

Ingredients:

The sauce

- ⅓ cup (85 ml) thinly cut white onion
- ⅔ cup (165 ml) chicken broth or vegetable broth for vegetarians
- 1½ tablespoons vegetable oil
- 12 ounces (340 g) tomatoes, broiled
- Salt to taste

The filling

- 1 cup (250 ml) cooked fresh peas, or defrosted uncooked
- 1 cup (250 ml) cooked green beans, cut into little pieces
- 1 cup (250 ml) cooked, diced carrot
- 12 5- to 6-inch (12.5- to fifteen-cm) tortillas, cut into strips and dried
- Vegetable oil for frying

To serve

- 4 ounces (115 g) chihuahua cheese or substitute grated (approximately 1 heaped cup/265 ml)

Directions:

1. Prepare a mildly greased ovenproof dish about 9 by 6 by 3 inches (23 by fifteen by 8 cm).
2. Heat the oil in a big frying pan and cook the onion gently until soft, approximately 3 minutes; do not brown.
3. Combine the unskinned tomatoes for a short period of time, then add, with the salt, to the onion in the pan. Cook over quite high heat while stirring occasionally, until it reduces—about three minutes. Put in the broth or vegetable water and cook for one minute or so longer, then set aside.
4. Heat the oil in a different frying pan and fry the tortilla pieces, approximately one third at a time so they fry uniformly, until just starting to stiffen, not brown. Drain thoroughly.
5. Preheat your oven to 375° f (190° c).
6. Spread half of the tortilla pieces over the bottom of the dish. Drizzle with approximately one third of the sauce, then cover with the vegetables, the remaining tortillas, and finally the remaining sauce. Cover the dish using foil and bake for approximately twenty minutes, or until the bottom tortillas are tender but not falling apart and the top ones are still slightly chewy. Take away the foil.

7. Drizzle the cheese over the top of the casserole and return the dish to the oven just until the cheese melts. Once this casserole is assembled it must be cooked and served, or it will become rather soggy.

CHILAQUILES

Fried tortillas immersed in a chile sauce and topped with delicious stuff. Who doesn't want that?

GREEN CHILAQUILES (CHILAQUILES VERDES TAMPIQUEÑOS)

Yield: Servings 6

Ingredients:

The sauce

- ⅓ medium white onion, roughly chopped
- 1 cup (250 ml) chicken broth
- 1 tablespoon vegetable oil
- 2 sprigs epazote
- 3 poblano chiles, charred, peeled, seeds and veins removed
- 3 sprigs cilantro
- 8 ounces (225 g) tomate verde, cooked and drained (approximately 1 cup/250 ml;)
- Salt to taste

The tortillas

- twelve tortillas, each cut into 6 triangular pieces and left to dry
- Vegetable oil for frying

To serve

- ½ cup (125 ml) roughly chopped white onion
- 2 hard-cooked eggs, cut
- 2 tablespoons roughly chopped cilantro
- 4 ounces (115 g) queso fresco, crumbled (about ⅔ cup/165 ml)

- 6 big radishes, thinly cut

Directions:

1. Combine the <u>tomate verde</u> with the chiles, epazote, cilantro, onion, and salt until the desired smoothness is achieved.
2. Heat the oil in a big frying pan and fry the sauce over moderate heat, stirring occasionally to prevent sticking, for five minutes. Put in the broth and carry on cooking for a minute more, then take out of the heat and save for later.
3. In a second frying pan, heat the oil and fry the tortilla pieces, approximately one third at a time so they will be uniformly cooked, until they barely start to stiffen but do not brown. Drain thoroughly.
4. Return the sauce to the heat and bring to its boiling point; mix in the tortilla pieces and cook them over moderate heat, scraping the bottom of the pan almost continuously, until most of the liquid has been absorbed and the tortillas are just tenderizing—5 to 8 minutes. Drizzle the cheese, onion, eggs, radishes, and cilantro over the top and serve instantly.

CHILAQUILES DE AGUASCALIENTES

Yield: Servings 4

Ingredients:

The sauce

- ⅛ teaspoon dried mexican oregano
- ¼ cup (65 ml) roughly chopped white onion
- ⅔ cup (165 ml) cooked and drained <u>tomate verde</u>
- 1½ tablespoons sesame seeds, toasted and crushed
- 2 garlic cloves, crushed
- 2 plum tomatoes (about 6 ounces/180 g), broiled
- 2 sprigs cilantro
- 2 tablespoons vegetable oil
- 4 canned chipotle chiles en adobo

- Salt to taste

The tortillas

- 12 stale tortillas, each cut into 6 triangular pieces
- Vegetable oil for frying

To serve

- ¾ cup (190 ml) thinly cut white onion
- 1 tablespoon roughly chopped cilantro (not necessary)
- 3 chorizos (approximately eight ounces/225 g), skinned, crumbled, and fried
- 8 ounces (225 g) queso fresco, crumbled (approximately 1⅓ cups/335 ml)

Directions:

1. In a blender, blend all the sauce ingredients apart from the oil until the desired smoothness is achieved.
2. Heat the oil in a frying pan and cook the sauce over a quite high heat while stirring and scraping the bottom of the pan for approximately five minutes. Turn off the heat and save for later. Preheat your oven to 350° f (180° c).
3. Heat the oil in a different frying pan and fry the tortilla pieces, approximately one third at a time so they are uniformly cooked, until they barely start to stiffen but do not brown. Drain thoroughly.
4. Put one third of the tortillas at the bottom of the dish, then put in half the chorizos and cheese and ⅓ cup (85 ml) of the sauce. Repeat the layers and top off with the remaining tortillas and sauce. Cover the dish using foil and bake for fifteen to twenty minutes, or until it is well thoroughly heated and the tortillas are just tender. Drizzle with the onion and cilantro and serve instantly.

CHILAQUILES VERACRUZANOS

Yield: Servings 4

Ingredients:

The chicken

- ¼ cup (65 ml) roughly cut white onion
- 1 big garlic clove
- 1 whole chicken breast, or 2 big legs, if you want
- 2 cups (500 ml) water
- 2 sprigs cilantro
- 2 sprigs fresh mint, or 1 small tablespoon dried
- Salt to taste

The sauce

- ¼ cup (65 ml) water
- 1 ancho chile, seeds and veins removed
- 1 big garlic clove
- 1 cup (250 ml) chicken broth
- 2 tablespoons vegetable oil
- 8 ounces (225 g) roughly chopped tomatoes (approximately 1½ cups/375 ml)
- Salt to taste

The tortillas

- 12 5-inch (12.5-cm) tortillas, each cut into 6 pieces and dried
- Vegetable oil for frying

To serve

- 1 cup (250 ml) prepared sour cream
- 1 cup (250 ml) thinly cut white onion
- 1 small avocado, peeled, cut into little squares, and dressed with a simple vinaigrette
- 3 ounces (85 g) queso fresco, crumbled (about ⅓ cup/85 ml)

Directions:

1. Place the chicken, salt, garlic, onion, cilantro, and mint with the water into a big deep cooking pan. Heat to a simmer, then reduce the heat and simmer until the chicken is just soft—about twenty minutes for breast, 25 or more for legs. Let the chicken cool off in the

broth. When the meat is sufficiently cool to handle, remove from bones and shred. Strain and reserve the broth.

2. Heat the oil in a frying pan. Fry the chile for approximately one minute on each side, flattening it down in the pan using a spatula. Take away the chile, cover with hot water, and let soak for five to ten minutes. Leave the oil in the pan.

3. Move the drained chile to a blender jar, put in the rest of the sauce ingredients apart from the broth, and blend until the desired smoothness is achieved.

4. Reheat the oil and fry the sauce over quite high heat for approximately three minutes, scraping the bottom of the pan to prevent sticking. Put in the broth and cook for a minute more. Adjust the seasoning, take out of the heat, and save for later.

5. In a separate frying pan, heat the oil and fry the tortilla pieces, approximately one third at a time so they cook uniformly, until they barely start to stiffen but do not brown. Drain thoroughly.

6. Return the sauce to the heat. As it starts to boil, mix in the tortillas and cook over moderate heat for five to 8 minutes, or until most of the sauce has been absorbed and the tortilla pieces are just starting to become tender. Stir almost continuously or the sauce and tortillas will stick and burn.

7. Place the chilaquiles into the dish, then top with the sour cream, chicken, avocado, onion, and cheese. Serve instantly.

CHILAQUILES DE GUANAJUATO

Yield: Servings 4

Ingredients:

The sauce

- ¼ cup (65 ml) roughly chopped white onion
- 12 ounces (340 g) tomate verde, cooked and partly drained (approximately 1½ cups/375 ml;)
- 2 garlic cloves, crushed
- 2 tablespoons vegetable oil
- 6 guajillo chiles, seeds and veins removed, mildly toasted and soaked

- Salt to taste

The tortillas

- 12 stale tortillas, each cut into 6 triangular pieces
- Vegetable oil for frying

To serve

- ½ cup (125 ml) finely chopped white onion
- 6 ounces (180 g) grated chihuahua cheese or muenster (approximately 1¼ cups/315 ml)

Directions:

1. Place the chiles into a blender jar. Put in the rest of the sauce ingredients apart from the oil and blend until fairly smooth.
2. Heat the oil in a frying pan, put in the sauce, and fry over moderate heat for approximately five minutes, scraping the bottom of the pan occasionally. Turn off the heat and save for later.
3. Heat the oil in a different frying pan and fry the tortillas, approximately one third at a time so they are cooked uniformly, until they barely start to stiffen but do not brown. Drain thoroughly.
4. Preheat your broiler or oven.
5. Heat the sauce, mix in the tortilla pieces, and cook over moderate heat, stirring occasionally to prevent sticking, for approximately five minutes, or until they are just starting to tenderize and some of the sauce has been absorbed. (take care, as the sauce sticks and burns easily.) Move the chilaquiles to the serving dish. Cover with the cheese, then run the dish under a hot broiler or into the oven until the cheese just starts to melt. Top with the onion and serve instantly.

TACOS, TOSTADAS, TAMALES, AND MORE

TACOS

When people from all over the world think of Mexican food, the first thing that comes to their mind is "Taco". To the world, a taco is a tortilla bent in half, stuffed with veggies, meats, sauces, etc. Tacos can be soft and they can be fried to a crunchy.

Now, I won't waste too much of your time describing the taco to you, as you've probably eaten more of these than you can count.

TOSTADAS

A tostada is basically a toasted of fried tortilla, and is usually flat or container shaped. This little description doesn't really do justice to the tostada through, as you will see the variety in the recipes that follow.

TAMALES

A tamale is a classic Mesoamerican dish, made of masa or dough, which is steamed in a corn husk or banana leaf.

Now that we're done with the intros, it is time to dive right into the recipes!

HOMEMADE TACO SHELLS

Yield: 8 Taco Shells

For the best results, use the taco shells instantly.

Ingredients:

- ¾ cup vegetable oil
- 8 corn tortillas

Directions:

1. In 8 inch frying pan, heat vegetable oil to 350 degrees. Using tongs, slip half of tortilla into hot oil and immerse using metal spatula. Fry until just set, but not brown, approximately half a minute.

2. Flip tortilla. Hold tortilla open approximately two inches while keeping bottom submerged in oil. Fry until a golden-brown colour is achieved, approximately 1½ minutes. Flip again and fry other side until a golden-brown colour is achieved.

3. Move shell, upside down, to paper towel–lined baking sheet to drain. Repeat with remaining tortillas, keeping oil between 350 and 375 degrees and serve.

DRESSED INDIANS (INDIOS VESTIDOS)

Yield: Servings 6

Ingredients:

The sauce

- ⅓ cup (85 ml) finely chopped white onion
- 1¼ pounds (565 g) tomatoes, broiled
- 2 canned chipotle chiles en adobo
- 2 tablespoons vegetable oil
- Salt to taste

The filling and frying

- 1 big avocado, thinly cut
- 1 pound (450 g) shredded, cooked pork (approximately 1⅓ cups/313 ml), or 8 ounces (225 g) queso fresco, crumbled (approximately 1⅓ cups/335 ml)
- 4 tablespoons finely grated queso añejo cheese
- 5 big eggs, separated
- About ½ cup (125 ml) all-purpose flour
- Salt to taste

To serve

- twelve tortillas, cut into halves
- Vegetable oil for frying

Directions:

1. Heat the oil in a big frying pan and fry the onion gently until translucent. Combine the unskinned tomatoes with the chiles, then put in to the pan, together with the salt. Cook the sauce over quite high heat for approximately 3 minutes so that it reduces a little. Season. Turn off the heat and keep warm.
2. Place a little of the filling onto each piece of tortilla. Fold in half and fasten using a toothpick, then dust mildly with flour.
3. Heat the oil, approximately ½ inch (1.5 cm) deep, in a frying pan.
4. In the meantime, beat the egg whites and salt until stiff but not dry, then put in the yolks, one at a time, and carry on beating until they are well blended. Immerse the tortilla "packages" into the beaten egg—they must be lightly but thoroughly coated—and fry until a golden-brown colour is achieved. Drain thoroughly, then put onto the serving platter, pour the heated sauce over, top with the avocado and cheese, and serve instantly.

SOUR CREAM TACOS (TAQUITOS DE NATA)

Yield: 12 tacos

Ingredients:

The filling

- ½ cup (125 ml) nata sour cream, commercial or homemade, at room temperature
- 1 fresh jalapeño chile, cut into fine strips
- 1 garlic clove
- 1 tablespoon vegetable oil
- 1½ to 2 cups (375 to 500 ml) cooked, shredded, and well-salted chicken
- 12 ounces (340 g) tomatoes, broiled
- 2 tablespoons finely chopped white onion
- 2 tablespoons vegetable oil
- Salt to taste

To serve

- ⅔ cup (165 ml) finely chopped white onion
- twelve tortillas

- Vegetable oil for frying

Directions:

1. Combine the tomatoes with the onion, garlic, and salt and split into two parts. Heat the oil in a frying pan and fry the shredded chicken and chile strips for one minute or so over quite hot heat while stirring occasionally to prevent sticking, until they barely start to brown. Put in half of the tomato puree and carry on cooking and stirring until almost dry. Set aside and keep warm.
2. Heat the oil in a different frying pan and fry the rest of the puree over quite high heat for approximately 3 minutes, stirring occasionally. Turn off the heat and mix in the sour cream. Set aside and keep warm.
3. Heat the oil in a frying pan and lightly fry the tortillas, a few at a time, on both sides.
4. Preheat your oven to 375° f (190° c).
5. Place a little of the filling on each of the tortillas, roll up, and place side by side on the serving dish. Pour the sauce down the center of the tacos and bake for about ten minutes. Drizzle with the onion and serve instantly.

BAJA FISH TACOS WITH PICKLED ONION AND CABBAGE

Yield: Servings 6

Ingredients:

- ¼ cup cornstarch
- ¾ cup all purpose flour
- 1 cup beer
- 1 cup fresh cilantro leaves
- 1 cup Mexican crema
- 1 quart peanut or vegetable oil
- 1 recipe Pickled Onion and Cabbage (recipe follows)
- 1 teaspoon baking powder
- 18 (6 inch) corn tortillas, warmed
- 2 pounds skinless whitefish fillets, such as cod, haddock, or halibut, cut crosswise into 4 by an inch strips
- Salt and pepper

Directions:

1. Adjust oven rack to middle position and heat oven to 200 degrees. Set wire rack in rimmed baking sheet. Pat fish dry using paper towels and sprinkle with salt and pepper. Whisk flour, cornstarch, baking powder, and 1 teaspoon salt together in big container. Put in beer and whisk until the desired smoothness is achieved. Put in fish to batter and toss to coat uniformly.

2. Put in oil to big Dutch oven until it measures about ¾ inch deep and heat over moderate high heat to 350 degrees.

3. Remove five or six pieces of fish from batter, allowing surplus to drip back into container, and put in to hot oil, for a short period of time dragging fish along surface of oil to stop sticking. Adjust burner, if required, to maintain oil temperature between 325 and 350 degrees. Fry fish, stirring slowly to stop pieces from clinging together and turning as required, until a golden-brown colour is achieved and crunchy, approximately eight minutes.

4. Move fish to readied wire rack and place in oven to keep warm. Return oil to 350 degrees and repeat with the rest of the fish, working with five or six pieces at a time. Serve with warm tortillas, cilantro, crema, and Pickled Onion and Cabbage.

PICKLED ONION AND CABBAGE

Yield: Servings 6

Ingredients:

- 1 cup white wine vinegar
- 1 small red onion, halved and cut thin
- 1 tablespoon sugar
- 2 jalapeño chiles, stemmed and cut into thin rings
- 2 tablespoons lime juice
- 3 cups shredded green cabbage
- Salt and pepper

Directions:

1. Mix onion and jalapeños in medium container. Bring vinegar, lime juice, sugar, and 1 teaspoon salt to boil in small deep cooking pan.

2. Pour vinegar mixture over onion mixture and allow it to sit for minimum 30 minutes, or place in your fridge for maximum 2 days.
3. Move ¼ cup pickling liquid to second medium container, put in cabbage, ½ teaspoon salt, and ½ teaspoon pepper and toss to blend.

BEEF TACOS (TACOS DE RES)

Yield: 12 tacos

Ingredients:

The filling

- ½ cup (125 ml) thinly cut white onion
- 1 pound (450 g) cooked and shredded beef (about 2 cups/500 ml;)
- 1½ tablespoons vegetable oil
- 12 strips of jalapeño chiles, with seeds

To serve

- ¾ cup (185 ml) prepared sour cream
- 1 cup (250 ml) salsa ranchera
- 3 ounces (85 g) queso fresco, crumbled (about ½ cup/125 ml)
- twelve tortillas
- Vegetable oil for frying

Directions:

1. Heat the oil in a big frying pan and fry the onion gently until translucent. Put in the meat and chiles and cook on moderate heat, stirring occasionally, until it is mildly browned. Set aside to cool a little.
2. Fill the tortillas and fry until mildly crunchy on the outside. Drain, then serve instantly topped with the sauce, sour cream, and cheese.

CARNITAS

Yield: Servings 6 to 8

Ingredients:

- ⅓ cup fresh orange juice, spent orange halves reserved
- 1 (3½ to 4 pound) boneless pork butt roast, fat cap trimmed to ⅛ inch thick and slice into 2 inch chunks
- 1 onion, peeled and halved
- 1 teaspoon dried oregano
- 1 teaspoon ground cumin
- 18–24 (6 inch) corn tortillas, warmed
- 2 bay leaves
- 2 cups water
- 2 tablespoons lime juice
- Fresh cilantro leaves
- Lime wedges
- Salt and pepper

Directions:

1. Adjust oven rack to lower middle position and heat oven to 300 degrees. Mix pork, water, onion, lime juice, oregano, cumin, bay leaves, 1 teaspoon salt, and ½ teaspoon pepper in Dutch oven (liquid should just barely cover meat). Put in orange juice and spent orange halves to pot. Bring mixture to simmer over moderate high heat while stirring once in a while. Cover pot, move to oven, and cook until meat is tender and falls apart when prodded with fork, approximately 2 hours, turning pieces of meat once during cooking.
2. Take the pot out of the oven and turn oven to broil. Using slotted spoon, move pork to container; discard orange halves, onion, and bay leaves (do not skim fat from liquid). Staying cautious of hot pot handles, place pot using high heat and simmer braising liquid, stirring frequently, until thick and syrupy, about eight to twelve minutes; you should have approximately 1 cup reduced liquid.
3. Move pork to cutting board and pull each piece in half with the help of two forks. Return pork to container, fold in reduced liquid, and sprinkle with salt and pepper to taste. Spread pork in even layer on wire rack set in rimmed baking sheet. Broil pork until thoroughly browned (but not charred) and edges are mildly crunchy on both sides, ten to 16 minutes, turning meat midway through broiling. Serve with warm tortillas, cilantro, and lime wedges.

CHICKEN TAMALES (TAMALES DE POLLO)

Yield: about 30 3-inch (8-cm) tamales

Ingredients:

The filling

- About 6 cups (1.5 l) well-seasoned chicken broth to cover
- One 3½-pound (1.575-kg) chicken cut into serving pieces, with skin and bone
- The chicken giblets

The sauce

- ¼ teaspoon cumin seeds, crushed
- 1 big garlic clove, roughly chopped
- 1 cup (250 ml) thinly cut white onion
- 1½ pounds (680 g) tomatoes, broiled
- 3 tablespoons vegetable oil or melted chicken fat
- 4 whole cloves, crushed
- 6 peppercorns, crushed
- Salt to taste

The masa

- 1½ pounds (675 g) tamale dough
- 8 ounces (225 g) pork lard
- About ½ cup (125 ml) of the reserved chicken broth, warm
- Salt to taste

To assemble the tamales

- 30 corn husks, soaked to tenderize and shaken dry
- 30 pitted green olives
- 30 strips of fresh jalapeños

Directions:

1. Make the filling: put the chicken, giblets, and broth into a big deep cooking pan, bring to a simmer, and carry on cooking using low heat until nearly soft—about 30 minutes. Take away the chicken and allow to cool. Strain the broth. There must be about 3 cups (750 ml). Shred the chicken roughly.

2. Make the sauce: place a few of the tomatoes into a blender jar with the garlic and spices and blend meticulously. Put in the remaining tomatoes and blend to a textured sauce.

3. Heat the oil in a big frying pan, put in the onion, and fry on moderate heat until translucent—about three minutes. Put in the mixed ingredients and cook over quite high heat until reduced and seasoned—about five minutes. Mix in the chicken pieces, adjust salt, and set aside to season.

4. Using an electric mixer, beat the lard about five minutes until well aerated—it will become very white and opaque. Slowly beat in the masa alternately with the warm broth as required (depending on how dry the masa), put in salt, and beat again for approximately five minutes or until a small ball of the mixture floats on the surface of a glass of water.

5. Bring a tamale steamer to heat.

6. Assembling the tamales: spread a big tablespoon of the dough finely over the inside of a corn husk. Put some of the sauced chicken down the middle with a strip of the chile and an olive. Fold the husk so that the masa is fully covered and turn the pointed end up to the back of the tamale—this will tighten up the seam.

7. Stack the tamales in the top of a tamale steamer, steam for approximately 1 hour, then test. If the dough separates easily from the husk the tamale is cooked.

CLASSIC GROUND BEEF TACOS

Yield: Servings 4

Ingredients:

- ¼ teaspoon cayenne pepper
- ½ cup canned tomato sauce
- ½ cup chicken broth
- ½ teaspoon dried oregano
- 1 onion, chopped fine
- 1 pound 90 percent lean ground beef

- 1 tablespoon vegetable oil
- 1 teaspoon ground coriander
- 1 teaspoon ground cumin
- 1 teaspoon packed light brown sugar
- 2 tablespoons chili powder
- 2 teaspoons cider vinegar
- 3 garlic cloves, minced
- 8 taco shells, warmed
- Salt

Directions:

1. Heat oil in 10 inch frying pan on moderate heat until it starts to shimmer Put in onion and cook until tender, approximately five minutes. Mix in chili powder, garlic, cumin, coriander, oregano, cayenne, and 1 teaspoon salt and cook until aromatic, approximately half a minute.
2. Mix in ground beef and cook, breaking up meat with wooden spoon, until no longer pink, approximately five minutes. Mix in tomato sauce, broth, vinegar, and sugar and simmer until it becomes thick, approximately ten minutes. Sprinkle with salt to taste. Split filling uniformly among taco shells before you serve.

CORN TORTILLAS

Yield: approximately 12 (6 inch) tortillas

Ingredients:

- ¼ teaspoon salt
- 1¼ cups warm tap water, plus extra as required
- 2 cups (8 ounces) masa harina or Maseca Brand Instant Masa Corn Flour
- 2 teaspoons vegetable oil

Directions:

1. Mix masa, 1 teaspoon oil, and salt together in medium container, then fold in water using a rubber spatula. Use your hands to knead mixture in container, putting in extra water, 1 tablespoon at a time, as required, until dough is tender and tacky but not clingy, and has

texture of Play Doh. Cover dough using a damp dish towel and allow it to sit for five minutes.

2. Cut sides of 1 quart zipper lock bag, leaving bottom seam undamaged. Line big plate with 2 damp dish towels. Split dough into 12 equivalent portions (1½ ounces each); keep covered. Working with 1 piece at a time, roll into ball, place on 1 side of zipper lock bag, and fold other side over top. Push dough flat into 6½ inch wide tortilla (approximately 1/16 inch thick) with the help of a tortilla press or pie plate; leave tortilla between plastic until frying pan is hot.

3. Heat remaining 1 teaspoon oil in 8 inch nonstick frying pan over moderate high heat until it starts to shimmer Use a paper towel to wipe out frying pan, leaving thin film of oil on bottom. Take the plastic off on top of tortilla, flip tortilla onto your palm, then remove plastic on bottom and lay tortilla in frying pan. Cook tortilla, without moving it, until it moves freely when pan is shaken and has shriveled slightly in size, approximately 45 seconds.

4. Turn the tortilla over and cook until edges curl and bottom is spotty brown, approximately one minute. Turn the tortilla back over and carry on cooking until first side is spotty brown and puffs up in center, thirty to 60 seconds. Lay toasted tortilla between damp dish towels. Repeat with the rest of the dough. (Tortillas can be placed in your fridge for maximum 5 days.)

CRISP-FRIED TORTILLA PIECES (TOTOPOS)

Totopos, squares or strips of crisped corn tortillas, are used as a topping for soups, added to scrambled eggs, and much more. Cut into bigger triangles, they are used as scoops with guacamole or refried beans.

It is a good idea to prepare your own totopos, since the commercially packaged ones, known as "fritos" in the USA, are too thin and highly seasoned. First, cut your corn tortillas into the required shapes and spread them onto a rack to dry out overnight—so they will absorb less oil in the frying process. Heat vegetable oil to the depth of approximately ½ inch (1.25 cm) in a smallish frying pan and fry a small quantity of the totopos until crunchy and a deep golden-brown in color. Drain thoroughly using paper towels. They are best used instantly, but if you have leftovers, freeze them and reheat using your oven.

SIMPLE CHIPOTLE CHICKEN TACOS

Yield: Servings 4

Ingredients:

- ½ cup orange juice
- ¾ cup chopped fresh cilantro
- 1 tablespoon Worcestershire sauce
- 1 teaspoon yellow mustard
- 1½ pounds boneless, skinless chicken breasts, trimmed
- 12 (6 inch) corn tortillas, warmed
- 2 teaspoons minced canned chipotle chile in adobo sauce
- 3 tablespoons unsalted butter
- 4 garlic cloves, minced
- Lime wedges
- Salt and pepper

Directions:

1. Melt butter in 12 inch frying pan over moderate high heat. Put in garlic and chipotle and cook until aromatic, approximately half a minute. Mix in ½ cup cilantro, orange juice, and Worcestershire and bring to simmer. Nestle chicken into sauce. Cover, decrease the heat to moderate low, and cook until chicken records 160 degrees, ten to fifteen minutes, turning chicken midway through cooking. Move chicken to plate and cover.
2. Increase heat to moderate high and cook liquid left in frying pan until reduced to ¼ cup, approximately five minutes. Remove the heat, whisk in mustard. Using 2 forks, shred chicken into bite size pieces and return to frying pan. Put in remaining ¼ cup cilantro and toss until well blended. Sprinkle with salt and pepper to taste. Serve with warm tortillas and lime wedges.

GORDITAS

Yield: 12 gorditas; serves four to 6

Ingredients:

- 1 recipe filling, warmed
- 1 teaspoon salt
- 1¾ cups hot tap water
- 2 cups (8 ounces) masa harina (Dried corn dougn)
- 2 cups vegetable oil

Directions:

1. Mix masa harina and salt in medium container, then fold in water using a rubber spatula. Use your hands to knead mixture in container until tender dough forms, one to two minutes. Cover dough using a damp dish towel and allow it to sit for five minutes.
2. Cut twenty four 8 inch squares of parchment paper. Knead dough for a short period of time, then split into 12 equivalent portions, roll into balls, and place on baking sheet. Cover dough using a damp dish towel.
3. Working with 1 piece dough at a time, press flat into 3½ inch wide disk between 2 pieces parchment with the help of a pie plate. Remove top piece parchment, softly push in edges to make a little thicker and smooth out any cracks, then flatten slightly to level; edges must be smooth, flat, and a little thicker than center. Move to plate, leaving bottom piece parchment in place, and cover using a damp dish towel; tortillas can be stacked.
4. Heat eleven-inch straight sided sauté pan on moderate heat until hot, two to three minutes. Put 1 tortilla parchment side up in your palm, remove parchment, then gently lay tortilla in hot, dry pan; repeat with 2 more tortillas. Cook until lightly golden on both sides, four to six minutes, turning midway through cooking; move to baking sheet. Repeat with remaining tortillas, lowering heat as required to stop scorching. (Gorditas can be stacked between parchment paper, wrapped using plastic wrap, and placed in the fridge for maximum 1 day or frozen for maximum three months; thaw completely before continuing.)
5. Coat second baking sheet with several layers of paper towels. Cautiously add oil to now empty pan and heat over moderate high heat to 375 degrees. Working in batches, fry tortillas, turning often, until they puff, two to three minutes. Move to readied baking sheet and allow to cool slightly. Use a paring knife to cut puffed tortillas open midway around edge. Stuff each tortilla with filling before you serve.

GRILLED CHICKEN TACOS

Yield: Servings 4

Ingredients:

- ¼ cup vegetable oil
- ½ cup chopped fresh cilantro
- 1 jalapeño chile, stemmed, halved, and seeded
- 1 onion, peeled and slice into ½ inch thick rounds
- 1 pound tomatillos, husks and stems removed, washed well and dried
- 1½ pounds boneless, skinless chicken breasts, trimmed
- 12 (6 inch) corn tortillas
- 2 tablespoons water
- 3 tablespoons lime juice (2 limes)
- 5 cloves garlic, minced
- Salt and pepper
- Sugar

Directions:

1. Whisk 3 tablespoons oil, 1 tablespoon lime juice, water, 1 teaspoon sugar, 1½ teaspoons salt, ½ teaspoon pepper, and half of garlic together in medium container. Put in chicken, cover, and refrigerate, turning once in a while, for half an hour Brush onion, jalapeño, and half of tomatillos with remaining 1 tablespoon oil and sprinkle with salt. Halve remaining tomatillos; set aside.
2. **For a Charcoal Grill:** Open bottom vent fully. Light big chimney starter filled with charcoal briquettes (6 quarts). When top coals are partly covered with ash, pour uniformly over grill. Set cooking grate in place, cover, and open lid vent fully. Heat grill until hot, approximately five minutes. **For A Gas Grill**: Set all burners to high, cover, and heat grill until hot, approximately fifteen minutes. Leave all burners on high.
3. Clean and oil cooking grate. Put chicken and oiled vegetables on grill. Cook (covered if using gas), turning as required, until chicken records 160 degrees and vegetables are mildlly charred and tender, ten to fifteen minutes. Move chicken and vegetables to cutting board and tent with aluminium foil.
4. Working in batches, grill tortillas, turning as required, until warm and soft, approximately half a minute; wrap firmly in foil to keep tender.

5. Chop grilled vegetables coarse, then pulse with remaining tomatillos, cilantro, remaining garlic, remaining 2 tablespoons lime juice, ½ teaspoon salt, and pinch sugar inside a food processor until slightly lumpy, 16 to 18 pulses. Slice chicken thin on bias and serve with tortillas and tomatillo salsa.

GRILLED FISH TACOS

Yield: Servings 6

Ingredients:

- ½ cup orange juice
- 1 jalapeño chile
- 1 pineapple, peeled, quartered along the length, cored, and each quarter halved along the length
- 1 red bell pepper, stemmed, seeded, and slice into ¼ inch pieces
- 1 tablespoon ancho chile powder
- 1 teaspoon dried oregano
- 1 teaspoon ground coriander
- 18 (6 inch) corn tortillas
- 2 garlic cloves, minced
- 2 pounds skinless swordfish steaks, an inch thick, cut along the length into an inch thick strips
- 2 tablespoons minced fresh cilantro, plus extra for serving
- 2 tablespoons tomato paste
- 2 teaspoons chipotle chile powder
- 3 tablespoons vegetable oil
- 6 tablespoons lime juice (3 limes)
- Salt

Directions:

1. Heat 2 tablespoons oil, ancho chile powder, and chipotle chile powder in 8 inch frying pan on moderate heat, stirring continuously, until aromatic and some bubbles form, two to three minutes. Put in garlic, oregano, coriander, and 1 teaspoon salt and carry on cooking until aromatic, approximately half a minute. Put in tomato paste and, using spatula,

purée tomato paste with spice mixture until blended, approximately twenty seconds. Mix in orange juice and 2 tablespoons lime juice. Cook while stirring continuously, until meticulously mixed and reduced slightly, approximately 2 minutes. Move chile mixture to big container and allow to cool for fifteen minutes.

2. Put in swordfish to chile mixture and stir slowly to coat. Cover and place in your fridge for minimum 30 minutes or maximum 2 hours. Brush pineapple and jalapeño with remaining 1 tablespoon oil.

3. **For a Charcoal Grill:** Open bottom vent fully. Light big chimney starter mounded with charcoal briquettes (7 quarts). When top coals are partly covered with ash, pour uniformly over grill. Set cooking grate in place, cover, and open lid vent fully. Heat grill until hot, approximately five minutes. **For A Gas Grill:** Set all burners to high, cover, and heat grill until hot, approximately fifteen minutes. Turn all burners to moderate high.

4. Clean and oil cooking grate. Put fish, pineapple, and jalapeño on grill. Cover and cook until fish, pineapple, and jalapeño have begun to brown, three to five minutes. Using thin spatula, turn fish, pineapple, and jalapeño. Cover and cook until pineapple and jalapeño are thoroughly browned and swordfish records 140 degrees, three to five minutes; move to platter and cover using aluminium foil.

5. Working in batches, grill tortillas, turning as required, until warm and soft, approximately half a minute; wrap firmly in foil to keep tender.

6. Chop pineapple and jalapeño fine and mix with bell pepper, cilantro, and remaining 4 tablespoons lime juice in container. Sprinkle with salt to taste. Using 2 forks, pull fish apart into big flakes and serve with pineapple salsa and tortillas.

GRILLED SHRIMP TACOS WITH JÍCAMA SLAW

Yield: Servings 6

Ingredients:

- ¼ cup thinly cut red onion
- 1 cup Mexican crema
- 1 pound jícama, peeled and slice into 3 inch long matchsticks
- 1 tablespoon minced fresh oregano or 1 teaspoon dried
- 1 teaspoon garlic powder
- 1 teaspoon grated orange zest plus ⅓ cup juice

- 18 (6 inch) corn tortillas
- 2 pounds extra big shrimp (21 to 25 per pound), peeled, deveined, and tails removed
- 2 teaspoons chipotle chile powder
- 3 tablespoons chopped fresh cilantro
- 3 tablespoons vegetable oil
- Lime wedges
- Salt

Directions:

1. Mix jícama, orange zest and juice, onion, cilantro, and ½ teaspoon salt in container, cover, and place in your fridge until ready to serve.
2. Whisk oil, oregano, chile powder, garlic powder, and ½ teaspoon salt together in big container. Pat shrimp dry using paper towels, put in to spice mixture, and toss to coat. Thread shrimp onto four 12 inch metal skewers, alternating direction of heads and tails.
3. **For a Charcoal Grill:** Open bottom vent fully. Light big chimney starter mounded with charcoal briquettes (7 quarts). When top coals are partly covered with ash, pour uniformly over grill. Set cooking grate in place, cover, and open lid vent fully. Heat grill until hot, approximately five minutes. **For A Gas Grill:** Set all burners to high, cover, and heat grill until hot, approximately fifteen minutes. Leave all burners on high.
4. Clean and oil cooking grate. Put shrimp on grill and cook (covered if using gas) until mildlly charred on first side, approximately 4 minutes. Flip shrimp, pushing them together on skewer if they separate, and cook until opaque throughout, approximately 2 minutes. Move to platter and cover using aluminium foil.
5. Working in batches, grill tortillas, turning as required, until warm and soft, approximately half a minute; wrap firmly in foil to keep tender.
6. Slide shrimp off skewers onto cutting board and slice into ½ inch pieces. Serve with tortillas, jícama slaw, crema, and lime wedges.

GRILLED SKIRT STEAK AND POBLANO TACOS

Yield: Servings 6

Ingredients:

- ½ teaspoon ground cumin

- 1 tablespoon vegetable oil
- 1½ pounds poblano chiles
- 18 (6 inch) corn tortillas
- 2 pounds skirt steak, trimmed
- 3 garlic cloves, minced
- 4 onions (3 cut crosswise into ½ inch thick rounds, 1 chopped coarse)
- 6 tablespoons lime juice (3 limes)
- Lime wedges
- Salt and pepper

Directions:

1. Process chopped onion, lime juice, garlic, cumin, and 1 teaspoon salt inside a food processor until the desired smoothness is achieved. Brush onion rounds and poblanos with oil and sprinkle with salt and pepper. Pat steak dry and sprinkle with salt and pepper.

2. **For a Charcoal Grill:** Open bottom vent fully. Light big chimney starter filled with charcoal briquettes (6 quarts). When top coals are partly covered with ash, pour uniformly over half of grill. Set cooking grate in place, cover, and open lid vent fully. Heat grill until hot, approximately five minutes. **For a Gas Grill:** Set all burners to high, cover, and heat grill until hot, approximately fifteen minutes. Leave primary burner on high and turn other burner(s) off.

3. Clean and oil cooking grate. Put poblanos on hotter side of grill and onion rounds on cooler side of grill. Grill (covered if using gas), turning as required, until poblanos are blistered and blackened and onions become tender and golden, 6 to twelve minutes. Move onions to platter and cover to keep warm. Move peppers to container, cover, and allow to steam while cooking steak and tortillas.

4. Put steak on hotter side of grill. Grill (covered if using gas), turning as required, until thoroughly browned on both sides and meat records 120 to 125 degrees (for medium rare), four to 8 minutes. Move steak to 13 by 9 inch pan and poke all over with fork. Pour pureed onion mixture over top, cover, and allow to rest for five to ten minutes.

5. Working in batches, grill tortillas, turning as required, until warm and soft, approximately half a minute; wrap firmly in aluminium foil to keep tender.

6. Peel poblanos, then slice thin. Separate onions into rings and cut coarse, then toss with poblanos. Take the steak out of the marinade, slice into four to 6 inch lengths, then slice thin against grain. Serve with warm tortillas, poblano onion mixture, and lime wedges.

GROUND PORK TACOS WITH ALMONDS AND RAISINS

Yield: Servings 4

Ingredients:

- ⅛ teaspoon ground cloves
- ¼ cup slivered almonds, toasted
- ½ cup canned tomato sauce
- ½ teaspoon ground cinnamon
- ½ teaspoon minced canned chipotle chile in adobo sauce
- 1 cup chicken broth
- 1 pound ground pork
- 1 small onion, chopped fine
- 1 tablespoon cider vinegar
- 1 tablespoon vegetable oil
- 2 garlic cloves, minced
- 2 tablespoons chopped raisins
- 8 taco shells, warmed
- Salt and pepper

Directions:

1. Heat oil in 12 inch nonstick frying pan on moderate heat until it starts to shimmer Put in onion and cook until tender, five to seven minutes. Mix in garlic, chipotle, cinnamon, and cloves and cook until aromatic, approximately half a minute. Mix in pork and cook, breaking up meat with wooden spoon, until no longer pink, approximately five minutes.
2. Mix in broth, tomato sauce, raisins, vinegar, ½ teaspoon salt, and ½ teaspoon pepper and simmer until it becomes thick, approximately ten minutes. Mix in almonds and sprinkle with salt and pepper to taste. Split filling uniformly among taco shells before you serve.

GUACAMOLE AND SOUR CREAM TOSTADAS (TOSTADAS DE GUACAMOLE Y CREMA)

Yield: twelve tostadas

Ingredients:

- 1 cup (250 ml) prepared sour cream
- 1½ cups (375 ml) finely shredded lettuce
- 12 corn tortillas
- 2 cups (500 ml) guacamole
- 4 to 6 jalapeño chiles en escabeche, cut into strips
- 8 ounces (225 g) chihuahua cheese (or any other cheese of your choice if you can't find it), cut into thin slices
- Vegetable oil for frying

Directions:

1. Heat the oil in a frying pan and fry the tortillas until crunchy. Drain thoroughly.
2. Cover the tortillas with the cut cheese and melt under a broiler or in your oven. Top each tostada with a big spoonful of the guacamole, a little sour cream, some shredded lettuce, and some chile strips. Serve instantly.

INDOOR STEAK TACOS

Yield: Servings 4

Ingredients:

- ½ cup fresh cilantro leaves, plus extra for serving
- ½ teaspoon ground cumin
- ½ teaspoon sugar
- 1 (1½ to 1¾ pound) flank steak, trimmed and cut with grain into 4 pieces
- 1 jalapeño chile, stemmed and chopped coarse
- 1 tablespoon lime juice
- 12 (6 inch) corn tortillas, warmed
- 3 garlic cloves, chopped coarse
- 3 scallions, chopped coarse
- 6 tablespoons vegetable oil
- Lime wedges
- Salt and pepper

Directions:

1. Pulse cilantro, scallions, garlic, jalapeño, and cumin inside a food processor until finely chopped, ten to 12 pulses. Put in ¼ cup oil and pulse until mixture is smooth, approximately fifteen seconds, scraping down container as required. Move 2 tablespoons herb paste to moderate container and mix in lime juice; set aside for serving.

2. Using dinner fork, poke each piece of steak ten to 12 times on each side. Put steaks in big baking dish, rub meticulously with 1½ teaspoons salt, then coat with remaining herb paste. Cover and place in your fridge for 30 minutes to an hour.

3. Scrape herb paste off steaks and drizzle with sugar and ½ teaspoon pepper. Heat remaining 2 tablespoons oil in 12 inch nonstick frying pan over moderate high heat until just smoking. Cook steaks, turning as required, until thoroughly browned on all sides and meat records 120 to 125 degrees (for medium rare), four to six minutes. Move steaks to cutting board and allow to rest for five minutes.

4. Slice steaks thin against grain, put in to container with reserved herb paste, and toss to coat. Sprinkle with salt and pepper to taste. Serve with warm tortillas, extra cilantro, and lime wedges.

LITTLE TACOS (TAQUITOS)

Yield: 12 tacos

Ingredients:

To prepare the tacos

- ¾ cup (185 ml) frijoles refritos (Mexican Refried Beans)
- 1 small avocado, cut into 12 slices
- 12 5- to 6-inch (12.5- to fifteen-cm) tortillas
- 12 thin slices white onion
- 4 ounces (115 g) chihuahua cheese or muenster (approximately 1 cup/250 ml)
- 4 to 6 canned chipotle chiles, each cut into 3 pieces
- Salt to taste

To serve

- 6 big radishes, thinly cut

- 6 romaine lettuce leaves, shredded
- Approximately 3 tablespoons roughly chopped cilantro sprigs
- Vegetable oil for frying

Directions:

1. On each tortilla place a slice of avocado, some strips of cheese, a piece or two of chile, a tablespoon of beans, and a thin slice of onion. Drizzle well with salt, roll the tortillas up, and secure using a toothpick.
2. Fry until golden but not too crunchy. Drain using paper towels and serve topped with the lettuce, radishes, and chopped cilantro.

MICHOACÁN FRESH CORN TAMALES (UCHEPOS)

Yield: 20 uchepos

Ingredients:

- ¼ cup (65 ml) milk (if required)
- 1 tablespoon natas, or crème fraîche or thick cream
- 1 tablespoon sugar
- 1 tablespoon unsalted butter
- 1 teaspoon salt
- 5 cups (1.25 l) white starchy field corn kernels
- About 20 fresh corn husks

Directions:

1. Prepare a tamale steamer. Put half of the corn into the container of a food processor, and pulse until the corn has been reduced to a textured consistency—approximately 1½ minutes. Put in the remaining corn and carry on grinding until you have a finely textured puree—about 2½ minutes more, putting in the milk only if required to blend. Put in the remaining ingredients and mix thoroughly.
2. Shake the husks once again to get rid of any surplus water. Put 1 heaped tablespoon of the mixture down the center of the husk, beginning just below the cupped top and extending approximately two inches (5 cm) down the husk. Being careful not to flatten

the mixture, or allow it to ooze out, roll, rather than fold, the husk over so that it overlaps the other side completely.

3. Fold the point end up to the back of the uchepo and instantly place it horizontally in the top of the steamer. (because of the loose consistency of the mixture they have to be cooked instantly and cannot sit around while you finish making them.)
4. To make sure that the bottom layer will not be squashed flat, steam for approximately ten minutes before you put in the rest. Don't forget to stir the mixture well before you continue with the subsequent layers. Steam for 1¼ hours and then test. The uchepos should barely separate from the husk. Set the uchepos aside to firm up for approximately 2 hours before you use.

MUSHROOM TACOS (TACOS DE HONGOS)

Yield: 12 tacos

Ingredients:

The filling

- ¼ cup (65 ml) finely chopped white onion
- 1 pound (450 g) mushrooms or cuitlacoche, roughly chopped (approximately four cups/1 l)
- 12 ounces (340 g) tomatoes, finely chopped (about 2 cups/500 ml)
- 2 garlic cloves, peeled and chopped
- 2 sprigs epazote or parsley, finely chopped
- 3 serrano chiles, cut into strips, with seeds and veins
- 3 tablespoons vegetable oil
- Salt to taste

To serve

- Prepared sour cream (not necessary)
- twelve tortillas
- Vegetable oil or melted lard for frying

Directions:

1. Heat the oil in a big frying pan and fry the onion and garlic gently for a few seconds; do not allow them to brown.
2. Put in the tomatoes, chiles, mushrooms, and salt. Cook on moderate heat, uncovered, stirring the mixture occasionally until the mushrooms are tender and the juices reduced—about fifteen minutes.
3. Put in the epazote and cook for a minute more. Set aside to cool a little.
4. Place a little of the mixture onto each of the tortillas, roll them up, and secure using a toothpick. Heat the fat and fry the tacos until they are just crisping but not hard. Drain them well and serve them instantly, either plain or with a little prepared sour cream.

NORTHERN BEAN TAMALES (TAMALES DE FRIJOL NORTEÑOS)

Yield: about 33 4-inch (10-cm) tamales

Ingredients:

The bean filling and chile sauce

- ¾ teaspoon cumin seeds, crushed
- 1 cup (250 ml) meat broth or water
- 2 garlic cloves
- 3 big ancho chiles, seeds and veins removed
- 3 tablespoons pork lard
- 4 peppercorns, crushed
- 8 ounces (225 g) flor de mayo or pinto beans
- Salt to taste

The masa

- 1 pound (450 g) tamale dough (about 2 cups/500 ml)
- 3 tablespoons reserved chile sauce
- 4½ ounces (130 g) pork lard (½ cup/125 ml, plus 2 tablespoons)
- About ⅓ cup (85 ml) meat broth or water
- About 36 halved corn husks—about 3 inches (8 cm) wide at the top, softened in water, drained, patted dry
- Salt to taste

Directions:

1. Prepare a tamale steamer.
2. Pick through the beans to ensure there are no small stones. Wash in cold water and skim the surface of any flotsam. Place the beans into a big deep cooking pan or slow cooker, cover with fresh water, and bring to its boiling point. Cook until the beans are fairly soft and most of the water has been absorbed—you should have approximately four cups (1 l).
3. In the meantime, prepare the chile sauce. Place the chiles and garlic into a small deep cooking pan, cover with water, bring to a simmer, and cook for approximately five minutes. Drain and save for later. Put ½ cup (125 ml) of the broth or water into your blender jar, put in the cumin and peppercorns, and blend well. Tear the chile into pieces and add, with the garlic and another ½ cup (125 ml) of the broth or water, to the blender jar and blend to a quite smooth sauce.
4. Heat the 3 tablespoons of lard in a deep frying pan, put in the beans, and purée on moderate heat to a rough-textured consistency. Mix in all but 3 tablespoons of the chile sauce and salt to taste and carry on cooking on moderate heat, stirring occasionally to prevent sticking until reduced—the bean paste should just plop off the spoon—and well seasoned, approximately fifteen minutes. Set aside to cool. You should have about 3½ cups (875 ml).
5. In a big container, combine the masa with the lard, the reserved 3 tablespoons chile sauce, and about ⅓ cup (85 ml) of the broth or water—with either your hand or an electric mixer—until all the ingredients are well blended. Put in salt as required.
6. Coat the top of the steamer with some of the corn husks and place an inverted soup plate in the center. Set on moderate heat.
7. Spread 1 rounded tablespoon of the dough super slimly over the whole width of the top of the corn husk and for approximately 4 inches (10 cm) down the husk. Put some of the bean paste down the center of the dough and fold one edge of the husk over the other to make a slender tamale—the overlapping masa will stick and help to close the husk more securely. Double the point of the husk up to cover the seam.
8. Stack the tamales in circular layers, the first layer supported at a gentle angle by the top of the plate. Cover the steamer and cook using high heat for approximately 50 minutes. The tamale is cooked when the dough separates cleanly from the husk.

NORTHERN PORK-FILLED TAMALES (TAMALES DE PUERCO NORTEÑOS)

Yield: about 33 4-inch (10-cm) tamales

Ingredients:

The meat filling

- ¾ teaspoon cumin seeds, crushed
- 1 pound (450 g) stewing pork with some fat, see note above, cut into ½-inch (1.5-cm) cubes
- 2 garlic cloves
- 3 big ancho chiles, seeds and veins removed
- 4 peppercorns, crushed
- Salt to taste

The masa

- 1 pound (450 g) tamale dough (about 2 cups/500 ml)
- 3 tablespoons of reserved chile sauce
- 4½ ounces (130 g) pork lard (½ cup/125 ml, plus 2 tablespoons)
- About 36 halved corn husks—about 3 inches (8 cm) wide at the top, softened in water, drained, patted dry
- Salt to taste

Directions:

1. Prepare a tamale steamer. Place the meat into a big deep cooking pan, cover with water, put in salt, and bring to a simmer. Carry on cooking until the meat is soft—thirty-five to forty minutes. Drain the meat and save for later. You will require minimum 2½ cups (625 ml) of broth; put in water if required to make up to that amount.
2. Place the chiles and garlic into a small deep cooking pan, cover with water, bring to a simmer, and cook for approximately five minutes. Strain and save for later.
3. Put ½ cup (125 ml) of the broth into your blender jar, put in the cumin and peppercorns, and blend well. Tear the chiles into pieces and put in to the blender jar together with the garlic and another ½ cup (125 ml) broth. Blend to a quite smooth sauce.

4. Place the meat into a frying pan, put in all but 3 tablespoons of the sauce and 1 cup (250 ml) of the broth, and cook on moderate heat, stirring occasionally, until well seasoned and the sauce is slightly reduced—to a medium consistency—about fifteen minutes. Adjust salt and allow to cool.

5. In a big container, combine the masa with the lard, the reserved 3 tablespoons of chile sauce, and about ⅓ cup (85 ml) of the rest of the broth with your hand, or an electric mixer, until all the ingredients are well blended—about five minutes. Put in salt as required.

6. Coat the top of the steamer with some of the corn husks and place an inverted soup plate in the center. Set on moderate heat.

7. Spread 1 rounded tablespoon of the dough super slimly over the whole width of the top and for approximately 4 inches (10 cm) down the corn husk. Put a few pieces of the meat and some of the sauce down the center of the dough and fold one edge of the husk over the other to make a slender tamale—the overlapping masa will stick and help to close the leaf securely. Double the point of the husk up to cover the seam.

8. Stack the tamales in circular layers, the first layer supported at a gentle angle by the top of the plate. Cover the steamer and cook using high heat for approximately 50 minutes. The tamale is cooked when the dough separates cleanly from the husk.

PANUCHOS

Yield: 12 panuchos; serves four to 6

Ingredients:

- 1 cup refried beans
- 1 recipe topping, warmed
- 1 teaspoon plus ¼ cup vegetable oil, plus extra as required
- 1¾ cups hot tap water
- 2 cups (8 ounces) masa harina
- Salt

Directions:

1. Mix masa harina and 1 teaspoon salt in medium container, then fold in water using a rubber spatula. Use your hands to knead mixture in container until tender dough forms,

one to two minutes. Cover dough using a damp dish towel and allow it to sit for five minutes.

2. Cut twenty four 8 inch squares of parchment paper. Knead dough for a short period of time then split into 12 equivalent portions, roll into balls, and place on baking sheet. Cover dough using a damp dish towel.

3. Working with 1 ball at a time, press dough flat into 4½ inch wide disk between 2 pieces parchment with the help of a pie plate. Remove top piece parchment and gently smooth out any cracks. Move to plate, leaving bottom piece parchment in place, and cover using a damp dish towel; tortillas can be stacked.

4. Coat baking sheet using paper towels. Heat 1 teaspoon oil in 12 inch nonstick frying pan over moderate high heat until just shimmering. Put 1 tortilla parchment side up in your palm, remove parchment, then gently lay tortilla in hot pan; repeat with 2 more tortillas. Cook until lightly golden on both sides, approximately 6 minutes, turning midway through cooking.

5. Flip again and press tightly around center of each tortilla with wad of paper towels until puffed; move to prepared sheet. Repeat with remaining tortillas, putting in 1 teaspoon oil to pan between batches and lowering heat as required to stop scorching.

6. Use a paring knife to cut 2 inch opening around edge of tortillas. Ladle 1 generous tablespoon beans inside each tortilla then softly push on tortilla to spread out beans. (Panuchos can be stacked between parchment paper, wrapped using plastic wrap, and placed in the fridge for maximum 1 day or frozen for maximum three months; thaw completely before continuing.)

7. Heat remaining ¼ cup oil in now empty frying pan over moderate high heat until it starts to shimmer Working in batches, fry panuchos until golden and crisp on each side, five to seven minutes, turning tortillas and putting in extra oil to pan between batches as required. Return to baking sheet and sprinkle lightly with salt. Ladle topping onto center of each panucho before you serve.

PIGS' FEET TOSTADAS (TOSTADAS DE MANITAS DE PUERCO)

Yield: twelve tostadas

Ingredients:

To prepare the pigs' feet

- ¼ teaspoon dried mexican oregano
- ⅓ cup (85 ml) thickly cut white onion
- 1 small mexican bay leaf
- 2 fresh pigs' feet, split in half
- 2 garlic cloves
- 3 sprigs fresh thyme or ⅛ teaspoon dried
- 6 peppercorns
- Freshly ground pepper
- Salt to taste

To serve

- 1 cup (250 ml) thinly cut purple onion
- 1 small avocado, cut
- 1½ cups (375 ml) finely shredded and dressed lettuce
- 1½ cups (375 ml) salsa ranchera, omitting the onion
- 3 tablespoons finely grated queso añejo
- The pigs' feet jelly
- twelve tortillas
- Vegetable oil for frying

Directions:

1. Put all the ingredients for the pigs' feet into a big deep cooking pan and immerse in cold water by ½ inch (1.5 cm). Bring slowly to its boiling point, then reduce the heat and simmer for approximately 2½ hours. (the meat must be soft but not too tender.) Set aside to cool in the broth.
2. When the pigs' feet are sufficiently cool to handle, remove all the bones cautiously and cut the meat, gelatinous gristle, and rind together into little pieces and put in a shallow dish and sprinkle with salt and pepper (bearing in mind that cooked foods served cold need to be more highly seasoned). Strain the broth and pour 1⅓ cups (335 ml) of it over the meat. Set the dish in your fridge until tightly set—approximately 1 hour.
3. Heat the oil in a frying pan and fry the tortillas until crunchy. Drain thoroughly.
4. Chop the pigs' feet jelly into little squares and put 2 to 3 heaped tablespoons onto each tostada. Cover with lettuce, some slices of avocado, sauce, cheese, and last of all the onion rings.

POTATO TACOS (TACOS DE PAPA)

Yield: 12 tacos

Ingredients:

The filling

- ½ medium white onion
- 12 ounces (340 g) cooked unpeeled and diced red bliss or other waxy potatoes (about 2¼ cups/563 ml)
- 4 ounces (115 g) queso fresco, crumbled (about ¾ cup/190 ml)
- Salt to taste

To serve

- ⅔ cup (165 ml) prepared sour cream
- 1 cup (250 ml) salsa ranchera, omitting the onion, warmed
- 1½ cups (375 ml) shredded lettuce
- 12 5- to 6-inch (12.5- to fifteen-cm) tortillas
- Jalapeño chiles en escabeche
- Vegetable oil for frying

Directions:

1. Combine the potatoes with the remaining filling ingredients.
2. Fill each tortilla with approximately 2 tablespoons of the mixture and secure with toothpicks.
3. Heat the oil and fry until the tortilla is just crisp on the outside. Drain thoroughly.
4. Serve instantly, topped with the sour cream, warm sauce, and lettuce. Serve the chiles separately.

SHREDDED BEEF TACOS

Yield: Servings 6

Ingredients:

- ½ cup cider vinegar
- ½ teaspoon ground cinnamon
- ½ teaspoon ground cloves
- 1 big onion, cut into ½ inch thick rounds
- 1 recipe Cabbage Carrot Slaw
- 1½ cups beer
- 18 (6 inch) corn tortillas, warmed
- 2 tablespoons tomato paste
- 2 teaspoons dried oregano
- 2 teaspoons ground cumin
- 3 bay leaves
- 3 pounds boneless beef short ribs, trimmed and slice into 2 inch cubes
- 4 dried ancho chiles, stemmed, seeded, and torn into ½ inch pieces (1 cup)
- 4 ounces queso fresco, crumbled (1 cup)
- 6 garlic cloves, lightly crushed and peeled
- Lime wedges
- Salt and pepper

Directions:

1. Adjust oven rack to lower middle position and heat oven to 325 degrees. Mix beer, vinegar, anchos, tomato paste, garlic, bay leaves, cumin, oregano, cloves, cinnamon, 2 teaspoons salt, and ½ teaspoon pepper in Dutch oven. Position onion rounds in single layer on bottom of pot. Put beef on top of onion rounds in single layer. Cover and cook until meat is thoroughly browned and soft, 2½ to three hours.

2. Using slotted spoon, move beef to big container and cover. Strain liquid through fine mesh strainer into 2 cup liquid measuring cup (do not wash pot). Discard onion rounds and bay leaves, then move remaining solids to blender. Allow strained liquid to settle for five minutes, then skim any fat off surface and put in water as required to equal 1 cup. Put in liquid to blender with solids and pulse until smooth, approximately 2 minutes; move to now empty pot.

3. Using 2 forks, shred beef into bite size pieces. Bring sauce to simmer on moderate heat. Mix in shredded beef and sprinkle with salt to taste. Serve with warm tortillas, queso fresco, slaw, and lime wedges.

SHREDDED PORK AND TOMATO FILLING FOR TACOS (PUERCO EN SALSA DE JITOMATE)

Yield: enough filling for twelve to fifteen small tacos, 1½ cups (375 ml)

Ingredients:

- ⅓ cup (85 ml) finely chopped white onion
- 1 garlic clove, roughly chopped
- 1⅓ cups (335 ml) cooked and shredded pork (approximately 12 ounces/340 g)
- 12 ounces (340 g) tomatoes, broiled
- 2 fresh jalapeño chiles, with seeds, thinly cut into thin strips
- 2 tablespoons lard or vegetable oil
- Salt to taste

Directions:

1. Combine the tomatoes with the garlic until almost smooth. Set aside.
2. Heat the lard in a big frying pan and cook the onion and chiles, without browning, until translucent. Put in the tomato mixture and cook on moderate heat for approximately five minutes; put in salt.
3. Put in the meat and carry on cooking the mixture for eight minutes, or until it is all well seasoned and the sauce moist but not juicy.

SOPES

Yield: 12 sopes; serves four to 6

Ingredients:

- 1 cup refried beans
- 1 recipe filling, warmed
- 1 teaspoon salt
- 1¾ cups hot tap water
- 2 cups (8 ounces) masa harina
- 2 cups vegetable oil

Directions:

1. Mix masa harina and salt in medium container, then fold in water using a rubber spatula. Use your hands to knead mixture in container until tender dough forms, one to two minutes. Cover dough using a damp dish towel and allow it to sit for five minutes.

2. Coat baking sheet using parchment paper. Cut sides of 1 quart zipper lock bag, leaving bottom seam undamaged. Knead dough for a short period of time, then split into 12 equivalent portions, roll into balls, and place on prepared sheet. Cover dough using a damp dish towel.

3. Working with 1 piece dough at a time, place on 1 side of zipper lock bag and fold other side over top. Push dough flat into 3½ inch wide disk with the help of a pie plate. Take the plastic off from top and pinch dough around edges as required to create ¾ inch tall sides. Take the plastic off from bottom of sope, return sope to baking sheet, and cover using a damp dish towel.

4. Adjust oven rack to middle position and heat oven to 200 degrees. Heat 1an inch straight sided sauté pan on moderate heat until hot, two to three minutes. Cautiously place 6 sopes in hot, dry pan. Using paper towels, press lightly in center of each sope to make sure contact with pan. Cook until bottoms start to brown, four to five minutes; return to baking sheet (do not cover). Repeat with remaining sopes. (Sopes can be wrapped firmly using plastic wrap and frozen for maximum three months; thaw completely before continuing.)

5. Coat baking sheet using paper towels. Cautiously add oil to now empty pan and heat over moderate high heat to 375 degrees. Put in 6 sopes, browned side down, and fry until bottom is crisp and golden, two to three minutes, adjusting heat as required to maintain oil temperature of 325 to 350 degrees. Lightly flip sopes and fry until sides are crisp and golden (center of sopes will not brown), two to three minutes.

6. Move sopes upright to prepared sheet and dab using paper towels to remove surplus oil; keep warm in oven. Repeat with remaining sopes. Spread refried beans uniformly into center of sopes, then top with filling before you serve.

SPONGY TAMALES FILLED WITH CHILE STRIPS AND CHEESE (TAMALES CERNIDOS DE RAJAS Y QUESO)

Yield: about 30 3-inch (8-cm) tamales

Ingredients:

The masa

- 1 pound (450 g) tamale flour
- 36 (to be safe) corn husks, soaked to tenderize and shaken dry
- 8 ounces (225 g) pork lard (approximately 1 cup/250 ml)
- About 1 cup (250 ml) warm chicken broth
- Salt to taste

The filling

- 12 ounces (340 g) chihuahua, mexican manchego, or muenster cheese, cut into strips about ½ inch (1.5 cm) wide
- 2 cups (500 ml) rajas of poblano chiles, approximately eight chiles
- 2 cups (500 ml) salsa de tomate verde

Directions:

1. Using an electric mixer, beat the lard until light and fluffy—about five minutes. Slowly beat in the flour alternately with the broth, beating meticulously after each addition. Put in salt. If beaten adequately, a small piece of dough should float on the surface of a glass of water.
2. Place a prepared tamale steamer using low heat.
3. Spread 1 heaped tablespoon of the masa finely over the upper part, and about 3 inches (8 cm) down the leaf. Put 2 strips of the chile, a strip of the cheese, and a tablespoon of the sauce over them. Fold the husk so that the filling is mostly covered by the masa and turn the spare part of the husk up the back of the tamale.
4. Set the tamales vertically in the top part of the steamer, cover well, and steam for approximately 1¼ hours. To test, open up a tamale; the masa should separate cleanly from the husk. Leave the tamales in the steamer until they are cool; they will become slightly firmer and less likely to break as you serve them.

SWEET FRESH CORN TAMALES (TAMALES DULCES DE ELOTE)

Yield: about 24 tamales

Ingredients:

- ¼ teaspoon salt
- ½ teaspoon baking powder
- 1 cup (250 ml) grated piloncillo or dark brown sugar
- 1 small tablespoon anise seeds
- 30 (to be safe) fresh corn husks, washed and shaken dry
- 4 cups (1 l) field or white starchy corn kernels
- 4 ounces (115 g) pork lard (½ cup/125 ml), melted and cooled
- 4 ounces (115 g) unsalted butter (½ cup/125 ml), melted and cooled
- 8-inch (20-cm) piece of cinnamon stick
- About ½ cup (125 ml) water

Directions:

1. Ready a tamale steamer and line the top part with fresh corn husks.
2. Use a food processor/blender to blend the corn with the water, in two batches, to a rough-textured consistency—you will have to keep stopping the machine and loosening the mixture using a spatula, but do not put in more liquid.
3. Grind the spices to a powder and put in with the sugar and salt to the corn, mixing meticulously. Slowly mix in the fats and lastly the baking powder. Again mix meticulously. The consistency must be that of a loose, textured paste.
4. Put approximately 1½ tablespoons of the corn mixture down the center of each husk to extend about 3 inches (8 cm) long. Curl one side of the leaf over the mixture, ensuring there is a good overlap and the mixture cannot ooze out. Push the leaf tightly where the mixture ends and fold the empty part, and pointed end, to the back of the tamale.
5. Ensure that the water is boiling in the steamer, then lay the tamales in horizontal layers in the top of the steamer. It is best to put one layer in first and allow it to firm up a little—about ten minutes—before stacking the other layers on top. Steam for approximately 1½ hours until, when tested, the dough separates cleanly from the husk.
6. Eat accompanied by a cup of atole or hot chocolate. Reheat this type of tamale, with the husk removed, on a comal or griddle on moderate heat.

SWEET TAMALES (TAMALES DE DULCE)

Yield: about 24 3-inch (8-cm) tamales

Ingredients:

- ⅓ cup (85 ml) chicken broth or water
- ½ cup (125 ml) sugar
- ½ teaspoon salt
- ⅔ cup (165 ml) roughly chopped pecans
- ¾ cup (185 ml) raisins
- 1 tablespoon ground cinnamon
- 1¼ pounds (570 g) tamale dough (about 2½ cups/625 ml)
- 7 ounces (200 g) pork lard
- About 24 corn husks (always do a few extra) soaked to tenderize and shaken dry

Directions:

Place a prepared tamale steamer using low heat.

1. Place the lard into a container and beat with an electric beater until the lard is very white and opaque—about five minutes. Slowly beat in the masa, broth, and salt, beating well after each addition. Continue beating for another five minutes, progressively putting in the cinnamon and sugar. Mix in the chopped pecans.
2. Spread a slim layer of the dough over the inside of the husk and place a teaspoon of raisins down the middle of the dough. Fold the husk over so that it covers the dough and turn the pointed end up to the back of the tamale.
3. When the water is boiling stack the tamales vertically in the top part, cover, and steam approximately 1 hour or until the pale pink dough comes cleanly away from the husk.

TACOS AL PASTOR

Yield: Servings 6

Ingredients:

- ⅛ teaspoon ground cloves
- ½ cup chopped fresh cilantro
- ½ pineapple, peeled, cored and slice into ½ inch thick rings
- ½ teaspoon ground cumin
- ¾ teaspoon sugar

- 1 lime, cut into 8 wedges
- 1¼ pounds plum tomatoes, cored and quartered
- 1½ cups water
- 12 dried guajillo chiles, stemmed, seeded and torn into ½ inch pieces (1½ cups)
- 18 (6 inch) corn tortillas
- 3 pounds boneless pork butt roast, fat cap trimmed to ¼ inch thick and cut against grain into ½ inch thick slabs
- 4 bay leaves
- 8 garlic cloves, peeled
- Salt and pepper
- Vegetable oil

Directions:

1. Toast guajillos in Dutch oven on moderate heat, stirring regularly, until aromatic, 2 to six minutes. Mix in water, tomatoes, garlic, bay leaves, 2 teaspoons salt, ½ teaspoon pepper, sugar, cumin, and cloves. Increase heat to moderate high and bring to simmer. Cover, decrease the heat to low, and simmer while stirring once in a while, until guajillos become tender and tomatoes purée easily, approximately twenty minutes.
2. Move mixture to blender and pulse until smooth, approximately one minute. Strain puree through fine mesh strainer, pushing on solids to extract as much liquid as you can; discard solids and return puree to pot.
3. Put in pork to pot, immerse in sauce, and bring to simmer on moderate heat. Partly cover, reduce heat, and gently simmer until pork is soft but still holds together, 1½ to 1¾ hours, turning and rearranging pork midway through cooking. (Pork and sauce can be placed in your fridge for maximum 2 days.)
4. Move pork to big plate, season both sides with salt, and cover firmly with aluminium foil. Whisk sauce to blend. Move ½ cup to container for grilling. Pour off all but ½ cup sauce left in pot (reserve surplus sauce for future use). Squeeze 2 lime wedges into sauce in pot and put in spent lime wedges; sprinkle with salt to taste. Brush pineapple with oil and sprinkle with salt.
5. **For a Charcoal Grill:** Open bottom vent fully. Light big chimney starter filled with charcoal briquettes (6 quarts). When top coals are partly covered with ash, pour uniformly over grill. Set cooking grate in place, cover, and open lid vent fully. Heat grill until hot,

approximately five minutes. **For a Gas Grill:** Set all burners to high, cover, and heat grill until hot, approximately fifteen minutes. Turn all burners to moderate.

6. Clean and oil cooking grate. Put pineapple on grill and cook, turning as required, until tender and caramelized, ten to fifteen minutes; move to cutting board. In the meantime, brush 1 side of pork with ¼ cup reserved sauce, then place on grill, sauce side down. Cook until thoroughly browned and crunchy, five to seven minutes. Repeat with second side using remaining ¼ cup reserved sauce; move to cutting board and tent using foil.

7. Working in batches, grill tortillas, turning as required, until warm and soft, approximately half a minute; wrap firmly in foil to keep tender.

8. Chop pineapple and move to serving container. Using tongs to stable pork, slice each piece crosswise into ⅛ inch pieces. Bring sauce left in pot to simmer on moderate heat. Remove the heat, put in cut pork and toss to coat with sauce. Serve with tortillas, cilantro, pineapple, and remaining 6 lime wedges.

TACOS OF CHILE STRIPS (TACOS DE RAJAS DE ZACATECAS)

Yield: 12 tacos

Ingredients:

The filling

- 2 tablespoons vegetable oil
- 3 big eggs
- 3 poblano chiles, charred, peeled, cleaned, and slice into thin strips
- 3 tablespoons roughly chopped white onion
- 8 ounces (225 g) tomatoes, broiled
- Salt to taste

To serve

- 1⅓ cups (335 ml) prepared sour cream
- twelve tortillas
- Vegetable oil for frying

Directions:

1. Heat the oil in a big frying pan. Put in the chile strips and cook using low heat for approximately 3 minutes.
2. Combine the tomatoes with the onion until the desired smoothness is achieved, then put in the puree to the chiles in the pan. Sprinkle with salt and cook on moderate heat for approximately five minutes, stirring and scraping the bottom of the pan occasionally.
3. Beat the eggs lightly and mix them into the mixture. Continue stirring until they are just set, then take out of the heat and keep warm.
4. Heat the oil in a frying pan and fry the tortillas on both sides. Fry slightly more than you would for enchiladas, but not allowing them to get so crisp that you cannot easily fold them over. Drain thoroughly, then fill each one with a little of the chile-egg filling. Double the tortillas over and set on the serving dish.
5. Pour the sour cream over the tacos and serve instantly.

TAMALES

Yield: 18

A tamale is a classic Mesoamerican dish, made of masa or dough, which is steamed in a corn husk or banana leaf. The wrapping can either be discarded before eating, or used as a plate.

Ingredients:

- ¾ teaspoon salt
- 1 cup (4 ounces) plus 2 tablespoons masa harina
- 1 cup plus 2 tablespoons quick grits
- 1 recipe filling
- 1 tablespoon sugar
- 1½ cups boiling water
- 1½ cups frozen corn, thawed
- 20 big dried corn husks
- 2¼ teaspoons baking powder
- 6 tablespoons lard, softened
- 6 tablespoons unsalted butter, cut into ½ inch cubes and softened

Directions:

1. Put grits in medium container, whisk in boiling water, and allow it to stand until water is mostly absorbed, approximately ten minutes. Mix in masa harina, cover, and let cool completely, approximately twenty minutes. In the meantime, place husks in big container, cover with hot water, and allow to soak until flexible, approximately 30 minutes.

2. Process masa dough, corn, butter, lard, sugar, baking powder, and salt together inside a food processor until mixture is light, sticky, and super smooth, approximately 1 minute, scraping down sides as required. Remove husks from water and pat dry using a dish towel.

3. Working with 1 husk at a time, lay on counter, cupped side up, with long side facing you and wide end on right side. Spread ¼ cup tamale dough into 4 inch square over bottom right hand corner, pushing it flush to bottom edge but leaving ¼ inch border at wide edge. Mound 2 small tablespoons filling in line across center of dough, parallel to bottom edge. Roll husk away from you and over filling, so that dough surrounds filling and makes a cylinder. Fold up the tapered end, leaving top open, and move seam side down to platter.

4. Fit big pot or Dutch oven with steamer basket, removing feet from steamer basket if pot is short. Fill pot with water until it just touches bottom of basket and bring to boiling point. Lightly lay tamales in basket with open ends facing up and seam sides facing out. Cover and steam, checking water level frequently and putting in extra water as required, until tamales easily come free from husks, approximately 1 hour. Move tamales to big platter. Reheat remaining sauce from filling in covered container in microwave, approximately half a minute, and serve with tamales.

TAMALE FILLINGS

Each filling makes enough for 18 tamales.

CHIPOTLE BEEF FILLING

- ⅛ teaspoon ground cloves
- ½ teaspoon ground cinnamon
- ¾ teaspoon ground cumin
- 1 big onion, chopped
- 1 teaspoon dried oregano
- 1 teaspoon sugar, plus extra as required
- 1½ tablespoons minced canned chipotle chile in adobo sauce

- 1½ tablespoons red wine vinegar
- 1¾ pounds top blade steaks, trimmed
- 3 cups beef broth
- 3 tablespoons vegetable oil
- 4 dried ancho chiles, stemmed, seeded, and torn into ½ inch pieces (1 cup)
- 6 garlic cloves, minced
- Salt and pepper

Directions:

1. Toast anchos in 12 inch frying pan on moderate heat, stirring regularly, until aromatic, 2 to six minutes; move to container.
2. Heat oil in now empty frying pan on moderate heat until it starts to shimmer Put in onion and cook until tender, five to seven minutes. Mix in garlic, chipotle, oregano, sugar, cumin, cinnamon, cloves, 1 teaspoon salt, and toasted chiles and cook for half a minute. Mix in broth and simmer until slightly reduced, approximately ten minutes. Move mixture to blender and pulse until smooth, approximately twenty seconds; return to frying pan.
3. Season beef with salt and pepper, nestle into frying pan, and bring to simmer on moderate heat. Cover, decrease the heat to low, and cook until beef is super soft, approximately 1½ hours.
4. Move beef to carving board and allow to cool slightly. Using 2 forks, shred beef into little pieces. Stir vinegar into sauce and sprinkle with salt, pepper, and sugar to taste. Toss shredded beef with 1 cup sauce. Reheat remaining sauce and serve with tamales.

RED CHILE CHICKEN FILLING

- ¾ teaspoon dried oregano
- ¾ teaspoon ground cumin
- 1 big onion, chopped
- 1¼ pounds boneless, skinless chicken thighs, trimmed
- 1½ tablespoons cider vinegar
- 3 cups chicken broth
- 3 tablespoons vegetable oil
- 4 dried ancho chiles, stemmed, seeded, and torn into ½ inch pieces (1 cup)
- 4 dried New Mexican chiles, stemmed, seeded, and torn into ½ inch pieces (1 cup)
- 6 garlic cloves, minced

- Salt and pepper
- Sugar

Directions:

1. Toast anchos and New Mexican chiles in 12 inch frying pan on moderate heat, stirring regularly, until aromatic, 2 to six minutes; move to container.
2. Heat oil in now empty frying pan on moderate heat until it starts to shimmer Put in onion and cook until tender, five to seven minutes. Mix in garlic, cumin, oregano, ½ teaspoon salt, and toasted chiles and cook for half a minute. Mix in broth and simmer until slightly reduced, approximately ten minutes. Move mixture to blender and pulse until smooth, approximately twenty seconds; return to frying pan.
3. Season chicken with salt and pepper, nestle into frying pan, and bring to simmer on moderate heat. Cover, decrease the heat to low, and cook until chicken records 160 degrees, twenty to twenty-five minutes.
4. Move chicken to carving board and allow to cool slightly. Using 2 forks, shred chicken into little pieces. Stir vinegar into sauce and sprinkle with salt, pepper, and sugar to taste. Toss shredded chicken with 1 cup sauce. Reheat remaining sauce and serve with tamales.

TORTILLA "SANDWICH" (TORTILLAS COMO SANDWICH)

Yield: 6 tortilla sandwiches

Ingredients:

- ½ cup (125 ml) finely chopped white onion
- ¾ cup (185 ml) prepared sour cream
- ¾ cup (185 ml) salsa de tomate verde, guacamole, or salsa ranchera
- 1½ cups (375 ml) finely shredded lettuce
- 6 ounces (180 g) chihuahua cheese or cheddar, finely cut
- 6 ounces (180 g) cooked ham, thinly cut
- 6 radishes, cut into flowers or cut
- twelve tortillas
- Vegetable oil for frying

Directions:

1. Lay 6 of the tortillas out flat; spread each one with some of the ham and cheese. Cover each with another tortilla to make a sandwich, then secure each pair of tortillas with 2 toothpicks, one on each side.
2. Heat the oil and fry each sandwich on either side until just starting to get crunchy, not hard. Drain thoroughly, then top with the sour cream, sauce, and chopped onion. Garnish each plate with the lettuce and radishes. Serve instantly.

TORTILLAS STACKED WITH GUACAMOLE AND TOMATO SAUCE (TORTILLAS PILADAS CON GUACAMOLE Y SALSA DE JITOMATE)

Yield: Servings four to 6

Ingredients:

The sauce

- 1 pound (450 g) tomatoes, roughly chopped (about 3 cups/750 ml)
- 2 garlic cloves
- 2 tablespoons vegetable oil
- 5 scallions, finely chopped
- Salt to taste

To serve

- ¾ cup (185 ml) prepared sour cream
- 1½ cups (375 ml) guacamole
- 4 ounces (115 g) chihuahua cheese or mild cheddar cheese, grated
- twelve tortillas, freshly made, if possible, and not too thin
- Vegetable oil for frying

Directions:

1. Heat the oil in a big frying pan and cook the scallions gently until they are tender but not browned.

2. Combine the tomatoes with the garlic. Put into the pan with the salt and fry the sauce over quite high heat while stirring and scraping the bottom of the pan almost continuously, until it has reduced and seasoned—about five minutes. Set aside and keep warm.
3. Heat the oil in a different frying pan and fry the tortillas for a short period of time on both sides. Drain thoroughly.
4. Make 3 piles. Immerse 3 of the tortillas into the sauce and lay them flat onto the serving dish. Spread them with approximately 2 tablespoons each of the guacamole, a little cheese, and some sour cream.
5. Immerse 3 more tortillas into the sauce and cover the filling. Repeat with an additional layer of tortillas on top of the first "sandwich," then repeat a layer of guacamole, cheese, and sour cream, ending with a layer of the rest of the tortillas.
6. Pour the remaining sauce over the stacks of tortillas and drizzle the rest of the cheese over the top. Cut into wedges and serve instantly.

TOSTADAS

Yield: twelve tostadas; serves four to 6

Ingredients:

- ¾ cup peanut oil
- 1 recipe topping, warmed
- 12 (6 inch) corn tortillas
- Kosher salt

Directions:

1. Using fork, poke center of each tortilla three to four times (to stop puffing and allow for even cooking). Heat oil in 8 inch frying pan on moderate heat to 350 degrees. Coat baking sheet with several layers of paper towels.
2. Working with one tortilla at a time, put in to hot oil and place metal potato masher on top to keep tortilla flat and submerged in oil. Fry until crunchy and mildly browned, 45 to 60 seconds (no flipping is necessary). Move fried tortilla to readied baking sheet. Repeat with remaining tortillas. Drizzle with salt. (Tostadas can be stored at room temperature for maximum 1 day.)

3. Ladle filling onto center of each tostada before you serve.

BAKED TOSTADAS

Spray tortillas meticulously with vegetable oil spray and spread out over 2 rimmed baking sheets. Bake on upper middle and lower middle racks in 450 degree oven until mildly browned and crisp, approximately ten minutes, switching and rotating sheets midway through baking. Drizzle lightly with salt.

TOSTADA FILLINGS

SPICY ZUCCHINI WITH SCALLIONS AND COTIJA CHEESE

Ingredients:

- ½ teaspoon dried oregano
- 1 cup vegetable broth
- 1 pound zucchini, cut into ½ inch pieces
- 1 serrano chile, stemmed, seeded, and minced
- 1 small onion, chopped fine
- 1 tablespoon chopped fresh cilantro
- 1 tablespoon vegetable oil
- 2 scallions, cut thin
- 2 tablespoons tomato paste
- 3 garlic cloves, minced
- 4 ounces Cotija cheese, crumbled (1 cup)
- Salt and pepper

Directions:

1. Heat oil in 12 inch nonstick frying pan on moderate heat until it starts to shimmer Put in onion and serrano and cook until mildly browned, approximately eight minutes. Mix in tomato paste, garlic, and oregano and cook until aromatic, approximately one minute. Mix in broth, 1 teaspoon salt, and ½ teaspoon pepper and simmer until slightly thickened, approximately 6 minutes.
2. Mix in zucchini, cover, and cook until zucchini is slightly softened, five to seven minutes. Remove the cover, increase heat to moderate high, and cook, stirring frequently, until

sauce has thickened and coats zucchini, approximately 4 minutes. Remove the heat, mix in cilantro and sprinkle with salt and pepper to taste. Decorate using scallions and Cotija.

CHICKEN WITH PICKLED ONION AND CABBAGE

Ingredients:

- ½ cup chicken broth
- ½ teaspoon dried oregano
- ½ teaspoon grated lime zest plus 1 tablespoon juice
- 1 avocado, halved, pitted, and cut thin
- 1 pound boneless, skinless chicken breasts, trimmed
- 1 recipe Pickled Onion and Cabbage
- 1 small onion, chopped fine
- 1 tablespoon ancho chile powder
- 1 tablespoon chopped fresh cilantro
- 2 garlic cloves, minced
- 2 ounces queso fresco, crumbled (½ cup)
- 2 tablespoons vegetable oil
- Salt and pepper

Directions:

1. Heat oil in medium deep cooking pan on moderate heat until it starts to shimmer Put in onion and cook until tender, approximately 4 minutes. Mix in chile powder, garlic, oregano, lime zest, and pinch salt and cook for half a minute. Mix in broth and bring to simmer. Nestle chicken into sauce. Cover, decrease the heat to moderate low, and cook until chicken records 160 degrees, ten to fifteen minutes, turning midway through cooking.

2. Move chicken to carving board and allow to cool slightly. Using 2 forks, shred chicken into little pieces. Return sauce to high heat and simmer until it becomes thick, approximately five minutes. Remove the heat, mix in shredded chicken, lime juice, and cilantro and sprinkle with salt and pepper to taste. Decorate using avocado, Pickled Onion and Cabbage, and queso fresco.

TOMATILLO CHICKEN WITH RADISHES AND QUESO FRESCO

Ingredients:

- ¼ cup chicken broth
- ½ small onion, chopped
- ¾ cup fresh cilantro leaves plus ¼ cup chopped
- 1 garlic clove, peeled
- 1 jalapeño chile, stemmed, halved, and seeded
- 1 pound boneless, skinless chicken breasts, trimmed
- 1 pound fresh tomatillos, husks and stems removed, washed well and dried
- 1 tablespoon lime juice
- 1 teaspoon vegetable oil
- 4 ounces queso fresco, crumbled (1 cup)
- 4 radishes, cut thin
- Salt and pepper

Directions:

1. Adjust oven rack 6 inches from broiler element and heat broiler. Coat rimmed baking sheet with aluminium foil. Toss tomatillos, onion, jalapeño, and garlic with oil and spread over prepared sheet. Broil, shaking sheet once in a while, until vegetables are well charred, ten to twelve minutes.
2. Move broiled vegetables to food processor and allow to cool slightly. Put in cilantro, broth, lime juice, and ¼ teaspoon salt and pulse until crudely chopped, approximately 7 pulses. Move to 10 inch nonstick frying pan, sprinkle with salt to taste, and bring to simmer.
3. Nestle chicken into sauce. Cover, decrease the heat to moderate low, and cook until chicken records 160 degrees, ten to fifteen minutes, turning midway through cooking. Move chicken to carving board and allow to cool slightly. Using 2 forks, shred chicken into little pieces. Toss chicken with sauce left in pan and sprinkle with salt and pepper to taste. Decorate using radishes, queso fresco, and cilantro.

PORK TINGA WITH AVOCADO AND QUESO FRESCO

- ¼ cup fresh cilantro leaves
- ½ teaspoon dried oregano
- 1 (fifteen ounce) can tomato sauce
- 1 avocado, halved, pitted, and diced
- 1 tablespoon minced canned chipotle chile in adobo sauce

- 2 bay leaves
- 2 onions (1 quartered, 1 chopped fine)
- 2 ounces queso fresco, crumbled (½ cup)
- 2 pounds boneless pork butt roast, trimmed and slice into an inch pieces
- 2 tablespoons olive oil
- 4 sprigs fresh thyme
- 5 garlic cloves (3 peeled and smashed, 2 minced)
- Lime wedges
- Salt

Directions:

1. Bring pork, quartered onion, smashed garlic, thyme sprigs, 1 teaspoon salt, and 6 cups water to simmer in big deep cooking pan over moderate high heat, skimming off any foam that rises to surface. Decrease the heat to moderate low, partly cover, and cook until pork is soft, 1¼ to 1½ hours.
2. Drain pork, saving for later 1 cup cooking liquid. Discard onion, garlic, and thyme. Return pork to now empty deep cooking pan and purée into rough ½ inch pieces using potato masher. (Pork can be placed in your fridge for maximum 2 days.)
3. Heat oil in 12 inch nonstick frying pan over moderate high heat until it starts to shimmer Put in oregano, shredded pork, and chopped onion and cook, stirring frequently, until pork is thoroughly browned and crunchy, 7 to ten minutes. Mix in minced garlic and cook until aromatic, approximately half a minute. Mix in tomato sauce, chipotle, bay leaves, and reserved pork cooking liquid and simmer until almost all liquid has vaporized, five to seven minutes. Discard bay leaves and sprinkle with salt to taste. Decorate using avocado, queso fresco, cilantro, and lime wedges.

VERACRUZ RANCH TAMALES (TAMALES VERACRUZANOS TIPO RANCHERO)

Yield: approximately twenty tamales

Ingredients:

The meat for the filling

- ¼ white onion, roughly chopped
- 1 garlic clove
- 1 pound (450 g) pork shoulder with some fat, cut into ¼-inch (.75-cm) cubes
- Salt to taste

The sauce for the filling

- 1 chipotle chile, dried or canned
- 1 cup (250 ml) reserved pork broth
- 1 garlic clove, roughly chopped
- 1 tablespoon roughly chopped white onion
- 1½ tablespoons pork lard or vegetable oil
- 4 ancho chiles, seeds and veins removed
- 6 ounces (180 g) tomatoes, broiled
- Salt to taste

The masa

- 1¼ pounds (565 g) tamale or tortilla dough (about 2½ cups/625 ml)
- 5 ounces (140 g) pork lard (approximately 1 heaped cup/265 ml)
- About ½ cup (125 ml) of the reserved broth, warm
- Salt to taste

Assembling the tamales

- 20 pieces of banana leaves, approximately 9 by 7 inches (23 by 18 cm)
- 5 big hoja santa leaves, cut into four equivalent portions

Directions:

1. Place the pork, onion, garlic, and salt into a big deep cooking pan. Barely cover with water and bring to its boiling point. Reduce the heat and simmer the pork for approximately thirty-five minutes. Allow the pork to cool off in the broth, then strain the meat, saving for later the broth, and set both aside. There must be approximately 1½ cups (375 ml) of broth; if not, make up to that amount with water.
2. Heat the comal and toast the chiles lightly, turning them occasionally so they do not burn.

3. Cover the chiles with hot water and allow them to soak for approximately ten minutes, then remove using a slotted spoon and put into a blender jar. Put in ½ cup of broth, the onion, garlic, and tomatoes and blend to a smooth sauce.

4. Heat the lard in a big frying pan, put in the chile sauce, and cook for approximately five minutes, stirring occasionally to prevent sticking. Put in salt to taste.

5. Put in the pork and ½ cup of broth to the sauce and allow the mixture to cook for approximately five minutes on moderate heat until it is all well seasoned and the liquid has reduced a little. Put in salt to taste. Set aside.

6. To prepare the dough, beat the lard until white and well aerated—about five minutes.

7. Beat the rest of the broth and dough alternately into the lard, putting in the salt. Continue beating for approximately five minutes more. (do not try to float a piece of the dough; it will be a much softer and damper consistency than that for ordinary tamales.)

8. Pass the leaves over a bare flame to make them slightly more flexible. Spread 1 big tablespoon of the dough over an area approximately four by 3 inches (10 by 8 cm) and ¼ inch (.75 cm) thick. Put two cubes of the meat and a little of the sauce into the center of the dough and cover with a piece of the hoja santa. Fold the edges of the banana leaf over until they completely cover the dough and filling. Stack the tamales horizontally in overlapping layers in the top of the steamer. Cover them with more leaves and then cover the top of the steamer with a thick cloth or piece of toweling and the steamer lid. Steam in the normal way for an hour.

YUCATECAN CHICKEN AND PORK TAMALE PIE (MUK-BIL POLLO)

Yield: Servings 6

Ingredients:

The fat for the dough

- 8 ounces (225 g) pork fat, cut into little cubes

The filling

- ¼ teaspoon dried mexican oregano, yucatecan if possible

- ¼ teaspoon peppercorns and 1 tablespoon achiote seeds (or 2 teaspoons recado rojo)
- ⅓ cup (85 ml) finely chopped white onion
- ½ medium green pepper, seeded and diced
- 1 big sprig epazote
- 1 habanero chile, whole
- 1 tablespoon mild white vinegar
- 1½ cups (375 ml) reserved meat broth
- 1½ teaspoons salt
- 2 garlic cloves, crushed
- 2 tablespoons tortilla masa
- 3 tablespoons of the rendered pork fat
- 4 garlic cloves, toasted
- 8 ounces (225 g) pork shoulder
- 8 ounces (225 g) tomatoes, finely chopped (approximately 1⅓ cups/333 ml)
- A 3-pound (1.35-kg) chicken
- Salt to taste

The dough

- ¼ teaspoon yucatecan chile seco or hot paprika
- 2 pounds (900 g) tortilla dough (approximately four cups/1 l)
- 2 teaspoons salt
- banana leaves to line the pan
- the rest of the rendered pork fat

Directions:

1. Lay two pieces of string—each 30 inches (76 cm) long—parallel across the length of a metal baking pan approximately eight by 8 by 2½ inches (20 by 20 by 6.5 cm) and two other pieces of string of the same length across the width—there will be a big overlap for tying.
2. Swiftly pass the banana leaves over a flame to make them more flexible, and line the dish with them, smooth, glossy side up, so that they overlap the pan by about 5 inches (13 cm) all the way around. Cut one leaf slightly bigger than the size of the pan.
3. Heat the fat in a frying pan on moderate heat, or in your oven, until the lard renders out of it. Turn the pieces occasionally so that they do not burn but become uniformly crisp

and brown. Ladle out 3 tablespoons fat for frying the filling and reserve the rest for the dough.

4. Chop the chicken into serving pieces and the pork into 1-inch (2.5-cm) cubes. Place them into a pan with the garlic, oregano, and salt and barely cover with water. Bring up to a simmer and cook using low heat until the meat is just soft—the chicken should take about 30 minutes; the pork a little longer.

5. Strain the meat, saving for later the broth. Take away the bones from the chicken. Set the meat aside. Return the broth to a clean pan; there must be minimum 1½ cups (375 ml).

6. Mix the masa progressively into the broth. Bring to its boiling point, reduce the heat, and stir the mixture until it thickens a little. Set the thickened broth aside.

7. Grind the peppercorns, achiote, and salt and mix with the crushed garlic and vinegar.

8. Heat the 3 tablespoons of rendered fat in a big pan and fry the onion, chile, green pepper, epazote, and tomatoes until tender and still slightly juicy—approximately eight minutes.

9. Put in the ground seasoning and carry on cooking the mixture for approximately 3 minutes.

10. Put in the cooked meats and carry on cooking the mixture for five minutes on moderate heat. Set aside.

11. Preheat your oven to 350° f (180° c).

12. To the dough put in the salt, chile seco or paprika, and remaining rendered fat and browned pieces and mix meticulously.

13. Push about two thirds of the dough into the readied baking pan to make a crust about ¼ inch (1 cm) thick on the bottom and sides of the pan. Put in the filling and pour the thickened broth over it.

14. Push the rest of the dough onto the smooth, glossy side of the reserved banana leaf. This will be the cover for the pie. Cautiously turn the leaf upside down so that the dough completely covers the pan, with enough of an overlap to secure the pie with the dough around the sides of the pan.

15. Fold the leaves over the top of the pie and tie them down tightly with the string.

16. Bake the muk-bil pollo for about ninety minutes and serve it instantly.

Soups

Personally, I feel Mexican soups are better than those from any other part of the world. Below are a few of my favorite Mexican sou recipes.

ANGEL HAIR PASTA IN TOMATO BROTH (SOPA DE FIDEO AGUADA)

Yield: Servings 6

This soup is easy to prepare, and easy on the wallet. Naturally, it is quite common on the Mexican dinner table.

Ingredients:

- ¼ cup (65 ml) roughly chopped white onion
- 1 garlic clove, roughly chopped
- 12 ounces (340 g) very ripe tomatoes, roughly chopped (2⅓ cups/585 ml)
- 2 sprigs flat-leaf parsley
- 3 to 4 tablespoons chicken fat or vegetable oil
- 4 ounces (115 g) angel hair pasta
- 7 cups (1.75 l) light chicken broth

Directions:

1. Heat the fat in a big frying pan and put in the whole bundles of pasta without breaking them up. Fry until the pasta is a deep golden brown, stirring all the time and ensuring not to burn. Drain off all but about 2 tablespoons of fat in the pan.
2. Combine the tomatoes with the garlic and onion until the desired smoothness is achieved. Put into the fried pasta and carry on cooking over very high heat approximately four minutes, stirring and scraping the bottom of the pan, until the mixture is almost dry. Put in the broth and the parsley and bring to its boiling point. Reduce the heat and simmer until the pasta is tender. Adjust the seasoning. (it should take about twenty minutes to cook and season well.)

AVOCADO SOUP (SOPA DE AGUACATE)

Yield: Servings 6

Ingredients:

- 2 big avocados, or enough to yield 2 cups (500 ml) pulp
- 6 cups (1.5 l) well-seasoned caldo de pollo
- Chipotle chiles adobados, torn into little pieces
- Small tortilla squares, fried crisp as for totopos

Directions:

1. Chop the avocados into halves. Take away the pits and scoop out the flesh.
2. Put 2 cups (500 ml) of broth in a blender jar, put in the avocado pulp, and blend to a smooth puree. Put into the remaining broth in the pan and just heat it through gently. Do not allow it to boil.
3. Serve the soup instantly, topped with the tortilla squares and pieces of chipotle chile.

BLACK BEAN CHILI

Yield: Servings 6 to 8

Ingredients:

- ⅛ teaspoon baking soda
- ½ cup minced fresh cilantro
- 1 (28 ounce) can crushed tomatoes
- 1 onion, chopped
- 1 pound (2½ cups) dried black beans, picked over and washed
- 1 pound white mushrooms, trimmed and broken into rough pieces
- 1 tablespoon minced canned chipotle chile in adobo sauce
- 1 tablespoon mustard seeds
- 1 tablespoon packed light brown sugar
- 2 bay leaves
- 2 red bell peppers, stemmed, seeded, and slice into ½ inch pieces
- 2 teaspoons cumin seeds

- 2½ cups vegetable broth
- 2½ cups water, plus extra as required
- 3 tablespoons chili powder
- 3 tablespoons vegetable oil
- 9 garlic cloves, minced
- Lime wedges
- Salt and pepper

Directions:

1. Adjust oven rack to lower middle position and heat oven to 325 degrees. Pulse mushrooms in food processor until consistently crudely chopped, approximately 10 pulses; set aside.
2. Toast mustard seeds and cumin seeds in Dutch oven on moderate heat, stirring continuously, until aromatic, approximately one minute. Mix in oil, onion, and processed mushrooms, cover, and cook until vegetables release liquid, approximately five minutes. Remove the cover and carry on cooking until liquid has vaporized and vegetables are browned, 5 to ten minutes.
3. Mix in garlic and chipotle and cook until aromatic, approximately half a minute. Mix in chili powder and cook, stirring continuously, until aromatic, approximately 1 minute (do not let mixture burn). Mix in broth, water, beans, sugar, bay leaves, and baking soda and bring to simmer, skimming foam from surface as required. Cover, move pot to oven, and cook for an hour.
4. Mix in tomatoes and bell peppers, cover, and carry on cooking in oven until beans are fully soft, approximately 1 hour longer. (If chili starts to cling to bottom of pot or looks too thick, mix in extra water as required.)
5. Take the pot out of the oven and discard bay leaves. Mix in cilantro and sprinkle with salt and pepper to taste. Serve with lime wedges.

BLACK BEAN SOUP

Yield: Servings 6

Ingredients:

- ⅛ teaspoon baking soda

- ½ teaspoon red pepper flakes
- 1 big carrot, peeled and chopped fine
- 1 pound (2½ cups) dried black beans, picked over and washed
- 1½ tablespoons ground cumin
- 2 bay leaves
- 2 big onions, chopped fine
- 2 tablespoons cornstarch
- 2 tablespoons lime juice
- 2 tablespoons water
- 3 celery ribs, chopped fine
- 3 tablespoons extra virgin olive oil
- 4 ounces ham steak, trimmed
- 5 cups water, plus extra as required
- 6 cups chicken broth
- 6 garlic cloves, minced
- Salt and pepper

Directions:

1. Put water, beans, ham steak, bay leaves, and baking soda in big deep cooking pan with tight fitting lid. Bring to boil over moderate high heat, skimming foam from surface as required. Mix in 1 teaspoon salt, decrease the heat to moderate low, cover, and simmer briskly until beans are soft, 1¼ to 1½ hours (if after 1½ hours beans are not soft, put in 1 cup more water and carry on simmering until soft); do not drain beans. Discard bay leaves. Move ham steak to cutting board, allow to cool slightly, then cut into ¼ inch pieces; set aside.

2. Heat oil in Dutch oven over moderate high heat until shimmering. Put in onions, carrot, celery, and ½ teaspoon salt and cook, stirring once in a while, until vegetables become tender and mildly browned, twelve to fifteen minutes. Decrease the heat to moderate low, put in garlic, cumin, and pepper flakes and cook, stirring continuously, until aromatic, approximately 3 minutes. Mix in broth, scraping up any browned bits. Mix in beans and bean cooking liquid, bring to simmer, and cook, stirring once in a while, until flavors meld, approximately 30 minutes.

3. Ladle 1½ cups beans and 2 cups liquid into food processor or blender, pulse until smooth, and return to pot. Mix together cornstarch and water in small container until blended,

then progressively stir half of cornstarch mixture into soup. Bring to boil over moderate high heat while stirring once in a while, until fully thickened. If soup is still thinner than desired once boiling, stir remaining cornstarch mixture to remix and progressively stir mixture into soup; return to boil to fully thicken. Remove the heat, mix in lime juice and ham. Sprinkle with salt and pepper to taste and serve.

BREAD SOUP (SOPA DE PAN)

Yield: Servings 6

Ingredients:

- ½ cup (125 ml) vegetable oil, more if required
- 1 cup (250 ml) thinly cut white onion
- 1 pound (450 g) tomatoes, thickly cut
- 10 peppercorns
- 2 garlic cloves, thinly cut
- 2 medium plantains (approximately 1 pound/450 g), peeled, quartered, and slice into 3-inch (8-cm) lengths
- 2 whole allspice
- 2 whole cloves
- 2-inch (5-cm) piece of cinnamon stick
- 4 cups (1 l) stale bread cubes, if possible sourdough
- 4 hard-cooked eggs, cut
- 4 ounces (115 g) carrots, scraped and thinly cut (approximately 1 cup/250 ml)
- 4 ounces (115 g) green beans, trimmed and slice into thirds
- 4 ounces (115 g) unsalted butter (approximately 1 cup/250 ml)
- 6 cups (1.5 l) chicken broth
- 6 sprigs fresh thyme or ¼ teaspoon dried
- 8 ounces (225 g) potatoes, peeled and slice into ½-inch (1.5-cm) slices (approximately 1¼ cups/315 g)
- Large pinch of saffron
- Salt to taste

Directions:

1. Preheat your oven to 300° f (150° c).
2. Put the bread cubes on a baking sheet in a single layer and bake until they are crisp on the outside but not dried all the way through—twenty minutes to half an hour.
3. Heat some of the oil in a big frying pan and melt a portion of the butter in it. Fry the bread cubes lightly until a golden-brown colour is achieved, putting in more oil and butter as required (if you put in it all at once, the bread cubes will absorb it and become soggy). Drain and set aside, saving for later the oil in the pan.
4. Heat the chicken broth, and when it comes to its boiling point, put in the beans and carrots and simmer until just soft—ten to fifteen minutes. Drain the vegetables and save for later. Put in the thyme, salt, and spices to the broth and simmer for approximately ten minutes. Strain and reserve the broth—there must be about 5 cups (1.25 l).
5. Reheat the oil in which the bread was fried, putting in about ½ cup (125 ml) more as required, and fry the cut potatoes on both sides until thoroughly browned; remove and drain. In the same oil, fry the plantain slices until a golden-brown colour is achieved; remove and drain. Fry the cut tomatoes, onion, and garlic together until soft, then remove and save for later.
6. Preheat your oven to 350° f (180° c). Grease an ovenproof dish, ideally 8½ by 13½ by 2 inches. Spread alternate layers of the vegetables and the tomato mixture in the dish. Cover with the bread cubes and top with the slices of egg. Pour the broth over and bake for approximately fifteen minutes.
7. Serve instantly in deep bowls.

CARNE ADOVADA

Yield: Servings 6

Popular in New Mexico, my hometown, this is the soup that I grew up with, and every slurp is one of nostalgia.

Ingredients:

- ¼ cup minced fresh cilantro
- ¼ cup raisins
- ⅓ cup chili powder
- ½ cup brewed coffee, hot
- 1 cup water

- 1 tablespoon minced canned chipotle chile in adobo sauce
- 1 teaspoon dried oregano
- 1 teaspoon grated lime zest plus 1 tablespoon juice
- 2 cups chicken broth
- 2 onions, chopped fine
- 3 tablespoons all purpose flour
- 3 tablespoons vegetable oil
- 4 pounds boneless pork butt roast, pulled apart at seams, trimmed, and slice into 1½ inch pieces
- 6 garlic cloves, minced
- Salt and pepper

Directions:

1. Adjust oven rack to lower middle position and heat oven to 325 degrees. Mix hot coffee and raisins in small container, cover, and allow it to sit until raisins are plump, approximately five minutes. Mix chili powder, flour, and oregano in separate small container. Pat pork dry using paper towels and sprinkle with salt and pepper.

2. Heat 1 tablespoon oil in Dutch oven over moderate high heat until just smoking. Brown half of pork on all sides, 7 to ten minutes; move to moderate container. Repeat with 1 tablespoon oil and remaining pork.

3. Pour off all but 2 tablespoons fat from pot and decrease the heat to moderate. Put in onions and cook until tender, approximately five minutes. Mix in garlic and chipotle and cook until aromatic, approximately half a minute. Mix in spice mixture and remaining 1 tablespoon oil and cook, stirring continuously, until aromatic, approximately 1 minute (do not let spices burn). Mix in broth, water, and raisin coffee mixture, scraping up any browned bits.

4. Process sauce in blender until the desired smoothness is achieved, one to two minutes. Return sauce to now empty pot. Mix in browned pork and any collected juices and bring to simmer. Cover, move pot to oven, and cook until pork is soft and sauce becomes thick, approximately 2 hours, stirring midway through cooking.

5. Take the pot out of the oven and mix in cilantro and lime zest and juice. Sprinkle with salt and pepper to taste and serve.

CHEESE BROTH (CALDO DE QUESO SONORENSE)

Yield: Servings 6

Ingredients:

- ⅓ cup (85 ml) cut white onion
- 1 anaheim chile, charred and peeled
- 1 pound (450 g) big tomatoes
- 1 small garlic clove, finely chopped
- 12 fine strips queso fresco or muenster cheese
- 12 ounces (340 g) red bliss or waxy new potatoes
- 2 tablespoons vegetable oil
- 5 cups (1.25 l) beef broth
- Salt to taste

Directions:

1. Peel the potatoes and cut them into 1-inch (2.5-cm) squares. Bring the broth to its boiling point, put in the potatoes, and allow them to cook on moderate heat for about ten minutes. They must be just cooked.
2. Cut a thin slice off the top of each tomato and grate the flesh on the coarse side of a grater. In a very short time you will have the skin of the tomato left flat in your hand. Do not forget to grate the flesh from the top slices.
3. Heat the oil in a big frying pan and lightly fry the onion and garlic, without browning, until translucent. Put in the tomato pulp and cook the sauce over brisk heat for five minutes, by which time it will have thickened fairly and be well seasoned. Put in the tomato sauce to the broth and potatoes.
4. Take away the seeds from the chile and cut it into strips. Put in the chile strips to the broth and allow it to cook on moderate heat for five minutes. Put in salt as required. Just before you serve, put in the cheese. Serve the soup as the cheese melts.

CHICKEN AND CHICKPEA SOUP

Yield: Servings 6 to 8

Ingredients:

- 1 (fifteen ounce) can chickpeas, washed
- 1 tablespoon vegetable oil
- 1 teaspoon minced fresh oregano
- 1½ pounds bone in split chicken breasts, trimmed
- 1½ teaspoons minced fresh thyme or ½ teaspoon dried
- 2 carrots, peeled and cut ½ inch thick
- 2 onions, chopped fine
- 2 tablespoons all purpose flour
- 2 teaspoons minced canned chipotle chile in adobo sauce
- 2 zucchini, cut into ½ inch pieces
- 3 tablespoons minced fresh cilantro
- 5 garlic cloves, minced
- 8 cups chicken broth
- Salt and pepper

Directions:

1. Pat chicken dry using paper towels and sprinkle with salt and pepper. Heat oil in Dutch oven over moderate high heat until just smoking. Brown chicken lightly, two to three minutes per side; move to plate.
2. Put in onions and carrots to fat left in pot and cook on moderate heat until tender and mildly browned, about eight to ten minutes. Mix in garlic, chipotle, and thyme and cook until aromatic, approximately half a minute. Mix in flour and cook for a minute. Slowly whisk in broth, scraping up any browned bits, and bring to simmer.
3. Return browned chicken and any collected juices to pot, decrease the heat to low, cover, and simmer gently until chicken records 160 degrees, fifteen to twenty minutes.
4. Move chicken to cutting board and allow to cool slightly. Using 2 forks, shred chicken into bite size pieces; discard skin and bones. In the meantime, stir zucchini and chickpeas into soup and simmer until zucchini is just soft, 5 to ten minutes.
5. Stir shredded chicken into soup and simmer until thoroughly heated, approximately 2 minutes. Remove the heat, mix in cilantro and oregano and sprinkle with salt and pepper to taste and serve.

CHICKEN AND VEGETABLE BROTH (CALDO TLALPEÑO)

Yield: Servings 6

Ingredients:

- ½ cup (125 ml) cooked and skinned chickpeas
- 1 avocado, cubed
- 1 cup (250 ml) cooked and shredded chicken
- 1 garlic clove, roughly chopped
- 1 tablespoon lard or vegetable oil
- 2 big sprigs epazote
- 2 chipotle chiles, dried or canned, torn into strips
- 2 tablespoons roughly chopped white onion
- 4 ounces (115 g) carrots (about 2 medium)
- 4 ounces (115 g) tomatoes, roughly chopped (approximately 1 cup/250 ml)
- 6 cups (1.5 l) caldo de pollo (Chicken Soup)
- 6 lime wedges
- 8 ounces (225 g) green beans

Directions:

1. Trim the beans and cut them in two. Trim and scrape the carrots and slice into rounds. Blend together the tomatoes, onion, and garlic. Heat the lard in a moderate-sized frying pan, put in the mixed ingredients, and fry on moderate heat for approximately 3 minutes.
2. Heat the caldo de pollo (Chicken Soup) in a big deep cooking pan, put in the vegetables, chickpeas, and tomato mixture, and cook on moderate heat until soft—about fifteen minutes.
3. Put in the epazote and chiles and cook for approximately five minutes more.
4. Serve the soup in deep bowls, putting in some of the shredded chicken and topping with the avocado. Lime wedges are passed separately.

CHICKEN POSOLE VERDE

Yield: Servings 6 to 8

Ingredients:

- 1 onion, chopped fine

- 1 tablespoon chopped fresh oregano or 1 teaspoon dried
- 12 ounces tomatillos, husks and stems removed, washed well, dried, and quartered
- 2 (fifteen ounce) cans white or yellow hominy, washed
- 2 jalapeños, stemmed, halved, and seeded
- 2 tablespoons vegetable oil
- 2½ cups fresh cilantro leaves and stems, trimmed (2 bunches)
- 3 garlic cloves, minced
- 4 pounds bone in chicken thighs, trimmed
- 4½ cups chicken broth
- Salt and pepper

Directions:

1. Adjust oven rack to lower middle position and heat oven to 300 degrees. Pat chicken dry using paper towels and sprinkle with salt and pepper. Heat 1 tablespoon oil in Dutch oven over moderate high heat until just smoking. Brown half of chicken, approximately five minutes per side; move to plate. Repeat with remaining 1 tablespoon oil and remaining chicken. Allow to cool slightly, then remove skin.
2. Pour off all but 1 tablespoon fat from pot; put in onion and ¼ teaspoon salt and cook on moderate heat until tender, approximately five minutes. Mix in garlic and oregano and cook until aromatic, approximately half a minute. Mix in 4 cups broth, scraping up any browned bits, and bring to simmer. Nestle browned chicken into pot together with any collected juices. Cover, move pot to oven, and cook until chicken is soft, approximately 1 hour.
3. Take the pot out of the oven, move chicken to cutting board, and allow to cool slightly. In the meantime, process tomatillos, jalapeños, cilantro, and remaining ½ cup broth in blender until the desired smoothness is achieved, approximately half a minute. Stir tomatillo mixture and hominy into stew, bring to simmer on moderate heat, and cook until flavors meld, ten to fifteen minutes.
4. Using 2 forks, shred chicken into bite size pieces; discard bones. Stir shredded chicken into stew and cook until thoroughly heated, approximately 2 minutes. Sprinkle with salt and pepper to taste and serve.

CHICKEN TORTILLA SOUP

Yield: Servings 6 to 8

Ingredients:

SOUP

- ½ jalapeño chile
- 1 big white onion, quartered
- 1 sprig fresh oregano
- 1 tablespoon minced canned chipotle chile in adobo sauce
- 1½ pounds bone in split chicken breasts, trimmed
- 2 tablespoons vegetable oil
- 2 tomatoes, cored and quartered
- 4 garlic cloves, peeled
- 8 (6 inch) corn tortillas, cut into ½ inch wide strips
- 8 cups chicken broth
- 8 sprigs fresh cilantro
- Salt

GARNISHES

- 1 ripe avocado, halved, pitted, and slice into ½ inch pieces
- 8 ounces Cotija cheese, crumbled (2 cups)
- Fresh cilantro
- Lime wedges
- Mexican crema
- Minced jalapeño chile

Directions:

1. Adjust oven rack to middle position and heat oven to 425 degrees. Toss tortilla strips with 1 tablespoon oil, spread onto rimmed baking sheet, and bake, stirring once in a while, until deep golden brown and crisp, approximately 14 minutes. Flavor mildly with salt and move to paper towel–lined plate.
2. In the meantime, bring broth, 2 onion quarters, 2 garlic cloves, cilantro sprigs, oregano sprig, and ½ teaspoon salt to simmer in Dutch oven over moderate high heat. Put in chicken, decrease the heat to low, cover, and simmer gently until chicken records 160 degrees, fifteen to twenty minutes. Move chicken to cutting board and allow to cool

slightly. Using 2 forks, shred chicken into bite size pieces; discard skin and bones. Strain broth through fine mesh strainer; discard solids.

3. Process tomatoes, jalapeño, chipotle, remaining 2 onion quarters, and remaining 2 garlic cloves in food processor until the desired smoothness is achieved, approximately half a minute, scraping down sides of container as required. Heat remaining 1 tablespoon oil in now empty pot over moderate high heat until shimmering. Put in tomato onion mixture and ⅛ teaspoon salt and cook, stirring regularly, until mixture has darkened in color and liquid has vaporized, approximately ten minutes.

4. Mix in strained broth, scraping up any browned bits, and bring to simmer. Cook until flavors meld, approximately fifteen minutes. Mix in shredded chicken and simmer until thoroughly heated, approximately 2 minutes. Remove the heat, sprinkle with salt and pepper to taste. Put some tortilla strips in bottom of individual bowls and ladle soup over top. Serve, passing garnishes separately.

CHILI CON CARNE

Yield: Servings 6

Ingredients:

- ⅓ cup masa harina
- 1 cup canned crushed tomatoes
- 1 onion, chopped fine
- 2 tablespoons cumin seeds
- 2 tablespoons lime juice
- 2 teaspoons dried oregano
- 3 dried ancho chiles, stemmed, seeded, and torn into ½ inch pieces (¾ cup)
- 3 dried New Mexican chiles, stemmed, seeded, and torn into ½ inch pieces (¾ cup)
- 4 jalapeño chiles, stemmed, seeded, and minced
- 4 pounds boneless beef chuck eye roast, pulled apart at seams, trimmed, and slice into an inch pieces
- 5 garlic cloves, minced
- 8 cups water
- 8 slices bacon, cut into ¼ inch pieces
- Salt and pepper

Directions:

1. Toast ancho and New Mexican chiles and cumin in Dutch oven on moderate heat, stirring regularly, until aromatic, 2 to six minutes; move to spice grinder. Put in oregano and grind to fine powder. Move spice mixture to container and mix in ½ cup water.
2. Cook bacon in now empty pot over moderate low heat until crisp, approximately ten minutes. Move bacon to paper towel–lined plate using slotted spoon. Pour off and reserve rendered fat in container.
3. Pat beef dry using paper towels and sprinkle with salt and pepper. Heat 1 tablespoon bacon fat in now empty pot over moderate high until just smoking. Brown half of beef on all sides, 7 to ten minutes; move to container. Repeat with 1 tablespoon bacon fat and remaining beef.
4. Heat 3 tablespoons bacon fat in now empty pot on moderate heat until shimmering. Put in onion and cook until tender, approximately five minutes. Mix in jalapeños and garlic and cook until aromatic, approximately one minute. Mix in chile paste and cook until aromatic, approximately 2 minutes. Mix in 7 cups water, tomatoes, and lime juice and bring to simmer. Mix in crisp bacon and browned beef and any collected juices and simmer until meat is soft and juices are dark, rich, and beginning to thicken, approximately 2 hours.
5. Mix masa harina and remaining ½ cup water in container to make paste. Increase heat to moderate, mix in masa harina mixture, and simmer until it becomes thick, 5 to ten minutes. Sprinkle with salt and pepper to taste and serve.

CHILLED TOMATO SOUP

Yield: Servings 4

Ingredients:

- ½ cup Mexican crema
- 1 garlic clove, quartered
- 1 shallot, peeled and halved
- 1 slice hearty white sandwich bread, crust removed, torn into an inch pieces
- 1 teaspoon sherry vinegar, plus extra for seasoning
- 1 teaspoon sugar, plus extra for seasoning
- 3 tablespoons minced fresh cilantro

- 3½ pounds tomatoes, cored and chopped coarse
- 5 tablespoons extra virgin olive oil
- Salt and pepper

Directions:

1. Toss tomatoes with ½ teaspoon salt and allow to drain in fine mesh strainer, set over container to reserve drained liquid, for an hour. Toss drained tomatoes with shallot, garlic, and sugar in separate container. Put in bread to drained tomato liquid, allow to soak for a minute, then mix into tomatoes.
2. Move half of mixture to blender and process for half a minute. With blender running, slowly sprinkle in 3 tablespoons oil until super smooth, approximately 2 minutes. Strain through fine mesh strainer into big container, using rubber spatula to help pass soup through strainer. Repeat with remaining mixture and remaining 2 tablespoons olive oil; strain into container.
3. Mix in vinegar and sprinkle with salt and pepper to taste. Cover and place in your fridge until chilled and flavors meld, minimum 2 hours or maximum 2 days.
4. Before serving, season soup with salt, pepper, extra sugar, and extra vinegar to taste. Mix in 2 tablespoons cilantro. Decorate individual portions with remaining 1 tablespoon cilantro and sprinkle with crema.

CREAM OF SQUASH FLOWER SOUP (CREMA DE FLOR DE CALABAZA)

Yield: Servings 6

Ingredients:

- ⅓ cup (85 ml) finely chopped onion
- ⅔ cup (165 ml) crème fraîche or heavy cream
- 1 big garlic clove, roughly chopped
- 1 pound (450 g) squash flowers, cleaned and finely chopped (approximately eight cups/2 l, tightly packed)
- 2 poblano chiles, charred, peeled, cleaned, cut into little squares, and lightly fried
- 3 tablespoons unsalted butter
- 3½ cups (875 ml) light chicken broth

- Salt to taste
- The reserved flowers

Directions:

1. Melt the butter, put in the onion and garlic in a deep deep cooking pan, and cook gently until translucent—do not brown. Put in the chopped flowers and salt, cover the pan, and cook using low heat until the flowers are fairly soft—ten to fifteen minutes. Set aside a scant ½ cup (125 ml) of the flowers.
2. Combine the remaining flowers with 1½ cups (375 ml) of the broth and return to the pan. Put in the remaining broth and cook using low heat for approximately 8 minutes.
3. Mix the cream into the soup and heat gently until it starts to simmer. Adjust seasoning and serve topped with the unblended flowers and the chile pieces.

DRIED FAVA BEAN SOUP (CALDO DE HABAS)

Yield: Servings 6

Ingredients:

- ⅔ cup (165 ml) roughly chopped white onion
- 10 sprigs fresh cilantro, roughly chopped
- 2 garlic cloves, roughly chopped
- 2 tablespoons vegetable oil
- 2 teaspoons salt, or to taste
- 8 ounces (225 g) dried, peeled yellow fava beans (approximately 1½ cups/375 ml)
- About 10 cups (2.5 l) hot water
- About 8 ounces (225 g) tomatoes, finely chopped (1⅓ cups/333 ml)

To serve

- 2 pasilla chiles, fried and crumbled
- 6 tablespoons fruity olive oil

Directions:

1. Wash the beans well, picking out any loose pieces of skin or fiber.

2. Heat the oil in a heavy-bottomed pot and fry the beans, with the onion and garlic, until they are mildly browned and the onion and garlic are translucent. Put in the tomatoes and fry using high heat, stirring continuously, until the mixture is almost dry—about three minutes. Put in the water, cilantro, and salt and let the soup cook using low heat until the beans are mushy and almost disintegrated—about 3½ hours.

3. Serve each container with a tablespoon of the olive oil and some crumbled pasilla chile on top.

DRIED SHRIMP CONSOMMÉ (CONSOMÉ DE CAMARÓN SECO)

Yield: Servings 6

Ingredients:

- 1 garlic clove, left whole
- 1 mulato or 2 pasilla chiles
- 4 to 5 cups (1 to 1.25 l) water
- 6 cascabel or 4 guajillo chiles
- 8 ounces (225 g) mexican dried shrimps

To serve

- Finely chopped white onion
- Lime quarters
- Roughly chopped cilantro sprigs

Directions:

1. Wash the uncleaned shrimps in cold water and drain, cover the shrimps with 2 cups (500 ml) of the water, and bring them to a simmer. Cook for a minute, then take out of the heat and set them aside to soak for five minutes longer—no more, as the shrimps soon lose their flavor. Drain the shrimps and reserve the cooking water.

2. Take away the stems from the chiles and veins and seeds from half of them. Place the chiles into a deep cooking pan, cover with water, and simmer for approximately five minutes, or until tender (time varies, depending on how dry the chiles are). Turn off the heat and set aside to soak for approximately five minutes longer. Drain, discard the water

in which they were cooked, and move to a blender jar with 1 cup (250 ml) of fresh water and the garlic. Blend until the desired smoothness is achieved.

3. Clean the shrimps by removing the legs, tails, and heads, but do not peel. Split the cleaned shrimps into two parts. Roughly break up or cut one half and save for later. Move the other half with the shrimp debris to the blender jar. Put in the water in which they were cooked and blend as smooth as you can.

4. Place the chile sauce and the mixed shrimps into a large, heavy deep cooking pan, bring to a simmer, and cook, stirring all the time and scraping the bottom of the pan, for approximately 3 minutes. Put in 1 more cup (250 ml) of the water, bring back to a simmer, and carry on cooking using low heat for approximately five minutes. Pass the mixture through a fine sieve. Put in the shrimp pieces and carry on cooking for five minutes, no longer. The soup must be rather thick, but dilute with water if you want.

5. Serve in small cups and pass the toppings separately.

FISH SOUP (CALDO MICHI)

Yield: Servings 6

Ingredients:

- ¼ cup (65 ml) vegetable oil
- ¼ teaspoon dried mexican oregano
- ½ cup (125 ml) thinly cut white onion
- ⅔ cup (165 ml) loosely packed frutas en vinagre or an equivalent amount of sour pickles plus 2 slices lime
- 10 ounces (285 g) cut tomatoes, approximately 1½ cups (375 ml)
- 2 zucchini (about 6 ounces/180 g), trimmed and slice into rounds
- 2½ pounds (1.125 kg) whole catfish or carp
- 3 garlic cloves, left whole
- 3 jalapeño chiles en escabeche, roughly chopped
- 3 medium carrots (approximately four ounces/115 g), scraped and cut
- 8 big sprigs cilantro, roughly chopped
- 8 cups (2 l) chicken broth
- Salt and freshly ground pepper to taste

Directions:

1. Wash and dry the fish well. Chop the body into 1-inch (2.5-cm) slices and the head, if used, into four pieces. Sprinkle with salt and freshly ground pepper.
2. Heat the oil in a large, heavy pan and fry the fish pieces very lightly; the flesh should just turn opaque. Remove and save for later.
3. In the same oil, fry the tomatoes, onion, and garlic together until the onion is tender and the mixture has a saucelike consistency. Put in the broth, carrots, zucchini, oregano, chiles, and frutas en vinagre (or substitutes) to the pan and cook until the vegetables are just soft, approximately twenty minutes. Put in the fish pieces and simmer until the flesh flakes easily from the bone—about ten minutes.
4. Take away the pan from the heat and put in the chopped cilantro. Serve the soup accompanied by freshly made tortillas.
5. Note: this soup may be prepared a few hours ahead of time, but put in the fish pieces about ten minutes before you serve. It will not freeze.

FRESH CORN AND POBLANO SOUP (SOPA DE ELOTE Y RAJAS)

Yield: Servings 6

Ingredients:

- ¾ cup (185 ml) whole corn kernels, for putting in later
- 2 tablespoons roughly chopped white onion
- 3 cups (750 ml) milk
- 3 small poblano chiles, charred, peeled, cleaned of veins and seeds
- 3 tablespoons butter
- 6 heaped tablespoons queso fresco or substitute, crumbled
- 8 ounces (225 g) tomatoes, broiled
- About 3 cups (750 ml) corn kernels, or 1½ 10-ounce (285-g) packages frozen corn
- Salt to taste

Directions:

1. Combine the tomatoes and onion and save for later.
2. Chop the cleaned chiles into thin strips. Melt the butter in a big deep cooking pan and fry the chiles gently for approximately 2 minutes—they should not brown. Put in the mixed

tomatoes to the chile strips and cook the mixture for approximately five minutes on moderate heat until the sauce has reduced a little.

3. Combine the 3 cups of corn, with the milk, at high speed to a very smooth consistency. This will probably have to be done in two stages. Place the corn mixture through the medium disk of a food mill or strainer and mix it in very progressively into the tomato sauce, stirring all the time.
4. Put in the whole kernels and salt and cook the soup using super low heat—it should just simmer—for approximately fifteen minutes.
5. Put in a little cheese to each container before pouring the hot soup into it.

FRESH CORN SOUP (SOPA DE ELOTE)

Yield: Servings 6

Ingredients:

- ¼ cup (65 ml) butter
- ½ teaspoon salt, or to taste
- 1 cup (250 ml) water
- 2 poblano chiles, charred, peeled, and cleaned, then diced and for a short period of time fried
- 3½ cups (875 ml) milk or light chicken broth
- 4 cups (1 l) fresh corn kernels (approximately 1½ pounds/675 g frozen corn)
- 6 small tortillas, cut into little squares, dried, and fried
- 6 tablespoons crumbled queso fresco

Directions:

1. Combine the corn with the water at high speed until you have a smooth puree. Place the puree through the medium disk of a food mill or a coarse strainer.
2. Melt the butter in a big deep cooking pan but do not allow it to get too hot. Put in the corn puree and allow it to cook on moderate heat for approximately five minutes, stirring all the time.
3. Put in the milk and the salt to the mixture and bring it to its boiling point. Reduce the heat and let the soup simmer for approximately fifteen minutes, stirring it occasionally to prevent sticking. By this time it will have thickened somewhat.

4. Put about ½ tablespoon diced chile and 1 tablespoon of crumbled cheese into each container. Pour the hot soup over them and put the crisp tortilla squares on top.

GARLIC AND BREAD SOUP (SOPA DE AJO Y MIGAS)

Yield: Servings 6

Ingredients:

- ⅓ cup (85 ml) vegetable or light olive oil, roughly
- 2 big eggs
- 2 big sprigs epazote
- 4 garlic cloves, cut
- 6 cups (1.5 l) strong chicken broth
- 6 thick slices french-type bread, if possible sourdough
- Salt to taste, if required
- Veins from 3 pasilla chiles, mildly toasted

Directions:

1. Preheat your oven to 300° f (150° c).
2. Put the bread slices on a baking sheet in a single layer and bake until they are crisp on the outside but not dried all the way through—about 30 minutes.
3. Heat a little of the oil in a heavy pan and fry the bread on both sides until very crisp and golden brown, putting in more oil as required. Drain on paper toweling and set aside to keep warm.
4. Put in or make up to 1 tablespoon of oil in the pan, and cook, rather than fry, the garlic on low heat so that it flavors the oil. Take away the garlic and discard. Pour a little of the broth into the pan, swirl it around, and put in to the remaining broth.
5. Heat the broth to a simmer in a deep cooking pan. Beat the eggs lightly with a teaspoon of oil and, stirring continuously in a circular motion, put in to the broth. Put in the epazote and simmer until the eggs are set. Adjust the seasoning, then put in the fried bread and simmer for half one minute, no longer.
6. Serve in deep soup bowls, with a crouton in each container, and top with chile veins to taste.

GREEN CORN SOUP (SOPA VERDE DE ELOTE)

Yield: Servings 6

Ingredients:

- ¼ cup (65 ml or about 2 ounces/60 g) unsalted butter
- ½ cup (125 ml) finely chopped white onion
- ⅔ cup (165 ml) green peas, fresh or frozen
- ⅔ cup (165 ml) tomate verde, cooked and drained
- 1 teaspoon salt, or to taste
- 2 small garlic cloves, finely chopped
- 2 small poblano chiles, charred and peeled
- 3 big romaine lettuce leaves, roughly chopped
- 4½ cups (1.125 l) corn kernels
- 5 cups (1.25 l) light chicken broth
- 6 big sprigs cilantro
- 6 tablespoons sour cream, commercial or homemade
- crisp-fried tortilla pieces

- **To serve**

Directions:

1. Melt the butter in a big deep cooking pan and fry the onion and garlic until translucent.
2. Combine the tomate verde until the desired smoothness is achieved. Put into the onion in the pan and fry using high heat for approximately 3 minutes, stirring continuously.
3. Place the corn kernels into a blender jar (one third at a time) with 2 cups (500 ml) of the chicken broth and the peas, cilantro, chiles, and lettuce leaves and blend until fairly smooth. Pass this puree through the medium disk of a food mill or strainer, then put in to the pan and cook over quite high heat for approximately 3 minutes, stirring and scraping the bottom of the pan continuously, since the mixture tends to stick.
4. Put in the remaining broth and the salt and cook the soup using low heat until it thickens and is well seasoned—about twenty minutes.
5. Serve in soup bowls with a big spoonful of the sour cream and a drizzling of tortilla pieces for each serving.

LEEK SOUP (SOPA DE PUERROS)

Yield: Servings 6

Ingredients:

- ¼ cup (65 ml) finely chopped flat-leaf parsley
- 2 tablespoons unsalted butter
- 2 tablespoons vegetable oil
- 4 cups (1 l) finely chopped leeks, white and soft green part only
- 5 hard-cooked eggs
- 6 cups (1.5 l) light chicken broth
- Salt and freshly ground pepper to taste

The topping

- Fried bread croutons or crisp-fried tortilla pieces

Directions:

1. Heat the butter with the oil in a large, heavy deep cooking pan and fry the leeks and parsley slowly until just soft, without browning—approximately eight minutes. Put in 5 cups (1.25 l) of the chicken broth and cook on moderate heat until the leeks are soft—approximately eight minutes.
2. Shell the eggs and separate the whites from the yolks. Cut the whites fine and save for later. Combine the yolks, with the remaining broth, until the desired smoothness is achieved and put in with the chopped whites to the soup. Season and carry on cooking for another ten minutes, or until the leeks are completely tender and well seasoned.
3. Serve the soup with croutons or crisp-fried tortilla pieces.

LENTIL AND CHORIZO SOUP

Yield: Servings 6 to 8

Ingredients:

- ⅛ teaspoon ground cloves
- 1 onion, chopped fine

- 1 pound (2¼ cups) brown lentils, picked over and washed
- 1 tablespoon all purpose flour
- 1 tablespoon red wine vinegar, plus extra for seasoning
- 1 teaspoon ground cumin
- 1½ pounds Mexican style chorizo sausage, pricked with fork multiple times
- 2 bay leaves
- 2 tablespoons ancho chile powder
- 2 tablespoons extra virgin olive oil
- 3 carrots, peeled and slice into ¼ inch pieces
- 3 garlic cloves, minced
- 3 tablespoons minced fresh cilantro
- 7 cups water
- Salt and pepper

Directions:

1. Put lentils and 2 teaspoons salt in heatproof container. Cover with 4 cups boiling water and allow to soak for half an hour Drain thoroughly.
2. Heat oil in Dutch oven over moderate high heat until just smoking. Brown chorizo on all sides, six to eight minutes; move to plate. Decrease the heat to low and put in onion, carrots, 1 tablespoon cilantro, and 1 teaspoon salt to fat left in pot. Cover and cook, stirring once in a while, until vegetables are very tender but not brown, fifteen to twenty minutes. If vegetables start to brown, put in 1 tablespoon water to pot.
3. Mix in chile powder, garlic, cumin, and cloves and cook until aromatic, approximately 2 minutes. Mix in flour and cook for a minute. Slowly whisk in water, scraping up any browned bits, and bring to simmer. Put in browned chorizo with any collected juices and bay leaves, decrease the heat to low, cover, and simmer gently until lentils are soft, fifteen to twenty minutes.
4. Discard bay leaves. Move chorizo to cutting board, allow to cool slightly, then halve along the length and slice ¼ inch thick. Stir chorizo into soup and simmer until thoroughly heated, approximately 2 minutes. Remove the heat, mix in vinegar and remaining 2 tablespoons cilantro. Sprinkle with salt, pepper, and extra vinegar to taste and serve.

LENTIL SOUP (SOPA DE LENTEJAS ESTILO QUERÉTARO)

Yield: Servings 6

Ingredients:

- ¼ cup (65 ml) finely chopped white onion
- 1 big scallion, green part included, quartered
- 1 cup (250 ml) chicken broth
- 1 garlic clove, roughly chopped
- 1 jalapeño chile, or 2 serrano chiles, or any fresh, hot green chile, thinly cut
- 2 tablespoons vegetable oil
- 3 big sprigs cilantro
- 4 to 6 ounces (1fifteen to 180 g or ½ rounded cup/125 ml) small brown lentils
- 6 cups (1.5 l) water, roughly
- 8 ounces (225 g) nopales (about 3 medium-size cactus paddles), cleaned of prickles and cut into little squares (approximately 1¾ cups/ 440 ml)
- 8 ounces (225 g) tomatoes, roughly chopped (1½ cups/375 ml)
- Salt to taste

Directions:

1. Wash the lentils well and drain. Place them into a pan with 6 cups (1.5 l) of cold water. Bring to its boiling point, then reduce the heat and cook on low heat until mushy—about three hours for mexican lentils, 2 hours for american.
2. Cover the cactus pieces with cold water, put in ½ teaspoon of the salt and the scallion, and simmer until just soft—about twenty minutes. Wash in cold water and drain, discarding the onion.
3. Combine the tomatoes with the garlic until the desired smoothness is achieved. Set aside.
4. Heat the oil in a frying pan and fry the onion and chile gently, without browning, until they are tender. Put in the tomato puree and fry for another three minutes or so over a high heat while stirring continuously, until the mixture is almost dry. Put into the lentils with the chicken broth and nopales. Cover the pan and cook using low heat for approximately twenty minutes, then put in the cilantro and cook for a minute longer. Salt to taste.

MEATBALL SOUP WITH RICE AND CILANTRO

Yield: Servings 6 to 8

Ingredients:

- ¼ teaspoon ground cumin
- ½ jalapeño chile, stemmed, halved, and seeded
- ½ onion, quartered
- 1 big egg
- 1 cup long grain white rice
- 1 small zucchini, cut into ½ inch pieces
- 1 tablespoon vegetable oil
- 1½ teaspoons minced fresh oregano or ½ teaspoon dried
- 2 carrots, peeled and slice into ½ inch pieces
- 2 tomatoes, cored and quartered
- 3 garlic cloves, minced
- 5 tablespoons minced fresh cilantro
- 8 cups chicken broth
- 8 ounces 90 percent lean ground beef
- 8 ounces ground pork
- Salt and pepper

Directions:

1. Bring 4 cups water to boil in Dutch oven. Put in rice and ¾ teaspoon salt and cook, stirring once in a while, for eight minutes. Drain rice through fine mesh strainer, wash with cold water, and drain once more.

2. Use your hands to mix half of parcooked rice, ground beef, ground pork, 3 tablespoons cilantro, egg, one third of garlic, oregano, cumin, 1 teaspoon pepper, and ½ teaspoon salt together in big container until meticulously blended. Pinch off and roll mixture into 1 tablespoon size meatballs (about 40 meatballs total) and position on rimmed baking sheet.

3. Process tomatoes, onion, jalapeño, and remaining garlic in food processor until the desired smoothness is achieved, approximately half a minute, scraping down sides of container as required. Heat oil in now empty pot over moderate high heat until shimmering. Put in tomato onion mixture and cook, stirring regularly, until mixture has darkened in color and liquid has vaporized, approximately ten minutes.

4. Mix in broth and carrots, scraping up any browned bits, and bring to simmer. Cook until carrots are nearly soft, approximately ten minutes. Mix in zucchini and remaining parcooked rice, then gently put in meatballs and simmer until meatballs are thoroughly cooked, ten to twelve minutes. Remove the heat, mix in remaining 2 tablespoons cilantro and sprinkle with salt and pepper to taste and serve.

MEXICAN BEEF AND VEGETABLE SOUP

Yield: Servings 6 to 8

Ingredients:

- ½ teaspoon ground cumin
- 1 (14.5 ounce) can diced tomatoes, drained
- 1 onion, chopped
- 1 pound boneless beef chuck eye roast, trimmed and slice into an inch pieces
- 1 tablespoon minced fresh oregano or 1 teaspoon dried
- 1 tablespoon vegetable oil
- 1 zucchini, cut into ½ inch pieces
- 10 ounces red potatoes, unpeeled, cut into an inch pieces
- 2 bay leaves
- 2 carrots, peeled and slice into ½ inch pieces
- 2 cups chicken broth
- 2 ears corn, husks and silk removed, cut into an inch rounds
- 2 tablespoons minced fresh cilantro
- 4 cups beef broth
- 5 garlic cloves, minced
- Salt and pepper

Directions:

1. Pat beef dry using paper towels and sprinkle with salt and pepper. Heat oil in Dutch oven over moderate high heat until just smoking. Brown beef on all sides, five to seven minutes; move to container.
2. Put in onion to fat left in pot and cook on moderate heat until tender, approximately five minutes. Mix in garlic, oregano, and cumin and cook until aromatic, approximately half a

minute. Mix in beef broth, chicken broth, tomatoes, and bay leaves, scraping up any browned bits, and bring to simmer. Mix in browned beef with any collected juices, decrease the heat to low, cover, and simmer gently for half an hour

3. Mix in carrots and potatoes and simmer, uncovered, until beef and vegetables are just soft, twenty to twenty-five minutes. Mix in zucchini and corn and simmer until corn is soft, 5 to ten minutes.

4. Remove the heat, discard bay leaves. Mix in cilantro and sprinkle with salt and pepper to taste and serve.

PORK POSOLE ROJO

Yield: Servings 8 to 10

Ingredients:

- 1 (14.5 ounce) can diced tomatoes
- 1 (5 pound) bone in pork butt roast
- 1 tablespoon minced fresh oregano or 1 teaspoon dried
- 1½ cups boiling water
- 2 big onions, chopped coarse
- 2 tablespoons vegetable oil
- 3 (fifteen ounce) cans white or yellow hominy, washed
- 3 dried ancho chiles, stemmed and seeded
- 5 garlic cloves, minced
- 6 cups chicken broth
- Salt and pepper

Directions:

1. Adjust oven rack to lower middle position and heat oven to 300 degrees. Trim thick skin and surplus fat from meat and cut along muscles to split roast into big pieces of various sizes; reserve bones. Season pork with salt and pepper.

2. Heat oil in Dutch oven on moderate heat until shimmering. Put in onions and ¼ teaspoon salt and cook until tender, approximately eight to ten minutes. Mix in garlic and cook until aromatic, approximately half a minute. Put in pork and bones and cook, stirring frequently, until meat is no longer pink on outside, approximately eight minutes. Mix in

broth, tomatoes and their juice, oregano, and ½ teaspoon salt and bring to simmer, skimming foam from surface as required. Cover, place pot in oven, and cook until pork is soft, approximately 2 hours.

3. In the meantime, soak anchos in container with boiling water until tender, approximately twenty minutes. Process anchos and soaking liquid in blender until the desired smoothness is achieved, approximately half a minute. Strain through fine mesh strainer into container, using rubber spatula to help pass chili mixture through strainer. Measure out and reserve ¼ cup ancho mixture for serving.

4. Take the pot out of the oven, move pork to cutting board, and allow to cool slightly; discard bones. While pork cools, stir hominy and remaining ancho mixture into pot and bring to simmer on moderate heat. Decrease the heat to low, cover, and simmer gently until flavors meld, approximately 30 minutes.

5. Using 2 forks, shred pork into bite size pieces. Stir shredded pork into stew and cook until thoroughly heated, approximately 2 minutes. Flavor it with reserved ancho mixture, salt, and pepper to taste and serve.

SOUP OF THE SEVEN SEAS

Yield: Servings 6 to 8

Ingredients:

- 1 onion, quartered
- 1 pound big shrimp (26 to 30 per pound), peeled, deveined, tails removed, and shells reserved
- 1 pound mussels, scrubbed and debearded
- 1 pound russet potatoes, peeled and slice into ½ inch pieces
- 1 tablespoon dried oregano
- 1½ pounds skinless catfish fillets, cut into 2 inch pieces
- 2 (8 ounce) bottles clam juice
- 2 bay leaves
- 2 ears corn, husks and silk removed, cut into an inch rounds
- 2 tablespoons minced fresh cilantro
- 2 teaspoons ground cumin
- 2 teaspoons sugar

- 3 dried ancho chiles, stemmed, seeded, and torn into ½ inch pieces (¾ cup)
- 3 garlic cloves, peeled
- 3 tablespoons vegetable oil
- 5 cups chicken broth
- Lime wedges
- Salt and pepper

Directions:

1. Toast anchos in Dutch oven over moderate high heat, stirring regularly, until aromatic, 2 to six minutes; move to food processor. Put in onion, garlic, oregano, cumin, sugar, bay leaves, and 1 teaspoon pepper to processor and pulse until crudely chopped, approximately fifteen pulses.
2. Heat oil in now empty pot over moderate high heat until shimmering. Put in ancho mixture, shrimp shells, and ½ teaspoon salt and cook, stirring regularly, until mixture has darkened in color and shrimp shells have turned bright pink, two to three minutes. Mix in broth and clam juice, scraping up any browned bits, and bring to simmer. Cook until flavors meld, approximately ten minutes. Strain broth through fine mesh strainer; discard solids. Return strained broth to again empty pot and bring to simmer.
3. Mix in corn and potatoes and simmer until potatoes are soft, about eight to ten minutes. Increase heat to moderate high, mix in mussels, cover, and simmer briskly until most mussels have opened, three to four minutes (discard any unopened mussels). Using slotted spoon, move mussels, potatoes, and corn to individual bowls.
4. Return broth to gentle simmer using low heat. Put in catfish and shrimp to pot, cover, and cook until catfish and shrimp are opaque throughout, approximately 3 minutes. Remove the heat, gently mix in cilantro and sprinkle with salt and pepper to taste. Ladle broth, shrimp, and catfish over mussels and vegetables. Serve with lime wedges.

SOUR "LIMA" SOUP (SOPA DE LIMA)

Yield: Servings 6

Ingredients:

- ¼ cup (65 ml) finely chopped chile dulce or green pepper
- ¼ teaspoon dried mexican oregano, yucatecan if possible, toasted

- ⅓ cup (85 ml) finely chopped white onion
- ½ lima agria or substitute fresh lime
- 10 garlic cloves, toasted
- 1½ tablespoons lard or chicken fat
- 2 chicken breasts with skin and bones
- 4 chicken gizzards
- 6 chicken livers (approximately eight ounces/225 g)
- 6 peppercorns
- 8 cups (2 l) water
- 8 ounces (225 g) tomatoes, finely chopped (1⅓ cups/335 ml)
- Salt to taste
- twelve tortillas, cut into strips and dried
- Vegetable oil for frying

To serve

- ⅓ cup (85 ml) habanero chiles, charred and finely chopped
- ¾ cup (185 ml) finely chopped white onion
- 6 thin slices lima agria

Directions:

1. Place the water into a soup pot. Put in the garlic, oregano, peppercorns, and salt. Heat to a simmer and cook for approximately ten minutes. Put in the gizzards and cook for fifteen more minutes.
2. Put in the chicken breasts and carry on cooking for another fifteen minutes. Put in the livers and cook for ten more minutes, or until the meats are soft.
3. Strain the broth and set it aside. Take away the meat from the breasts and shred. Cut the livers, remove the gristle from the gizzards, and cut them. Keep the meats hot.
4. Heat the lard in a frying pan and lightly fry the onion and pepper until they are soft, but not browned. Put in the tomatoes to the mixture in the pan, and cook for approximately five minutes on moderate heat. Put into the broth and allow it to simmer uncovered for approximately five minutes. Put in salt as required. Put in a little of the chopped and shredded meats to each container.
5. Squeeze the juice of the ½ lima agria into the broth. Drop the squeezed lima shell into the broth for a few seconds only, then remove. Keep the broth warm.

6. Heat the oil in a frying pan and fry the tortilla strips until they are crunchy. Drain them on the toweling, and while they are still super hot, drop some of them into the broth in each soup container.
7. Pass the chopped onion, the chiles, and slices of lima separately.

SPICY BUTTERNUT SQUASH SOUP WITH CHIPOTLE

Yield: Servings four to 6

Ingredients:

- ¼ cup pepitas, toasted
- ½ cup heavy cream
- ½ teaspoon ground cumin
- 1 (3 pound) butternut squash, halved along the length and widthwise, seeds and fibers removed and reserved
- 1 big shallot, chopped fine
- 1 tablespoon honey
- 2 tablespoons minced fresh cilantro
- 2 teaspoons minced canned chipotle chile in adobo sauce
- 4 tablespoons unsalted butter
- 6 cups water, plus extra as required
- Salt and pepper

Directions:

1. Melt 2 tablespoons butter in Dutch oven on moderate heat. Put in shallot and cook until tender, two to three minutes. Put in squash seeds and fibers and cook, stirring once in a while, until butter turns orange, approximately 4 minutes.
2. Mix in water and 1 teaspoon salt and bring to boil. Reduce to simmer, place squash cut side down in steamer basket, and lower basket into pot. Cover and steam squash until it is completely soft, thirty to forty minutes.
3. Using tongs, move cooked squash to rimmed baking sheet. When sufficiently cool to handle, use big spoon to scrape cooked squash from skin; discard skin. Strain steaming broth through fine mesh strainer into 4 cup liquid measuring cup. You should have minimum 3 cups of broth; if short, put in water.

4. Working in batches, puree cooked squash with 3 cups broth until the desired smoothness is achieved, one to two minutes. Return puree to clean pot. Mix in heavy cream, honey, chipotle, cumin, and remaining 2 tablespoons butter. Return to brief simmer, putting in additional broth (or water) as required to adjust soup's consistency. Mix in cilantro and sprinkle with salt and pepper to taste. Decorate individual bowls with pepitas before you serve.

SPICY PINTO BEAN SOUP

Yield: Servings 6

Ingredients:

- 1 jalapeño chile, stemmed, halved, and seeded
- 1 onion, quartered
- 1 tablespoon dried oregano
- 1 tablespoon minced canned chipotle chile in adobo sauce
- 2 bay leaves
- 2 tomatoes, cored and quartered
- 3 dried ancho chiles, stemmed, seeded, and torn into ½ inch pieces (¾ cup)
- 3 garlic cloves, peeled
- 3 tablespoons vegetable oil
- 7 cups chicken broth, plus extra as required
- 8 ounces (1¼ cups) dried pinto beans, picked over and washed
- Salt and pepper

Directions:

1. Dissolve 1½ tablespoons salt in 2 quarts cold water in big container or container. Put in beans and soak at room temperature for minimum 8 hours or maximum one day.
2. Drain beans and wash well. Toast anchos in Dutch oven over moderate high heat, stirring regularly, until aromatic, 2 to six minutes; move to blender. Put in tomatoes, onion, garlic, jalapeño, chipotle, and oregano and pulse until smooth, approximately half a minute.
3. Heat oil in now empty pot over moderate high heat until shimmering. Put in ancho mixture and 1 teaspoon salt and cook, stirring regularly, until mixture has darkened in

color and liquid has vaporized, approximately ten minutes. Mix in broth, scraping up any browned bits. Mix in beans and bay leaves and bring to simmer. Decrease the heat to low, cover, and simmer gently until beans are soft, one to 1½ hours.

4. Discard bay leaves. Working in batches, process soup in clean, dry blender until the desired smoothness is achieved, one to two minutes. Return soup to again empty pot, adjust consistency with extra broth as required, and sprinkle with salt and pepper to taste and serve.

TARASCAN BEAN AND TORTILLA SOUP (SOPA TARASCA TIPO CONDE)

Yield: Servings 6

Ingredients:

- ¼ teaspoon dried mexican oregano
- 1 garlic clove
- 1 pound (450 g) tomatoes, broiled
- 2 tablespoons roughly chopped white onion
- 2½ cups (625 ml) chicken or pork broth
- 3 ancho chiles, cleaned of seeds and then cut into thin strips and fried
- 3 small tortillas cut into strips, fried crisp as for totopos
- 3 tablespoons lard or vegetable oil
- 6 ounces (180 g) queso fresco, thinly cut
- 8 ounces (225 g) cooked pink or pinto beans (about 3½ to 4 cups; 875 ml to 1 l) with broth
- Salt as required
- thick sour cream

Directions:

1. Combine the beans, with their broth, to a smooth consistency and move to a large, heavy deep cooking pan.
2. Combine the tomatoes, garlic, and onion together to a smooth sauce. Melt the fat in a frying pan and cook the tomato mixture using high heat for approximately five minutes,

then mix into the bean puree and allow it to cook on moderate heat for approximately 8 minutes, stirring it all the time.

3. Put in the broth and let the soup cook for an extra five minutes using low heat. Put in salt to taste and put in the oregano just before you serve.

4. Place a few pieces of the cheese into each container. Pour the hot soup over them and top with the chiles, some tortilla strips, and a spoonful of sour cream.

5. Note: this soup will become thick considerably as it stands and will have to be diluted with broth or water. It freezes well.

TORTILLA BALL SOUP (SOPA DE BOLITAS DE TORTILLAS)

Yield: Servings 6

Ingredients:

The soup

- ½ cup (125 ml) finely grated queso añejo (approximately 1½ ounces/45 g)
- ½ cup (125 ml) hot whole milk
- 1 big egg, well beaten
- 12 stale tortillas, dried
- 6 cups (1.5 l) tomato-chicken broth (see Next recipe)
- Approximately ¼ cup (65 ml) whole milk, cold
- Melted lard or vegetable oil for frying
- Sea salt to taste

To serve

- ⅓ cup (85 ml) prepared sour cream
- Finely chopped fresh cilantro or parsley

Directions:

1. Break the tortillas into little pieces and blend until they are like fine bread crumbs; this amount will make approximately 1 cup (250 ml). Put in the hot milk, cheese, egg, and salt and knead the dough well, then set it aside for quite a few hours or place in your fridge it overnight, to allow the tortilla particles to become tender.

2. Again knead the dough well, putting in the cold milk. Roll the dough uniformly into one long piece; split this into 12 pieces, and each piece in half once more. Roll the 24 pieces into little balls approximately 1 inch (2.5 cm) in diameter.

3. Heat the lard in a frying pan and fry the balls very gently, turning them occasionally until they are a golden brown—about five minutes. Drain thoroughly. Place the balls into the heated broth, bring to its boiling point, then decrease the heat and simmer for approximately 2 minutes.

4. Serve in individual bowls—four balls per serving—and top each using a spoonful of the cream and some chopped cilantro.

TORTILLA SOUP (SOPA DE TORTILLA)

Yield: Servings 6

Ingredients:

- ¼ cup (65 ml) roughly chopped white onion
- 1 garlic clove
- 12 ounces (340 g) tomatoes, broiled
- 12 small tortillas, cut into strips and dried
- 2 big sprigs epazote
- 3 pasilla chiles, fried crisp and crumbled
- 6 cups (1.5 l) caldo de pollo (Chicken Soup)
- 6 heaped tablespoons grated chihuahua cheese or muenster
- Vegetable oil for frying

Directions:

1. Heat the oil in a big frying pan and fry the tortilla strips until they are mildly browned but not too crunchy. Drain them on paper toweling. Pour off all but 1 tablespoon of the oil.

2. Combine the tomatoes, onion, and garlic to a smooth sauce, then put in to the oil and fry for approximately five minutes, until the sauce is well seasoned and has reduced fairly.

3. Put in the sauce to the caldo de pollo and bring to its boiling point. Adjust seasoning. Put in the tortilla strips and cook them for approximately 3 minutes.

4. Just before you serve, put in the epazote. Cook for a minute more.

5. Serve each portion topped with pieces of crumbled chile and grated cheese.

6. Note: the base could be prepared (and even stored frozen) hours ahead but the final steps, putting in tortillas and epazote, must be done a few minutes before you serve.

WHITE CHICKEN CHILI

Yield: Servings 6 to 8

Ingredients:

- ¼ cup minced fresh cilantro
- 1 pound onions, cut into an inch pieces
- 1 tablespoon ground cumin
- 1½ teaspoons ground coriander
- 2 (fifteen ounce) cans cannellini beans, washed
- 2 tablespoons vegetable oil
- 3 Anaheim chiles, stemmed, seeded, and slice into an inch pieces
- 3 cups chicken broth
- 3 jalapeño chiles, stemmed, seeded, and minced
- 3 poblano chiles, stemmed, seeded, and slice into an inch pieces
- 3 pounds bone in split chicken breasts, trimmed
- 3 tablespoons lime juice (2 limes)
- 4 scallions, cut thin
- 6 garlic cloves, minced
- Salt and pepper

Directions:

1. Pulse half of poblanos, half of Anaheims, and half of onions in food processor until consistency of lumpy salsa, ten to 12 pulses, scraping down sides of container as required; move to moderate container. Repeat with remaining poblanos, Anaheims, and onions; move to container (do not clean food processor).
2. Pat chicken dry using paper towels and sprinkle with salt and pepper. Heat 1 tablespoon oil in Dutch oven over moderate high heat until just smoking. Brown half of chicken, approximately five minutes per side; move to plate. Repeat with remaining 1 tablespoon oil and remaining chicken. Allow to cool slightly, then remove skin.

3. Pour off all but 2 tablespoons fat from pot and decrease the heat to moderate. Put in chile mixture, two thirds of jalapeños, garlic, cumin, coriander, and ¼ teaspoon salt. Cover and cook, stirring once in a while, until vegetables become tender, approximately ten minutes. Remove pot from heat.

4. Move 1 cup cooked vegetable mixture to now empty food processor. Put in 1 cup beans and 1 cup broth and pulse until smooth, approximately twenty seconds. Put in vegetable bean mixture and remaining 2 cups broth to pot and bring to simmer over moderate high heat. Nestle browned chicken into pot together with any collected juices. Decrease the heat to low, cover, and simmer gently until chicken records 160 degrees, fifteen to twenty minutes.

5. Move chicken to cutting board and allow to cool slightly. In the meantime, stir remaining beans into chili and simmer, uncovered, until beans are thoroughly heated and chili has thickened slightly, approximately ten minutes.

6. Using 2 forks, shred chicken into bite size pieces; discard bones. Stir shredded chicken and remaining jalapeño into chili and cook until thoroughly heated, approximately 2 minutes. Remove the heat, mix in lime juice, cilantro, and scallions. Sprinkle with salt and pepper to taste and serve.

Stews

PREPARATION OF CORN FOR POZOLE, MENUDO, AND GALLINA PINTA

In this section, you will find recipes for pozole, menudo, and gallina pinta. All of these recipes call for an ingredient called "prepared and cooked white corn". Dried corn with broad, white kernels is commonly known as "cacahuazintle or maiz pozolero" and is easily found in the freezer section of Latin American grocery stores. If you can't find it, or have the time and patience to make your own, here's how you go about it:

Directions:

1. Allow 1 pound (450 g) of corn to soak in cold water overnight. This step is not essential, but it helps reduce the final cooking time. Remove any bits that float to the top of the water, then strain.
2. Place the corn into a deep pot, cover well with water, put in 1 tablespoon powdered lime, and bring to a simmer—it will turn yellow. Carry on cooking uncovered using low heat for approximately fifteen minutes. Turn off the heat and set aside to cool and soak for approximately twenty minutes. When sufficiently cool to handle, wash in fresh water and rub the kernels through your hands until the rather slimy skin has been removed—you may need several changes of water until it is clean and white. With a paring knife—or strong fingernails—remove the pedicels at the top of the kernels.
3. Return the cleaned kernels to the pot and cover with water to come about 3 inches (8 cm) above the level of the corn—a little difficult because the kernels tend to float. Cook on moderate heat, covered, until the kernels open up like a flower—about three hours depending on how old and dry the corn is. Put in salt to taste.

CHICKEN STEW MIX

Yield: Servings 6 to 8

Ingredients:

- ¼ cup unsalted dry roasted peanuts

- 1 (fifteen ounce) can pinto beans, washed
- 1 jalapeño chile, stemmed
- 1 onion, quartered
- 1 pound sweet potatoes, peeled and slice into ½ inch pieces
- 1 tablespoon red wine vinegar
- 2 cups ½ inch pineapple pieces
- 2 ripe plantains, peeled, quartered along the length and cut an inch thick
- 3 dried ancho chiles, stemmed, seeded, and torn into ½ inch pieces (¾ cup)
- 3 garlic cloves, peeled
- 3 tablespoons sesame seeds, toasted, plus extra for serving
- 3 tablespoons vegetable oil
- 4 pounds bone in chicken thighs, skin removed, trimmed
- 4 scallions, cut thin
- 4½ cups chicken broth
- Salt and pepper

Directions:

1. Adjust oven rack to lower middle position and heat oven to 300 degrees. Toast anchos in Dutch oven over moderate high heat, stirring regularly, until aromatic, 2 to six minutes; move to blender. Put in ½ cup broth, 1 cup pineapple, onion, peanuts, sesame seeds, garlic, and jalapeño and pulse until smooth, approximately 60 seconds.
2. Heat oil in now empty pot over moderate high heat until shimmering. Put in ancho mixture and 1 teaspoon salt and cook, stirring regularly, until mixture has darkened in color and liquid has vaporized, approximately ten minutes. Mix in remaining 4 cups broth, scraping up any browned bits. Mix in sweet potatoes and beans and bring to simmer. Season chicken with salt and pepper and nestle into pot. Cover, move pot to oven, and cook until chicken is soft, approximately 1 hour.
3. Take the pot out of the oven and move chicken to cutting board. Let chicken cool slightly, then, using 2 forks, shred into bite size pieces; discard bones. Stir shredded chicken, plantains, and remaining 1 cup pineapple into stew and bring to simmer on moderate heat. Mix in vinegar and sprinkle with salt and pepper to taste. Serve with scallions and extra sesame seeds.

CHILE DE ÁRBOL SAUCE

Ingredients:

- 3 ounces (85 g) árbol chiles (about 2 cups/500 ml, stems only removed
- Water to cover

Directions:

1. Wash the chiles for a short period of time in cold water, drain, and cover with fresh water. Set aside to soak overnight.
2. Combine the whole chiles with the water in which they were soaking. Run the sauce through a strainer, discarding the debris. Do not put in salt (conventionally no salt is added).

MEXICAN BEEF STEW

Yield: Servings 6 to 8

Ingredients:

- ¼ cup minced fresh cilantro
- ¼ teaspoon ground cinnamon
- 1 (14.5 ounce) can diced tomatoes
- 1 cup pitted green olives, chopped coarse
- 1 jalapeño chile, stemmed, seeded, and minced
- 1 tablespoon dried oregano
- 1½ pounds red potatoes, unpeeled, cut into 1½ inch pieces
- 1½ teaspoons ground cumin
- 2 dried ancho chiles, stemmed and seeded
- 2 onions, chopped fine
- 2 red or green bell peppers, stemmed, seeded, and slice into an inch pieces
- 2 tablespoons all purpose flour
- 2 tablespoons vegetable oil
- 3 cups beef broth
- 3 garlic cloves, minced

- 4 pounds boneless beef chuck eye roast, pulled apart at seams, trimmed, and slice into 1½ inch pieces
- Salt and pepper

Directions:

1. Adjust oven rack to lower middle position and heat oven to 325 degrees. Toast anchos in Dutch oven over moderate high heat, stirring regularly, until aromatic, 2 to six minutes; move to container.
2. Pat beef dry using paper towels and sprinkle with salt and pepper. Heat 1 tablespoon oil in now empty pot over moderate high heat until just smoking. Brown half of beef on all sides, 7 to ten minutes; move to plate. Repeat with remaining 1 tablespoon oil and remaining beef.
3. Put in onions and ¼ teaspoon salt to fat left in pot and cook on moderate heat until tender, approximately five minutes. Mix in garlic, jalapeño, oregano, cumin, and cinnamon and cook until aromatic, approximately half a minute. Mix in flour and cook for a minute. Slowly whisk in broth, scraping up any browned bits. Mix in tomatoes and their juice and toasted anchos and bring to a simmer. Mix in browned beef and any collected juices, cover, move pot to oven, and cook for an hour.
4. Mix in potatoes and bell peppers, cover, and cook in oven until beef and potatoes are soft, one to 1½ hours.
5. Take the pot out of the oven and discard anchos. Mix in olives and allow it to sit until thoroughly heated, two minutes. Adjust stew consistency with hot water as required. Mix in cilantro and sprinkle with salt and pepper to taste and serve.

MOLE COOKED IN A POT (MOLE DE OLLA)

Yield: Servings 6

Ingredients:

The meat

- 2 quarts (2 l) water
- 2 teaspoons salt, or to taste
- 3 pounds (1.35 kg) pork neck bones or 3 pounds (1.35 kg) boiling beef (brisket or a shoulder cut), with bone

The seasoning sauce

- ⅛ teaspoon cumin seeds, crushed
- ½ medium white onion, roughly chopped
- 1 cup (250 ml) tomate verde, cooked and drained
- 2 garlic cloves, roughly chopped
- 3 tablespoons vegetable oil
- 4 ancho chiles, wiped clean, seeds and veins removed
- 4 pasilla chiles, wiped clean, seeds and veins removed

The vegetables

- 1 big ear of corn
- 1 small chayote (approximately eight ounces/225 g)
- 1 xoconostle, peeled and center with seeds removed
- 3 sprigs epazote
- 4 ounces (115 g) green beans
- 8 ounces (225 g) potatoes
- 8 ounces (225 g) zucchini

The garnish

- Wedges of lime and finely chopped white onion

Directions:

1. Have the butcher chop the meat and bones into serving pieces. Cover them with the water, put in the salt, and bring to its boiling point. Reduce the heat and simmer the meat, uncovered, until nearly soft—about forty minutes for the pork and 1 hour for the beef.
2. In the meantime prepare the chiles. Heat the comal and toast the chiles on both sides, ensuring not to burn. When cool they must be easy to crumble into your blender. Combine the chiles with the remaining seasoning ingredients apart from the oil until the desired smoothness is achieved.
3. Heat the oil in a frying pan and fry the sauce for approximately five minutes. Put in it to the meat.
4. Clean and trim the squash and slice into halves, then into four along the length. Trim the beans and slice into halves. Chop the corn into six pieces. Chop the chayote open and

remove the core, then cut into ¼-inch (.75-cm) wedges. Skin the potatoes and slice into cubes.

5. When the meat is soft, put in the vegetables and cook the mole slowly, uncovered, for approximately 30 minutes, or until the vegetables are cooked. Put in the epazote about five minutes before the mole is ready, and put in salt as required.

6. Serve in large, deep soup bowls, with hot tortillas, wedges of lime, and finely chopped onion on the side.

NORTHERN TRIPE SOUP (MENUDO BLANCO NORTEÑO)

Yield: Servings approximately 16

Ingredients:

- 1 head of garlic, unpeeled, cut in half horizontally
- 1½ pounds (675 g) calf's feet, cut into 4 pieces
- 5½ pounds (2.5 kg) tripe of different textures
- Optional: 3 pigs' feet, approximately 1 pound (450 g)
- Salt to taste

The corn

- 1 pound 2 ounces (500 g) pozole corn, cooked and "flowered"

The seasoning

- ⅓ cup (85 ml) water
- 1 heaped tablespoon dried mexican oregano, if possible
- 1 teaspoon cumin seeds, crushed
- 3 garlic cloves (not necessary)

To serve

- ½ cup (125 ml) toasted and powdered ancho chile
- Crumbled, dried mexican oregano
- Finely chopped white onion
- Slices of lime

Directions:

1. Wash the tripe twice in cold water, drain, and slice into two-inch (5-cm) squares. Wash the calf's and pigs' feet and drain. Put into a big stockpot or mexican earthenware olla. Fill the pot with water almost to the top—the level must be several inches above the meats. Put in the garlic and salt and put using low heat, uncovered, until it comes to a simmer. Carry on cooking for an hour, then cover and carry on cooking until the tripe and feet are soft—anywhere from 2 to 4 hours depending on the quality of the tripe.
2. Meantime, the corn must be cooking. When it is soft and has opened up, or "flowered," drain, saving for later about 3 cups (750 ml) of the broth.
3. Place the ⅓ cup (85 ml) of water into your blender jar, put in the cumin, oregano, and optional garlic, and blend until the desired smoothness is achieved.
4. When the meats are soft, put in the seasoning mixture and corn with the reserved broth. Adjust the salt, and carry on cooking uncovered until the meats are soft—approximately 1 hour more.
5. Take away the pieces of calf's foot from the broth and chop the gelatinous parts into little cubes. Return them to the pot.
6. Serve the menudo—about 2 cups (500 ml) per person is a healthy portion—in deep bowls and pass the toppings separately.

OXTAIL, PORK, AND BEAN SOUP (GALLINA PINTA)

Yield: Servings 6 to 8

Ingredients:

- ½ cup (125 ml) pinto beans
- ½ white onion, roughly cut
- 1 oxtail (1½ to 2 pounds/675 to 900 g), cut into little pieces with most of the fat removed
- 1 pound (450 g) country-style pork spareribs, cubed
- 1½ cups (375 ml) prepared and cooked white corn for pozole
- 2 ancho chiles, seeds and veins removed and mildly toasted
- 2 garlic cloves
- 2 quarts (2 l) water
- 6 peppercorns
- Salt to taste

Directions:

1. Place the oxtail into a big deep cooking pan with the onion, garlic, salt, pinto beans, and peppercorns. Cover with the water and bring to its boiling point. Reduce the heat and simmer for an hour.
2. Put in the spareribs and white corn and carry on cooking using low heat, uncovered, for another one to 1½ hours, until the meat is super soft and the beans tender. Put in salt to taste.
3. About twenty minutes before the soup is done, blend one of the chiles with a little of the broth and put in the mixture to the soup. Tear the other chile into fine strips and put in to the soup.
4. Serve in deep bowls.

PORK AND WHITE CORN SOUP (POZOLE DE JALISCO)

Yield: Servings twelve to 14

Ingredients:

- ½ pig's head, approximately 3 pounds (1.35 kg)
- 1 pound (450 g) pork neck bones
- 1 pound (450 g) white corn kernels for pozole
- 1½ pounds (675 g) boneless stewing pork
- 1½ tablespoons salt
- Approximately 14 cups (3.5 l) water

To serve

- 1 cup (250 ml) cut radishes
- 1 cup (250 ml) finely chopped white onion
- 2 cups (500 ml) finely shredded lettuce or cabbage
- chile de árbol sauce
- Wedges of lime

Directions:

1. Two days before you serve, put the corn to soak, as indicated.

2. One day before you serve, clean and prepare the white corn for cooking.
3. Chop the pork into big serving pieces and put it, with the head and bones, in cold water to soak overnight. Change the water as frequently as is practical.
4. On serving day, cover the white corn with the cold, unsalted water. Bring to its boiling point and cook, uncovered, over brisk heat until it opens up like a flower—approximately 1 hour. Do not stir the corn during this time, but, if required, skim the surface of the water occasionally.
5. Drain and cover the head with cold, unsalted water. Bring to its boiling point, then reduce the heat and allow it to simmer, uncovered, until the flesh can be removed from the bone—but do not overcook—approximately 1 hour. Set it aside to cool.
6. When the head is sufficiently cool to handle, remove all the meat and skin and cut it into serving pieces. Chop the ear up (there must be a piece for everyone) and set the eyes aside for the honored guest. Put in the pieces of head, and the broth in which it was cooked, to the corn in its pot.
7. Put in the salt. Put the meat on top of the corn and let the pozole cook, uncovered, over gentle heat for approximately 4 hours. Throughout the cooking time skim the fat from the surface. Keep some water boiling in a kettle at the side to put in to the liquid in the pan. On no account should cold water be added. The liquid must be maintained at almost the same level from start to finish.
8. Put the meat onto a serving dish so it can be divided up more easily and everyone can have the part that he likes best. Serve the pozole with the corn in large, deep bowls, with the following small side dishes to which everyone can help himself: the chile de árbol sauce, finely chopped onion, cut radishes, finely shredded lettuce, and wedges of lime.

TRIPE IN A SPICY, PICANTE BROTH (MONDONGO EN KABIK)

Yield: Servings 6

Ingredients:

The meats

- ½ head garlic, toasted and unpeeled
- 1 small calf's foot, cut into 8 pieces
- 1 tablespoon salt
- 1 teaspoon dried mexican oregano, toasted, yucatecan if possible

- 2 cups (500 ml) seville orange juice or substitute
- 2 pounds (900 g) tripe, cut into two-inch (5-cm) squares

The tomato seasoning

- ⅓ cup (85 ml) finely chopped white onion
- 1 small green pepper, cleaned and chopped into little squares
- 1 teaspoon simple recado rojo
- 2 tablespoons vegetable oil
- 3 yucatecan green chiles, güero chiles, or any fresh, hot green chiles, toasted
- 4 sprigs epazote, leaves and soft stems only, roughly chopped
- 8 ounces (225 g) tomatoes, finely chopped (about ⅓ cup/85 ml)
- Salt to taste

To serve

- ⅓ cup (85 ml) finely chopped chives
- ½ cup (125 ml) finely chopped white onion
- 6 yucatecan green chiles or any fresh, hot green chiles, cut into rounds
- Slices of lima agria or lime

Directions:

1. Rinse the tripe well, cover with the orange juice, and let soak for minimum 4 hours flipping the pieces once in a while. Scrub the pieces of calf's foot. Put into a big deep cooking pan with the garlic, oregano, and salt, and cover well with water. Bring to its boiling point, then reduce the heat and allow to cook gently for approximately three hours, or until the meat is just starting to get soft. Set aside, in the cooking liquid, in your fridge overnight.
2. The next day, drain the tripe, wash, and put in to the calf's foot, in its broth. Bring to its boiling point and cook slowly until both meats are soft—2½ to three hours.
3. In the meantime, heat the oil in a heavy pan and put in the tomatoes, onion, green pepper, and chopped epazote. Fry on moderate heat until the mixture is reduced and seasoned, approximately eight minutes. Put in the chiles and recado rojo, together with 2 tablespoons of the meat broth, and cook for a few minutes more. Season and save for later.

4. When the meats are soft, drain, saving for later the broth. Take away the bones from the calf's foot and cut the meat, gristle, and skin (all edible) into big pieces. Place the pieces, together with the tripe, onto a warmed serving dish and set aside in a warm place.

5. If required, put in water to the reserved broth to make up to 8 cups (2 l). Put in the tomato seasoning and simmer for approximately five minutes, or until well flavored. (if there is too much fat on top of the broth, skim as required.) Serve the broth in big soup bowls; serve the meat separately.

TRIPE SOUP WITH CHILE (MENUDO COLORADO NORTEÑO)

Yield: Servings approximately 16

Ingredients:

- 1 head of garlic, unpeeled, cut in half horizontally
- 1½ pounds (675 g) calf's foot, cut into 4 pieces
- 5½ pounds (2.5 kg) tripe of different textures
- Optional: 3 pigs' feet, approximately 1 pound (450 g), each one cut into 3 pieces
- Salt to taste

The corn

- 1 pound 2 ounces (500 g) pozole corn, cooked and "flowered"

The chile

- 1 heaped tablespoon dried mexican oregano, long-leafed from nuevo león if possible
- 1 teaspoon cumin seeds, crushed
- 2 ancho chiles, seeds removed (leave the veins)
- 3 garlic cloves (not necessary)
- 3 guajillo chiles, seeds removed (leave the veins)
- About 1¼ cups (315 ml) water

To serve

- Crumbled, dried mexican oregano
- Finely chopped serrano chile
- Finely chopped white onion

- Slices of lime

Directions:

1. Wash the tripe twice in cold water, drain, and slice into two-inch (5-cm) squares. Wash the calf's and pigs' feet and drain. Put into a big stockpot or mexican earthenware olla. Fill the pot with water almost to the top—the level must be several inches above the meats. Put in the garlic and salt and set using low heat, uncovered, until it comes to a simmer. Carry on cooking for an hour, then cover and carry on cooking until the tripe and feet are soft—anywhere from two to three hours, depending on the quality of the tripe.
2. Meantime, the corn must be cooking. When it is soft and has opened up, or "flowered," drain, saving for later about 3 cups (750 ml) of its broth.
3. Place the chiles into a container, cover with cold water, and let soak for a little more than half an hour. Drain and tear into pieces.
4. Put ¼ cup (65 ml) of the water into your blender jar, put in the cumin, oregano, and optional garlic, and blend until the desired smoothness is achieved. Put in the remaining 1 cup (250 ml) of water and blend the chiles, a few at a time, until the desired smoothness is achieved. If some pieces of guajillo skin remain, pass the sauce through a strainer, pushing down hard to extract as much of the chile as you can.
5. When the meats are soft, remove the pieces of calf's foot from the broth, remove the bones, and chop the gelatinous parts into little cubes. Return them to the pot. Put in the chile sauce and corn with the reserved broth. Adjust the salt, and carry on cooking uncovered until the meats are soft—approximately 1 hour more.
6. Serve with toppings on the side.

APPETIZERS AND DRINKS

Mexicans love appetizers to nibble on, simply because there are so many awesome appetizers available to them to nibble on.

FLAMED CHEESE (QUESO FLAMEADO)

Yield: Servings 6

This robust mexican version of a cheese fondue is best served with picante tomato sauce and a stack of flour tortillas.

Ingredients:

- 1½ dozen flour tortillas
- 12 ounces (340 g) chihuahua cheese or muenster, thinly cut
- 6 ounces (180 g) mexican chorizos, skinned, crumbled, and fried (not necessary)

Directions:

1. Put the cheese in two layers in a shallow, flameproof dish.
2. Melt the cheese either on top of the stove or in your oven, drizzling the chorizo over it.
3. Heat the tortillas and serve instantly, with the sauce on the side.

FRIED PUMPKIN (CALABAZA FRITA)

Yield: about 5 cups (1.25 l)

A delicious recipe for all pumpkin lovers out there!

Ingredients:

- ⅓ to ½ cup (85 to 125 ml) olive oil (not extra virgin)
- 1 green pepper, seeded and finely chopped (1 scant cup/235 ml)
- 1 small white onion, finely chopped (½ cup/125 ml)
- 12 ounces (340 g) tomatoes, finely chopped (about 2 cups/500 ml)
- 2 pounds (900 g) unpeeled pumpkin, cut into little pieces

- Salt to taste

To serve

- ⅓ cup (85 ml) finely grated queso seco de chiapas or añejo or romano cheese

Directions:

1. Place the pumpkin pieces into a big pot, cover with water, bring to its boiling point, reduce the heat, and cook, covered, until still slightly firm, approximately twenty minutes depending on the kind of pumpkin. Drain, peel, and slice into ½-inch (1.5-cm) cubes. Set aside.
2. Heat the oil in a deep flameproof casserole; put in the onion, pepper, and tomatoes with salt to taste and cook on moderate heat, stirring occasionally to prevent sticking, until well seasoned and still slightly juicy—approximately eight minutes.
3. Put in the cubed pumpkin and mix thoroughly. Carry on cooking over low heat while stirring occasionally to prevent sticking, putting in a little water if mixture is too dry, for approximately fifteen minutes. Examine for salt, then set aside to season for minimum 30 minutes.
4. Serve sprinkled with the cheese and accompanied by tostadas.

7 LAYER DIP

Yield: Servings 8 to 10

Although not a traditional Mexican dish, this recipe is loaded with Mexican ingredients, and make a great appetizer!

Ingredients:

- ¾ teaspoon chili powder
- 1 (fifteen ounce) can black beans, drained but not washed
- 1 pound pepper Jack cheese, shredded (4 cups)
- 1 recipe (3 cups) Chunky Guacamole
- 1½ cups sour cream
- 2 garlic cloves, minced
- 2 jalapeño chiles, stemmed, seeded, and minced

- 2 tablespoons plus 2 teaspoons lime juice (2 limes)
- 3 tablespoons minced fresh cilantro
- 4 big tomatoes, cored, seeded, and chopped fine
- 6 scallions (2 minced; 4, green parts only, cut thin)
- Salt

Directions:

1. Mix tomatoes, minced scallions, jala peños, cilantro, 2 tablespoons lime juice, and ⅛ teaspoon salt in container. Allow to sit until tomatoes start to tenderize, approximately 30 minutes. Drain mixture, discard liquid, and return to container.
2. In the meantime, pulse beans, garlic, chili powder, remaining 2 teaspoons lime juice, and ⅛ teaspoon salt in food processor to crude paste, approximately fifteen pulses. Spread bean mixture uniformly into 8 inch square baking dish or 1 quart glass container.
3. In clean, dry workbowl, pulse 2½ cups pepper Jack and sour cream until the desired smoothness is achieved, approximately fifteen pulses. Spread sour cream mixture uniformly over bean layer. Top uniformly with remaining 1½ cups pepper Jack, followed by guacamole and, finally, drained tomato mixture. (Immerse can be placed in your fridge for maximum one day; bring to room temperature before you serve.) Drizzle with cut scallion greens before you serve.

AGUAS FRESCAS

Yield: 8 cups; serves 8 to 10

These delicious non-alcoholic beverages are usually made by blending fruits, grains, seeds, or flowers with sugar and water.

HIBISCUS AGUA FRESCA

Keep the flowers placed in the fridge in an airtight container.

Ingredients:

- 1 cup sugar
- 2 cups dried hibiscus flowers, washed
- 8 cups water
- Pinch salt

Directions:

1. Bring 4 cups water to boil in medium deep cooking pan. Off heat, mix in hibiscus flowers, cover, and allow to steep for an hour. Strain mixture into 2 quart pitcher; discard solids.
2. Mix in sugar and salt until blended, then mix in remaining 4 cups water.
3. Place in your fridge until completely chilled, approximately 2 hours. Serve over ice. (Agua Fresca can be placed in your fridge for maximum 5 days; stir to remix before you serve.)

WATERMELON LIME AGUA FRESCA

If you can't find seedless watermelon, remove as many seeds as you can before processing.

Ingredients:

- ⅛ teaspoon salt
- ⅓ cup lime juice (3 limes), plus extra as required
- 2 cups water
- 2 tablespoons agave nectar or honey, as required
- 8 cups seedless watermelon, cut into an inch pieces
- Mint leaves (not necessary)

Directions:

1. Working in 2 batches, process watermelon and water in blender until the desired smoothness is achieved, approximately half a minute.
2. Strain mixture through fine mesh strainer into 2 quart pitcher; discard solids. Mix in lime juice, agave, and salt into watermelon mixture. Mix in extra lime juice and agave to taste.
3. Serve over ice with mint, if using. (Agua Fresca can be placed in your fridge for maximum 5 days; stir to remix before you serve.)

BEAN AND BEEF TAQUITOS

Yield: Servings four to 6

These large tortillas taste absolutely amazing with Avocado Sauce!

Ingredients:

- ½ cup water

- 1 (8 ounce) can tomato sauce
- 1 big egg, lightly beaten
- 1 cup canned pinto beans, washed
- 1 cup plus 4 teaspoons vegetable oil
- 1 onion, halved and cut thin
- 1 teaspoon chili powder
- 1 teaspoon ground cumin
- 12 (6 inch) corn tortillas
- 2 jalapeño chiles, stemmed, seeded, and minced
- 3 garlic cloves, minced
- 3 tablespoons minced fresh cilantro
- 8 ounces 90 percent lean ground beef
- Salt and pepper

Directions:

1. Heat 1 teaspoon oil in 12 inch nonstick frying pan over moderate high heat until just smoking. Put in ground beef and cook, breaking up meat with wooden spoon, until no longer pink, approximately five minutes. Drain beef in colander. In separate container, purée beans to paste with potato masher.

2. Heat 1 tablespoon oil in now empty frying pan on moderate heat until shimmering. Put in onion and cook until tender and mildly browned, five to seven minutes. Mix in jalapeños, garlic, cumin, and chili powder and cook until aromatic, approximately half a minute. Mix in tomato sauce, water, cilantro, ½ teaspoon salt, ½ teaspoon pepper, drained beef, and mashed beans. Cook while stirring frequently, until mixture has thickened and starts to sizzle, approximately ten minutes. Sprinkle with salt and pepper to taste, move to container, and allow to cool for about twenty minutes.

3. Adjust oven rack to middle position and heat oven to 200 degrees. Coat rimmed baking sheet using parchment paper. Set wire rack in second rimmed baking sheet. Stack 6 tortillas, wrap in damp dish towel, and place on plate; microwave until warm and flexible, approximately one minute.

4. Working with one tortilla at a time, brush edges of top half with beaten egg. Spread 3 tablespoons filling in tight row across lower half of tortilla, fold bottom of tortilla over filling, then pull back on tortilla to tighten around filling. Roll firmly, place seam side down on parchment covered sheet, and cover with second damp towel. Microwave remaining 6

tortillas and repeat with rest of the filling. (Taquitos can be covered with damp towel, wrapped firmly using plastic wrap, and placed in the fridge for maximum one day.)

5. Put in remaining 1 cup oil to clean, dry 12 inch nonstick frying pan and heat over moderate high heat to 350 degrees. Using tongs, place 6 taquitos, seam side down, in oil. Fry taquitos until golden on all sides, approximately eight minutes, turning as required and adjusting heat as required to maintain oil temperature between 300 and 325 degrees. Move to prepared wire rack and place in oven to keep warm while repeating with remaining 6 taquitos and serve.

BLACK BEAN DIP

Yield: about 2 cups

Black beans are a staple in the Mexican kitchen, and can be use to make some insanely delicious and smooth dips, such as this one.

Ingredients:

- ½ onion, chopped
- ½ teaspoon ground cumin
- 1 garlic clove, minced
- 1 tablespoon extra virgin olive oil
- 1 teaspoon minced canned chipotle chile in adobo sauce
- 1 teaspoon minced fresh oregano
- 2 (fifteen ounce) cans black beans, washed
- 2 tablespoons lime juice
- 2 tablespoons minced fresh cilantro
- Salt

Directions:

1. Mix lime juice, garlic, and oregano in small container; set aside for minimum fifteen minutes.
2. Pulse beans, onion, oil, chipotle, cumin, ¼ teaspoon salt, and lime juice mixture in food processor until fully ground, 5 to 10 pulses. Scrape down sides of container with rubber spatula. Continue to pulse until uniform paste forms, approximately 1 minute, scraping down container a couple of times.

3. Move dip to container, cover, and allow it to sit at room temperature for minimum 30 minutes. (Immerse can be placed in your fridge for maximum one day; bring to room temperature before you serve.) Mix in cilantro and sprinkle with salt to taste before you serve.

CHILE-SEASONED PORK (CHILORIO)

Yield: enough to fill twelve tortillas

Ingredients:

- ⅛ teaspoon cumin seeds, crushed
- ¼ teaspoon dried mexican oregano
- ⅓ cup (85 ml) mild vinegar; make up to ½ cup (125 ml) of liquid by putting in water
- 2 pounds (900 g) pork shoulder, without bone but with some fat
- 2 teaspoons salt
- 8 ancho chiles, seeds and veins removed
- 8 garlic cloves, roughly chopped
- Lard as required
- Salt to taste

Directions:

1. Chop the meat into 1-inch (2.5-cm) cubes and cook with salt as for <u>carnitas</u>. When the water has vaporized and the fat has rendered out of the meat but the meat hasn't browned—about forty-five minutes—take the meat out of the dish and pound it in the molcajete until it is completely shredded, or shred it finely using two forks.
2. In the meantime, make the sauce. Cover the chiles with hot water. Soak for about ten minutes and drain.
3. Place the diluted vinegar into your blender jar with the garlic and spices and blend as smooth as you can. Slowly put in the chiles and blend after each addition. The sauce must be thick, more like a paste. You will have to keep stopping the blender to release the blades. Only put in more liquid if required to release the blades of the blender.
4. There must be about ¼ cup (65 ml) of fat in the dish in which the meat was cooked; if not, make up to that amount with lard. Put in the meat and blend the chile sauce thoroughly

into it. Cook using low heat for fifteen to twenty minutes, or until the meat is well seasoned and the mixture rather dry, scraping the bottom of the dish to prevent sticking.

5. Chilorio will keep for months in your fridge.

CHILIED PEANUTS (CACAHUATES ENCHILADOS)

Yield: approximately 1 cup (250 ml)

These fiery little snacks are commonly enjoyed in Mexican bars with tequila.

Ingredients:

- 1 cup (250 ml) raw shelled peanuts, with or without brown papery skins
- 1 tablespoon vegetable oil
- 1 teaspoon salt, or to taste
- 1 to 1½ teaspoons powdered chile de árbol, or to taste
- 10 small garlic cloves

Directions:

1. In a frying pan just big enough to accommodate the peanuts in a single layer, heat the oil. Put in the peanuts and garlic cloves and fry for approximately 2 minutes, flipping them over continuously.
2. Reduce the heat a little, put in the powdered chile and salt, and cook for one minute or two longer, stirring occasionally to prevent sticking; take care that the chile powder does not burn.
3. Set aside to cool before you serve with drinks.

CHUNKY GUACAMOLE

Yield: about 3 cups

A chunky version of the classic guacamole which goes great with homemade chips!

Ingredients:

- ¼ cup minced fresh cilantro
- ½ teaspoon ground cumin

- 1 jalapeño chile, stemmed, seeded, and minced
- 2 garlic cloves, minced
- 2 tablespoons finely chopped red onion
- 2 tablespoons lime juice
- 3 ripe avocados
- Salt

Directions:

1. Halve 1 avocado, remove pit, and scoop flesh into moderate container. Put in cilantro, jalapeño, onion, lime juice, garlic, ¾ teaspoon salt, and cumin and purée with potato masher (or fork) until mostly smooth.
2. Halve, pit, and dice remaining 2 avocados. Put in cubes to container with mashed avocado mixture and gently purée until mixture is well blended but still coarse. (Guacamole can be placed in your fridge for maximum one day using plastic wrap pressed directly against its surface.) Sprinkle with salt to taste before you serve.

DRIED SHRIMP FRITTERS (BOTANAS DE CAMARÓN SECO)

Yield: about 24 botanas

Ingredients:

- ½ cup (125 ml) finely chopped white onion
- ¾ cup (190 ml) small dried shrimps, cleaned
- 1 cup (250 ml) cold water
- 1 egg white
- 4 ounces (115 g) flour (approximately 1 scant cup)
- 5 serrano chiles, finely chopped
- Salt to taste
- Vegetable oil for frying

Directions:

1. Combine the flour, water, and salt together for a couple of minutes and leave the batter to stand for minimum 1 hour.

2. Wash the shrimps to remove surplus salt. Cover with warm water and leave them to soak for approximately five minutes—no longer.
3. Beat the egg white until stiff and fold it into the batter.
4. Drain the shrimps (if large, cut into 2) and put in them, with the chopped onion and chiles, to the batter.
5. Heat the oil in a frying pan and drop tablespoons of the mixture into it, a few at a time. Fry the botanas until they become golden brown, flipping them over once. Drain them on the paper towelling and serve instantly.

EMPANADAS

Yield: 24 empanadas

These filled pastries are a quite popular all over Mexico.

Ingredients:

- 1 recipe filling, chilled
- 1 tablespoon sugar
- 1¼ cups ice water
- 1½ teaspoons salt
- 12 tablespoons unsalted butter, cut into ½ inch pieces and chilled
- 2 tablespoons extra virgin olive oil
- 3¾ cups (18¾ ounces) all-purpose flour

Directions:

1. Process flour, sugar, and salt together in food processor until blended, approximately 3 seconds. Spread butter pieces over flour mixture and pulse until mixture resembles coarse cornmeal, approximately 16 pulses. Move mixture to big container. Working with ¼ cup ice water at a time, drizzle water over flour mixture and, using stiff rubber spatula, stir and press dough together until dough sticks together and no small bits of flour remain (you may not need to use all of water).
2. Turn dough onto clean, dry counter and softly push into consistent ball. Split dough into 2 even pieces. Turn each piece of dough onto sheet of plastic wrap, flatten into 6 inch disks, wrap firmly, and place in your fridge for an hour. Allow the chilled dough to sit on counter to tenderize slightly, approximately ten minutes, before rolling.

3. Adjust oven racks to upper middle and lower middle positions and heat oven to 425 degrees. Coat 2 baking sheets using parchment paper. Roll 1 dough disk into 18 inch circle, approximately ⅛ inch thick, on mildly floured counter. Using 4 inch round biscuit cutter, cut out 12 rounds, discarding dough scraps. Put 1 tablespoon filling in center of each dough round. Brush edges of dough with water and fold dough over filling. Push to secure, and crimp edges with tines of fork. Move to 1 prepared sheet, cover, and place in your fridge Repeat with the rest of the dough disk and rest of the filling. (Filled empanadas can be wrapped firmly using plastic wrap and placed in the fridge for maximum one day or frozen for maximum 1 month. After empanadas are completely frozen, approximately eight hours, they can be moved to zipper lock freezer bags to save space in freezer. Move back to parchment paper covered sheet before you bake. Increase baking time by about five minutes.)

4. Brush tops of empanadas with oil and bake until a golden-brown colour is achieved, twenty minutes to half an hour, switching and rotating sheets midway through baking. Allow to cool for five minutes before you serve.

EMPANADA FILLINGS

These fillings should be chilled at the time of using, and hence should be prepared in advance. Each filling makes enough for 24 empanadas.

BEEF AND CHEESE FILLING

Ingredients:

- ⅛ teaspoon cayenne pepper
- ⅛ teaspoon ground cloves
- ½ cup beef broth
- 1 onion, chopped fine
- 1 tablespoon extra virgin olive oil
- 1 tablespoon tomato paste
- 1 teaspoon ground cumin
- 1 teaspoon minced fresh oregano or ¼ teaspoon dried
- 12 ounces 85 percent lean ground beef
- 2 tablespoons minced fresh cilantro
- 3 garlic cloves, minced
- 4 ounces Monterey Jack cheese, shredded (1 cup)

- Salt and pepper

Directions:

1. Heat oil in 12 inch frying pan on moderate heat until just shimmering. Put in onion and cook until tender, approximately five minutes.
2. Mix in garlic, tomato paste, oregano, cumin, clove, and cayenne and cook until aromatic, approximately one minute.
3. Put in ground beef and cook, breaking up meat with wooden spoon, until beef is no longer pink, approximately five minutes.
4. Mix in broth, bring to simmer, and cook until mixture is moist but not wet, approximately eight minutes. Sprinkle with salt and pepper to taste.
5. Move mixture to container, allow to cool slightly, then cover and place in your fridge until completely cool, approximately 1 hour.
6. Mix in Monterey Jack and cilantro. (Filling can be placed in your fridge for maximum 2 days.)

POBLANO AND CORN FILLING

Ingredients:

- ¾ cup frozen corn, thawed
- 1 teaspoon ground coriander
- 1 teaspoon ground cumin
- 1 teaspoon minced fresh oregano or ¼ teaspoon dried
- 12 ounces (2 to 3) poblano chiles, stemmed, seeded, and chopped fine
- 2 garlic cloves, minced
- 2 tablespoons unsalted butter
- 3 scallions, white parts minced, green parts cut thin
- 4 ounces pepper Jack cheese, shredded (1 cup)
- 4 ounces queso fresco, crumbled (1 cup)
- Salt and pepper

Directions:

1. Melt butter in 12 inch frying pan on moderate heat. Put in poblanos and scallion whites and cook until tender and mildly browned, approximately eight minutes.

2. Mix in garlic, oregano, cumin, coriander, and ¼ teaspoon salt and cook until aromatic, approximately half a minute.
3. Mix in corn and sprinkle with salt and pepper to taste. Move mixture to container, allow to cool slightly, then cover and place in your fridge until completely cool, approximately 1 hour.
4. Mix in pepper Jack, queso fresco, and scallion greens. (Filling can be placed in your fridge for maximum 2 days.)

FRESH MARGARITAS

Yield: approximately four cups; serves four to 6

The best Margaritas are those made at home!

CLASSIC MARGARITAS

It is a good idea to steep for full one day, if possible. If you need to serve margaritas instantly, omit the zest and skip the steeping process altogether.

Ingredients:

- ¼ cup superfine sugar
- 1 cup 100 percent agave tequila, if possible reposado
- 1 cup triple sec
- 2 cups crushed ice
- 4 teaspoons finely grated lemon zest plus ½ cup juice (3 lemons)
- 4 teaspoons finely grated lime zest plus ½ cup juice (4 limes)
- Pinch salt

Directions:

1. Mix lime zest and juice, lemon zest and juice, sugar, and salt in 2 cup liquid measuring cup; cover and place in your fridge until flavors meld, minimum 4 hours or maximum one day.
2. Split 1 cup crushed ice among four to 6 margarita or twofold old fashioned glasses. Strain juice mixture into 1 quart pitcher or cocktail shaker; discard solids. Put in tequila, triple sec, and remaining 1 cup crushed ice; stir or shake until meticulously blended and chilled, 20 to 60 seconds. Strain into ice filled glasses and serve instantly.

STRAWBERRY MARGARITAS

The strawberry flavor in this variation makes the zest and steeping process redundant.

Ingredients:

- ¼ cup superfine sugar
- ½ cup Chambord
- ½ cup lemon juice (3 lemons)
- ½ cup lime juice (4 limes)
- 1 cup 100 percent agave tequila, if possible reposado
- 1 cup triple sec
- 2 cups crushed ice
- 5 ounces strawberries, hulled (1 cup)
- Pinch salt

Directions:

1. Process strawberries, lime juice, lemon juice, sugar, and salt in blender until the desired smoothness is achieved, approximately half a minute.
2. Split 1 cup crushed ice among four to 6 margarita or twofold old fashioned glasses. Strain juice mixture into 1 quart pitcher or cocktail shaker; discard solids. Put in tequila, triple sec, Chambord, and remaining 1 cup crushed ice; stir or shake until meticulously blended and chilled, 20 to 60 seconds. Strain into ice filled glasses and serve instantly.

GROUND MEAT MARINATED IN LIME JUICE (CARNE COCIDA EN LIMÓN)

Yield: Servings 4

A great snack to go with drinks!

Ingredients:

- ½ cup (125 ml) fresh lime juice
- 2 tablespoons finely chopped white onion
- 4 ounces (115 g) tomatoes, finely chopped (⅔ cup/165 ml)
- 4 serrano chiles, finely chopped

- 8 ounces (225 g) freshly ground sirloin, absolutely free of fat
- Salt to taste

Directions:

1. Combine the lime juice well into the ground meat and set it aside to "cook" in your fridge for minimum 4 hours in a nonreactive container.
2. Stir in the remaining ingredients and set the meat aside to season for minimum 2 hours more.
3. Serve with crisp tortillas, either toasted or fried.

HOMEMADE BAKED TORTILLA CHIPS

Yield: 2½ ounces; serves 2 to 3

Tortilla chips for when you're looking to cut your oil intake.

Ingredients:

- 5 (6 inch) corn tortillas
- Kosher salt
- Vegetable oil spray

Directions:

1. Adjust oven rack to middle position and heat oven to 350 degrees. Spray both sides of tortillas liberally with oil spray, then cut each tortilla into 6 wedges. Sprinkle with salt and spread into single layer on baking sheet.
2. Bake tortillas, stirring once in a while, until golden and crunchy, fifteen to twenty minutes. Remove chips from oven and allow to cool before you serve. (Cooled chips can be stored at room temperature for maximum four days.)

HOMEMADE FRIED TORTILLA CHIPS

Yield: 4 ounces; serves 4

These super crisp tortilla chips are exactly how they are meant to be enjoyed.

Ingredients:

- 5 cups peanut oil
- 8 (6 inch) corn tortillas
- Kosher salt

Directions:

1. Cut each tortilla into 6 wedges. Coat 2 baking sheets with several layers of paper towels. Heat oil in Dutch oven over moderate high heat to 350 degrees.
2. Put in half of tortillas and fry until golden and crisp around edges, 2 to 4 minutes. Move fried chips to prepared sheet, drizzle lightly with salt, and allow to cool. Repeat with remaining tortillas and serve. (Cooled chips can be stored at room temperature for maximum four days.)

LITTLE PIECES OF BROWNED PORK (CARNITAS)

Yield: Servings 6

This succulent and delicious recipe is loved all over Mexico!

Ingredients:

- 2 teaspoons salt, or to taste
- 3 pounds (1.35 kg) boneless pork shoulder, with fat

Directions:

1. Chop the meat, with the fat, into strips about 2 by ¾ inches (5 by 2 cm). Barely cover the meat with water in a heavy, wide pan. Put in the salt and bring to its boiling point, uncovered. Reduce the heat and allow the meat to carry on cooking briskly until all the liquid has vaporized—by this time it must be thoroughly cooked but not falling apart.
2. Reduce the heat a little and carry on cooking the meat until all the fat has rendered out of it. Keep turning the meat until it is mildly browned all over—total cooking time is approximately 1 hour and ten minutes.
3. Serve instantly for best flavor and texture.

MEXICAN STYLE SHRIMP COCKTAIL

Yield: Servings 6

A cool, stylish, and mildly spicy appetizer for all the shrimp lovers!

Ingredients:

- ¼ cup chopped fresh cilantro, stems reserved
- ½ cup ketchup
- 1 avocado, halved, pitted, and slice into ½ inch pieces
- 1 cucumber, peeled, halved along the length, seeded, and slice into ½ inch pieces
- 1 small red onion, chopped fine
- 1 tablespoon hot sauce
- 1 tablespoon sugar
- 1 teaspoon black peppercorns
- 1½ pounds medium shrimp (41 to 50 per pound), peeled, deveined, and tails removed
- 2 cups Clamato juice
- 2 tablespoons lime juice, plus lime wedges for serving
- 3 tomatoes, cored and slice into ½ inch pieces
- Salt and pepper

Directions:

1. Mix shrimp, 3 cups water, cilantro stems, peppercorns, sugar, and 1 teaspoon salt in big deep cooking pan. Put deep cooking pan on moderate heat and cook, stirring once in a while, until shrimp are pink and firm to touch, about eight to ten minutes (water must be just bubbling around edge of deep cooking pan and register 165 degrees). Remove deep cooking pan from heat, cover, and let shrimp sit in cooking liquid for a couple of minutes.
2. In the meantime, fill big container with ice water. Drain shrimp into colander, discarding cilantro stems and spices. Instantly move shrimp to ice water to stop cooking and chill meticulously, approximately 3 minutes. Remove shrimp from ice water and meticulously pat dry using paper towels.
3. Mix tomatoes, cucumber, onion, Clamato juice, ketchup, lime juice, and hot sauce together in serving container. Mix in shrimp, cover, and place in your fridge for minimum 30 minutes. (Shrimp cocktail can be placed in your fridge for maximum one day; allow it

to sit at room temperature for about ten minutes before you serve.) Mix in avocado and chopped cilantro and sprinkle with salt and pepper to taste and serve.

MOLLETES

Yield: Servings 6

A popular snack common in Mexican restaurants and coffee shops, as well as many street food stalls.

Ingredients:

- ½ cup finely chopped onion
- ½ cup fresh cilantro leaves
- 1 (16 inch) loaf French or Italian bread
- 1 cup refried beans
- 1 garlic clove, minced
- 1 jalapeño chile, stemmed, seeded, and minced
- 2 tablespoons lime juice
- 3 tomatoes, cored and chopped
- 4 tablespoons unsalted butter, softened
- 8 ounces mild cheddar cheese, shredded (2 cups)
- Salt and pepper

Directions:

1. Toss tomatoes with ¼ teaspoon salt in colander and allow to drain for half an hour As tomatoes drain, layer onion, cilantro, jalapeño, and garlic on top. Shake colander to drain off and discard surplus tomato juice. Move mixture to container, mix in lime juice, and sprinkle with salt and pepper to taste.
2. Adjust oven rack to middle position and heat oven to 400 degrees. Coat baking sheet with aluminum foil. Slice bread in half horizontally, then remove all but ¼ inch of interior crumb; reserve removed crumb for future use. Spread butter uniformly inside hollowed bread and place cut side up on prepared sheet. Bake until mildly toasted and browned, approximately eight minutes.

3. Allow the bread to cool slightly, spread refried beans uniformly inside toasted bread and top with cheese. Bake until cheese is just melted, five to seven minutes. Move bread to cutting board, top with salsa, and slice crosswise into 2 inch pieces. Serve warm.

PEPPERED OYSTERS (OSTIONES PIMENTADOS)

Yield: Servings 6 to 8

I know I know, oysters are best enjoyed raw, but hold your judgments until you try this recipe!

Ingredients:

- ½ teaspoon salt, or to taste
- 1 tablespoon fresh lime juice, more if you wish
- 2 mexican bay leaves
- 2 tablespoons olive oil
- 2 teaspoons whole peppercorns
- 4 dozen oysters, shucked, shells and liquid reserved
- 6 garlic cloves

Directions:

1. Heat the liquid from the oysters to the simmering point, then put in the oysters and poach until the edges start to curl, approximately 2 minutes. Drain the oysters, saving for later the broth.
2. Crush the peppercorns with the salt in a molcajete or mortar. Pound in the garlic and progressively put in the lime juice. Last of all, put in about 3 tablespoons of the reserved oyster broth. Mix thoroughly.
3. Heat the olive oil in a frying pan. Put in the bay leaves and the peppercorn mixture and cook using high heat for approximately 3 minutes. Take away the pan from the heat and put in the oysters. Adjust the seasoning, then put in a squeeze of lime juice and slightly more of the oyster liquid if you wish.
4. Serve warm or at room temperature in half shells.

PICKLED PORK RIND (CHICHARRÓN EN ESCABECHE)

Yield: Servings 6

Ingredients:

- ¼ cup (65 ml) vegetable oil
- ½ teaspoon dried mexican oregano
- ½ teaspoon salt, or to taste
- 1 avocado, peeled and cut
- 1½ cups (375 ml) vinegar, mild or diluted with ½ cup (125 ml) water, roughly
- 2 jalapeño chiles en escabeche, cut into strips
- 2 medium purple onions, thickly cut
- 3 sprigs fresh thyme or ⅛ teaspoon dried
- 6 garlic cloves, left whole
- 8 ounces (225 g) chicharron (Fried pork belly), the thinner the better, broken into two-inch (5-cm) squares
- Freshly ground pepper

Directions:

1. Heat the oil and lightly fry the onions and garlic without browning for approximately 2 minutes. Put in the vinegar, oregano, thyme, salt, and pepper to the pan and bring to its boiling point. Put in the chicharrón pieces and chiles and cook over quite high heat while stirring occasionally to prevent sticking, until the chicharrón has tenderized and absorbed almost all the vinegar—about five minutes. Set aside to cool, then serve, topped with slices of avocado.
2. To my mind, chicharrón en escabeche is best served the moment it has cooled off, but it will keep indefinitely in your fridge (although it congeals and must be brought up to room temperature before you serve).

PUMPKIN SEED DIP (SIKIL P'AK)

Yield: about 3 cups

A classic hummus-like dip that is enjoyed in the Yucatán peninsula.

Ingredients:

- ¼ cup extra virgin olive oil

- 1 habanero chile, stemmed, seeded, and chopped
- 1 onion, chopped
- 1 pound tomatoes, cored and halved
- 1½ cups roasted, unhulled pumpkin seeds
- 2 ounces queso fresco, crumbled (½ cup)
- 2 tablespoons chopped fresh cilantro
- 2 tablespoons lime juice
- Salt and pepper

Directions:

1. Adjust 1 oven rack to middle position and second rack 6 inches from broiler element. Heat oven to 400 degrees. Wash pumpkin seeds under warm water and dry meticulously. Spread seeds on rimmed baking sheet, place sheet on lower rack, and toast seeds until a golden-brown colour is achieved, stirring once in a while, twelve to fifteen minutes. Set aside to cool down a little and heat broiler.
2. Coat second rimmed baking sheet with aluminum foil. Toss tomatoes with 1 tablespoon oil and position cut side down on prepared sheet. Put sheet on upper rack and broil until tomatoes are spotty brown, 7 to ten minutes. Move tomatoes to blender and let cool to room temperature.
3. Put in onion, lime juice, habanero, pumpkin seeds, and remaining 3 tablespoon oil to blender and pulse until smooth, approximately 1 minute, scraping down sides of blender as required. Move dip to serving container and place in your fridge until completely chilled, minimum 2 hours or maximum one day. Sprinkle with salt and pepper to taste. Drizzle with queso fresco and cilantro before you serve.

QUESO FUNDIDO

Yield: Servings 6 to 8

An insanely delicious table dip of Mexican table cheese served with toppings.

Ingredients:

- ½ small onion, cut thin
- 1 poblano chile, stemmed, seeded, and cut thin
- 1 teaspoon vegetable oil

- 4 ounces Mexican style chorizo sausage, casings removed
- 6 (8 inch) corn or flour tortillas, warmed and slice into wedges
- 8 ounces queso de Oaxaca, cut into ½ inch pieces

Directions:

1. Adjust oven rack to lower middle position and heat oven to 375 degrees. Heat oil in 12 inch nonstick frying pan over moderate high heat until shimmering. Put in chorizo and cook, breaking up meat with wooden spoon, until fat starts to render, approximately one minute. Mix in poblano and onion and cook until chorizo and vegetables are thoroughly browned, five to seven minutes. Drain chorizo mixture in colander.
2. Spread queso Oaxaca uniformly into 9 inch pie plate, then drizzle with drained chorizo mixture. Move pie plate to oven and bake until cheese is just melted, about eight to ten minutes. Serve instantly with tortillas.

RICH WELL-FRIED BEANS FROM JALISCO (FRIJOLES PUERCOS ESTILO JALISCO)

Yield: Servings 6

My personal favourite variation of the classic frijoles puercos.

Ingredients:

- 1 chorizo, approximately 3 ounces (85 g)
- 2 jalapeño chiles en escabeche
- 2 tablespoons finely grated queso ranchero or romano
- 20 small, pitted green olives, chopped
- 6 strips bacon
- 8 ounces (225 g) pinto or pink beans, cooked—3½ to 4 cups (875 ml to 1 l) with broth
- Lard as required
- toasted tortillas or totopos

Directions:

1. Skin and crumble the chorizo, and cut the bacon. Cook in a frying pan using low heat, covered, until most of the fat has rendered out. Be careful not to allow them to burn. Remove chorizo and bacon and save for later.
2. There must be about ⅓ cup (85 ml) fat in the pan. Take out or make up to that amount with lard. Put in the beans and broth and cook them using high heat, mashing them. If they start to dry out and cling to the pan, put in slightly more lard.
3. Once the beans are mashed to a coarse texture and are almost dry, ready to roll, put in the bacon and about two thirds of the olives, chiles, and chorizo.
4. Roll the beans, then turn onto the serving dish and top with the rest of the olives, chiles, and chorizo.
5. Drizzle the roll with the cheese and serve with the toasted tortillas or totopos.

ROE SNACK (CAVIAR DE CHAPALA CARP)

Yield: Servings 6

A delicious Mexican appetizer usually served with hot tortillas other small sides to nibble on.

Ingredients:

- ¼ cup (65 ml) vegetable or olive oil
- 1 garlic clove, finely chopped
- 1 pound (450 g) carp roe
- 1 tablespoon salt
- 2 tablespoons finely chopped white onion
- About 6 ounces (180 g) tomatoes, finely chopped (approximately 1 cup/250 ml)

The toppings

- ⅓ cup (85 ml) finely chopped cilantro
- ⅓ cup (85 ml) finely chopped green, unripe tomatoes or tomate verde
- ⅓ cup (85 ml) finely chopped serrano chiles or any other fresh, hot green chiles
- ½ cup (125 ml) finely chopped white onion

Directions:

1. Place the salt and enough water to cover the roe in a shallow pan and bring to the simmering point. Put in the roe and allow it to simmer for eight to ten minutes, depending on thickness, then remove and drain. When it is sufficiently cool to handle, take off the skin and crumble the roe.

2. Heat the oil in a heavy pan. Put in the tomatoes, onion, and garlic and fry over quite high heat while stirring occasionally and scraping the bottom of the pan, until the onion is tender and the mixture is almost dry. Put in the crumbled roe with salt to taste and carry on frying the mixture on moderate heat, flipping it over continuously, until dry and crumbly, approximately five minutes.

3. Serve hot, accompanied by the onion and the other finely chopped toppings, in small different bowls, and a pile of hot corn tortillas.

SEAFOOD COCKTAIL (MARISCOS A LA MARINERA)

Yield: Servings 6

Any seafood ingredient of your choice will do the job here: raw clams or scallops, abalone, conch, or cooked shrimps.

Ingredients:

- ½ cup (125 ml) fresh lime juice
- 1 big avocado, cubed
- 1 small white onion, finely chopped (about ¼ cup/65 ml)
- 2 heaped tablespoons finely chopped cilantro
- 3 dozen big raw clams or scallops or medium-size cooked shrimps
- 3 tablespoons olive oil
- 3 to 4 serrano chiles or any fresh, hot green chiles, finely chopped with seeds
- About 12 ounces (340 g) tomatoes, finely chopped (about 2 cups/500 ml)
- Salt and freshly ground pepper to taste

Directions:

1. If you are using clams, open them or have them opened for you, saving both the clams and their juice. If you are using scallops, allow them to marinate in the lime juice for about 1 hour or so.

2. Mix the clams (and their liquid) or other seafood with the remaining ingredients, tweak the seasoning, and serve slightly chilled.

SHREDDED CRABMEAT AND VEGETABLES (SALPICÓN DE JAIBA)

Yield: enough to fill 12 small tortillas

This salpicón makes a scrumptious filling for small tacos and can also be served with plain white rice.

Ingredients:

- ¼ cup (65 ml) vegetable oil
- ⅓ cup (85 ml) finely chopped white onion
- ½ cup (125 ml) finely chopped celery
- 1 cup (250 ml) cooked, shredded crabmeat
- 3 tablespoons finely chopped cilantro
- 5 serrano chiles, finely chopped, with seeds
- Salt to taste

Directions:

1. Heat the oil in a frying pan and cook the onion gently until translucent.
2. Put in the celery, chiles, and crabmeat and fry until they barely start to brown mildly. The mixture must be rather dry. Finally, put in the cilantro and salt and cook for a minute more.
3. Serve with hot tortillas.

SHRIMP AND LIME CEVICHE

Yield: Servings 6

Usually served with crispy tortilla chips or used as a topping for tostadas, this simple and delicious seafood appetizer is quite uplifting.

Ingredients:

- ¼ cup extra virgin olive oil
- ½ cup lemon juice (3 lemons)
- ½ teaspoon sugar
- 1 garlic clove, minced
- 1 jalapeño chile, stemmed, seeded, and minced
- 1 pound extra big shrimp (21 to 25 per pound), peeled, deveined, tails removed, and halved along the length
- 1 teaspoon grated lime zest plus ½ cup juice (4 limes)
- 1 tomato, cored, seeded, and chopped fine
- 3 tablespoons minced fresh cilantro
- 4 scallions, cut thin
- Salt and pepper

Directions:

1. Mix tomato, lemon juice, jalapeño, lime zest and juice, garlic, and ½ teaspoon salt in medium container. Mix in shrimp, cover, and place in your fridge until shrimp are firm and opaque throughout, forty-five minutes to an hour, stirring midway through refrigerating.
2. Drain shrimp mixture in colander, leaving shrimp slightly wet, and move to serving container. Mix in oil, scallions, cilantro, and sugar. Sprinkle with salt and pepper to taste and serve.

SINALOAN SHREDDED BEEF (MOCHOMOS SINALOENSES)

Yield: about 6 cups (1.5 l)

An insanely popular dish from Sinaloa, made of carne machaca, or machacada.

Ingredients:

- ½ cup (125 ml) lard or vegetable oil
- 1 poblano chile, charred, peeled, cleaned, and cut into little squares
- 1½ tablespoons coarse sea salt
- 2 pounds (900 g) round steak (with some fat on)
- 8 ounces (225 g) white onions, roughly cut

Directions:

1. Chop the meat into 1-inch (2.5-cm) cubes. Put the meat in a single layer in a big pan. Put in the salt and water to barely cover. Bring the water to its boiling point, reduce the heat, and cook slowly, uncovered, until the water has vaporized and the meat is soft but not too soft—thirty-five to forty minutes. Continue drying the meat out using low heat so that it is dried and slightly crusty on the outside. Let cool.
2. Put 3 pieces of the meat into a blender and blend at moderate speed until meat is finely shredded. Continue in similarly until all the meat has been shredded.
3. Heat half of the lard in a frying pan, put in the onions, and fry for a short period of time for approximately 1 minute—they must be crisp and still opaque. Take away the onions using a slotted spoon and drain. Set aside.
4. Put in the rest of the lard to the frying pan, heat, put in the shredded meat and chile, and stir until the meat is well thoroughly heated and just browning—5 to 8 minutes.
5. Mix in the onions, heat through, and serve instantly.

STUFFED JALAPEÑOS

Yield: Servings 6 to 8

The only thing better than jalapeños are stuffed jalapeños.

Ingredients:

- 1 big egg yolk
- 1 teaspoon ground cumin
- 12 jalapeño chiles, halved along the length with stems left undamaged, seeds and ribs removed
- 2 scallions, cut thin
- 2 tablespoons panko bread crumbs
- 2 teaspoons lime juice
- 3 tablespoons minced fresh cilantro
- 4 ounces cream cheese, softened
- 4 ounces mild cheddar cheese, shredded (1 cup)
- 4 ounces Monterey Jack cheese, shredded (1 cup)
- 6 slices bacon

- Salt

Directions:

1. Adjust oven rack to upper middle position and heat oven to 500 degrees. Set wire rack in rimmed baking sheet. Cook bacon in 12 inch nonstick frying pan on moderate heat until crunchy, 7 to 9 minutes. Using slotted spoon, move bacon to paper towel–lined plate. When bacon is sufficiently cool to handle, cut fine and save for later.
2. Season jalapeños with salt and place cut side down on prepared rack. Bake until just starting to tenderize, approximately five minutes. Remove jalapeños from oven and reduce oven temperature to 450 degrees. When sufficiently cool to handle, flip jalapeños cut side up.
3. Mix cheddar, Monterey Jack, cream cheese, scallions, cilantro, panko, egg yolk, lime juice, cumin, and bacon together in container until meticulously blended. Split cheese mixture among jalapeños, pushing into cavities. (Filled jalapeños can be covered and placed in the fridge for maximum one day.)
4. Bake jalapeños until soft and filling is mildly browned, 9 to 14 minutes. Allow to cool for five minutes and serve.

TOMATILLO AND PINTO BEAN NACHOS

Yield: Servings four to 6

Try this recipe when you're in mood for a crunchy vegetarian snack!

Ingredients:

- ½ cup sour cream
- 1 (fifteen ounce) can pinto beans, washed
- 1 cup Fresh Tomato Salsa
- 1 cup frozen corn, thawed
- 1 onion, chopped fine
- 1 tablespoon vegetable oil
- 1 teaspoon ground coriander
- 1 teaspoon salt
- 1½ cups Chunky Guacamole
- 12 ounces pepper Jack cheese, shredded (3 cups)

- 12 ounces tomatillos, husks and stems removed, washed well, dried, and slice into ½ inch pieces
- 2 jalapeño chiles, stemmed and cut thin
- 2 teaspoons minced fresh oregano or ½ teaspoon dried
- 3 garlic cloves, minced
- 3 radishes, trimmed and cut thin
- 8 ounces tortilla chips
- Lime wedges

Directions:

1. Adjust oven rack to middle position and heat oven to 400 degrees. Heat oil in 12 inch nonstick frying pan on moderate heat until shimmering. Put in onion and cook until tender, approximately five minutes. Mix in garlic, coriander, salt, and oregano and cook until aromatic, approximately half a minute. Put in tomatillos and corn, decrease the heat to moderate low, and cook until tomatillos have released all their moisture and mixture is nearly dry, approximately ten minutes. Allow to cool slightly.
2. Spread half of tortilla chips uniformly into 13 by 9 inch baking dish. Drizzle 1½ cups pepper Jack uniformly over chips, then top uniformly with half of tomatillo mixture, followed by half of beans and, finally, half of jalapeños. Repeat layering with remaining chips, pepper Jack, tomatillo mixture, beans, and jalapeños. Bake until cheese is melted and just starting to brown, 7 to ten minutes.
3. Let nachos cool for a couple of minutes, then drizzle with radishes. Drop scoops of guacamole, salsa, and sour cream around edges of nachos. Serve instantly, passing lime wedges separately.

BEEF NACHOS

Yield: Servings four to 6

The name pretty much says it all!

Ingredients:

- ⅛ teaspoon salt
- ¼ teaspoon cayenne pepper
- ½ cup sour cream

- ½ teaspoon ground coriander
- ½ teaspoon ground cumin
- 1 cup Fresh Tomato Salsa
- 1 garlic clove, minced
- 1 pound cheddar cheese, shredded (4 cups)
- 1 small onion, chopped fine
- 1 tablespoon chili powder
- 1 teaspoon minced fresh oregano or ¼ teaspoon dried
- 1½ cups Chunky Guacamole
- 2 big jalapeño chiles, stemmed and cut thin
- 2 scallions, cut thin
- 2 teaspoons vegetable oil
- 8 ounces 90 percent lean ground beef
- 8 ounces tortilla chips
- Lime wedges

Directions:

1. Adjust oven rack to middle position and heat oven to 400 degrees. Heat oil in 12 inch frying pan on moderate heat until shimmering. Put in onion and cook until tender, approximately 3 minutes. Mix in chili powder, garlic, oregano, cumin, coriander, cayenne, and salt and cook until aromatic, approximately half a minute. Put in ground beef and cook, breaking up meat with wooden spoon, until beef is no longer pink, approximately five minutes.
2. Spread half of tortilla chips uniformly into 13 by 9 inch baking dish. Drizzle 2 cups cheddar uniformly over chips, then top uniformly with half of beef mixture, followed by half of jalapeño slices. Repeat layering with remaining chips, cheddar, beef mixture, and jalapeños. Bake until cheese is melted and just starting to brown, 7 to ten minutes.
3. Let nachos cool for a couple of minutes, then drizzle with scallions. Drop scoops of guacamole, salsa, and sour cream around edges of nachos. Serve instantly, passing lime wedges separately.

YUCATECAN PICKLED LIMA BEANS (IBIS ESCABECHADOS)

Yield: about 3 cups (750 ml)

Ibis, both fresh and dried, are common ingredients in the food of the yucatán peninsula. They are quite similar to lima beans.

Ingredients:

- ¼ cup (65 ml) bitter orange juice or fresh lime juice
- ⅓ cup (85 ml) tightly packed, finely chopped cilantro
- ½ habanero chile, finely chopped
- 1 cup (250 ml) loosely packed, thinly cut white onion
- 12 ounces (340 g) ibis or lima beans (about 2½ cups/625 ml)
- Boiling water to cover
- Salt to taste

Directions:

1. Cover the onion with the boiling water and leave to soak for a minute. Drain, put in salt to taste, and mix in the bitter orange juice and chile. Set aside in a nonreactive container at room temperature to macerate while you cook the beans.
2. Put enough water into a small deep cooking pan to cover the beans. Bring the water to its boiling point, put in the beans, and cook on moderate heat until just soft—about ten minutes. Drain, and while still warm put in to the onion. Mix in the cilantro and put in salt as required. Serve at room temperature.

YUCATECAN PICKLED POTATOES (PAPAS ESCABECHADAS)

Yield: about 2⅔ cups (665 ml)

A popular snack serve in Mexican bars, usually free of charge.

Ingredients:

- ¼ cup (65 ml) bitter orange juice or fresh lime juice
- ⅓ cup (85 ml) tightly packed, finely chopped cilantro
- ½ habanero chile, finely chopped
- 1 cup (250 ml) loosely packed, thinly cut white onion
- 12 ounces (340 g) waxy potatoes, cut into ¾-inch (2-cm) cubes
- Boiling water to cover

- Salt to taste

Directions:

1. Cover the onion with the boiling water and leave to soak for a minute. Drain, put in salt to taste, and mix in the bitter orange juice and chile. Set aside in a nonreactive container at room temperature to macerate while you cook the potatoes.
2. Put enough water into a small deep cooking pan to cover the potatoes. Bring the water to its boiling point, put in the potatoes, and cook on moderate heat until just soft—approximately eight minutes. Drain, cool off a little, and peel—but while still slightly warm put in to the onion. Mix in the cilantro and put in more salt as required. Serve at room temperature.

YUCATECAN SHREDDED MEAT (SALPICÓN YUCATECO OR DZIK DE VENADO)

Yield: Servings 6

Any meat can be used in this recipe. This recipe is a great way to use any leftover meat you might have from a previous meal.

Ingredients:

- ½ cup (125 ml) seville orange juice
- ⅔ cup (165 ml) radishes cut into fine strips
- 1 cup (250 ml) cooked and shredded meat
- 3 tablespoons very finely chopped cilantro
- Salt to taste

Directions:

1. Mix all the ingredients and allow them to season for approximately 30 minutes before you serve.

ABOUT THE AUTHOR

Marissa Marie is a cook, a nutritionist, and a restaurant owner. She was raised in a small city called Los Alamos in New Mexico. Her parents loved to cook, and as a result she too fell in love with the art. Although she learnt a lot from her mother, most of her knowledge comes from self-teaching and experimentation.

Made in the USA
Las Vegas, NV
20 October 2024